The One and the Many

THE
One AND THE
Many

A Contemporary
Thomistic Metaphysics

W. NORRIS CLARKE, S.J.

University of Notre Dame Press

Notre Dame, Indiana

Reprinted in 2002, 2005, 2006, 2007

Manufactured in the United States of America

Library of Congress Cataloging-in-Publication Data
Clarke, W. Norris (William Norris), 1915–
The one and the many : a contemporary Thomistic metaphysics / W. Norris Clarke.
p. cm.
Includes bibliographical references and index.
ISBN 0-268-03706-x (cloth: alk. paper)
ISBN 13: 978-0-268-03707-9(pbk. : alk. paper)
ISBN 10: 0-268-03707-8 (pbk. : alk. paper)
1. Metaphysics. 2. Thomists. I. title.

B945.C483   054   2001
110—dc21   00-055987

∞ *This book is printed on acid-free paper.*

Contents

Introduction

My aim here is to provide an advanced textbook of systematic meta-physics in the Thomistic tradition, one which is alert not only to developments within Thomism but also to contemporary problems and other movements in philosophy. Its inspiration is primarily St. Thomas's own rich and profound metaphysical "system"—in the loose, general meaning of the term—which I think is still unsurpassed in its depth, comprehensiveness of vision, and coherence not only with direct human experience but with what is known in other fields of knowledge. But my own adaptation of his system for contemporary readers also draws upon various fruitful developments in philosophy since Aquinas's time and so is not merely a repetition of his own thought but a "creative retrieval" of it (to use a term from Heidegger) and sometimes a "creative completion" of themes implicit in Aquinas but never explicitly developed by him.

Hence this is not intended as a work of historical scholarship aimed at distilling the exact thought in Thomas's texts. It is, rather, a creative appropriation of his central metaphysical themes, gathered into a systematic order—partly traditional and partly my own—which he himself did not have the occasion to do. It is presented as far as possible in simplified, streamlined terms more accessible to a contemporary reader than Thomas's own writings with their heavy technical apparatus taken over from Aristotle, which was his chosen medium of expression but is not easy for us to be at home in today without a long apprenticeship. Hence I prefer to call my presentation a "Thomistically inspired metaphysics," taking my own responsibility for its philosophical validity. There is always risk involved in transposing a philosopher's thought into the framework of a different language and cultural background. But the risk is worth it, I think, if Thomas's own profound seminal insights and rich integrating vision of reality are to enter effectively into the bloodstream of contemporary thought and be made available to those, young and old, who are seeking to appropriate for themselves our rich medieval cultural heritage, and especially to develop for themselves some kind of holistic vision of the intelligibility and meaningfulness of our universe as a whole and our human life within it.

The *need* for such a contemporary rethinking and representation of the core of Aquinas's philosophical wisdom, his metaphysics, has become more and more evident. In the recent past, in what has been called the "heyday of American Thomism," there were a number of distinguished textbooks of Thomistic metaphysics available; but most have now gone out of print and few new ones are available, at least at a price accessible to students. Outside of the Thomistic and Scholastic traditions, textbooks in "Metaphysics" today usually mean something quite different from the great classical tradition of systematic metaphysics in the style of Aristotle, Aquinas, Duns Scotus, Spinoza, Leibniz, Hegel, Whitehead, etc. The very notion of constructing a unified systematic philosophical inquiry into being as a whole, distinct from other philosophical disciplines, has been abandoned by most contemporary philosophers (Whiteheadian Process philosophy is one of the few exceptions still flourishing). This is largely due to the many attacks on the very possibility of such a systematic metaphysics stemming from modern philosophers like Hume and the empiricists, Kant and analytic philosophers generally—for whom, like Strawson, "descriptive metaphysics is in; explanatory metaphysics is out." Not to mention the latest phase of deconstruction and postmodernism, which, according to Prof. Miller of Yale, "has dismantled the entire engine of Western metaphysics beyond hope of repair"—a premature epitaph for a discipline which, as Gilson puts it graphically, "has always buried its undertakers."

As a result, what goes by the name of "Metaphysics" in most contemporary American textbooks bearing the name is not a systematic study of being at all, but a grab bag of diverse particular philosophical problems whose only common bond is that they cannot be solved by scientific inquiry, logical analysis, or the descriptive methods of phenomenology. Examples are the mind-body problem, realism vs. idealism in epistemology, free will, the existence of God, and the like.

The present text is, therefore, a return to a systematic metaphysics of being in the classical Thomistic tradition. The need to make this tradition available to our own day is more urgent now than ever, in the face of the growing tendency of our culture toward specialization and fragmentation of inquiry into "careful piecemeal work," as the well-known American philosopher Sidney Hook approvingly described the current fashion in American philosophy (in the editorial preface to his *American Philosophers at Work*). But with no integrating vision of reality and human life as a whole to balance off this piecemeal approach, we tend to become fragmented people, with our lives "in pieces," so to speak, "perpetually condemned to fragmentary perspectives," as one former student of mine and lover of metaphysics recently expressed it colorfully. This textbook, therefore, is dedicated to the search for an integrated vision of reality as a whole, to fulfill the need "to balance off the fascination of the part with the vision of the whole," as someone described the role of philosophical inquiry within a liberal education. I present it, accordingly, as a "Thomistically inspired" exploration of the central problems of such a metaphysics in the classical tradition, for which I am indebted principally, but not exclusively, to the profound insights and disciplined method of inquiry of St. Thomas himself (but for whose contemporary transposition and expression I alone take full responsibility). Now let us validate the project, we hope, by its execution!

I must end by warning my readers, lest their expectations be disappointed, that this does not pretend to be a history of metaphysical systems in any way, nor does it regularly compare the position of St. Thomas with that of other rival systems on each point. That is in itself an important and illuminating part of one's philosophical education, especially for graduate students. But it would make the book impossibly long to attempt to do this adequately in a single volume. I believe anyway that metaphysical systems are more properly compared as wholes, not as parts abstracted from the whole. Hence, my purpose is to offer only a systematic exposition of Thomistic metaphysics in itself. A teacher using it will have to provide historical background and comparisons with other resources. I believe also that the best method to train anyone in metaphysical thinking is not to stand back and compare brief snapshots of many different thinkers, none in depth. Rather, it is to engage the subject like an apprentice, going deeply and thoroughly into one great system of thought, seeing how the problems and solutions are systematically connected, so that if one holds something in one area, one cannot implicitly deny it in another and remain consistent. Having once learned how a metaphysical system is put together and holds together, one can then step back and evaluate it critically, compare it with others, and decide how much one wants to accept, adapt, revise more radically, or reject for some other position. One can learn metaphysical thinking only by first *doing it* under the guidance of some master, somewhat like the apprentices in any skilled trade or art.

CHAPTER ONE

What Is Metaphysics and Why Do It?

I. Role of Philosophy and How Metaphysics Fits into It

Since every philosopher to some extent, especially in our age of pluralism, works out of a personal view of what the philosophical enterprise is all about, let me lay out first how I understand the philosophical project as a whole and then how metaphysics fits into it. Philosophy is the critically reflective, systematically articulated attempt to illumine our human experience in depth and set it in a vision of the whole. Thus, it is not primarily a search for new experience or new facts—although some may turn up along the way—but a second-level enterprise, so to speak, where we take the experience (including the vicarious experience of others) and data we already have and try to illumine them in depth, i.e., to search out their ultimate grounding or necessary conditions of possibility, their ultimate meaning, and their connections with the rest of reality. And although particular areas of philosophy will focus on particular domains of our experience, e.g., philosophical anthropology on human beings, philosophy of art on the domain of human art, etc., the philosophical eye will always look further to discover how this particular domain fits into an integrated vision of the universe as a whole. This, at least, is what philosophy is all about according to St. Thomas and the classical tradition as a whole, from Plato on.

Role of metaphysics. Metaphysics fits into the overall project of philosophy as its innermost ground, as that part which focuses its inquiry explicitly on the *vision of the whole,* that is, what is common to all real beings and what constitutes their connectedness to the universe as a meaningful whole. It is the ultimate framework or horizon of inquiry, into which all other investigations, including all the sciences, fit as partial perspectives. Its work will then be to try to discern the great universal properties, constitutive principles, and governing laws of all that is real, in a word, the laws of intelligibility of *being as such*, including how all real beings interrelate to form an intelligible whole, that is, a *universe* (the term "universe" comes from the Latin *universum*, which means "turned toward unity"). This is the meaning of the ancient classical definition of metaphysics descending from Aristotle—the first to explicitly define metaphysics—namely, "Metaphysics is the study of *being qua being*" or being as such. Spelled out, this means the study of *all beings* precisely insofar as they are *real*, which means for St. Thomas *actually existent*. It also includes the whole realm of *mental beings* of various kinds, such as possibles, abstractions, mathematical and logical entities, theoretical and imaginative constructions, etc., precisely insofar as their very being consists in their being-thought-about by the activity of real minds.

In practice, however, we humans cannot directly inspect all beings as immediately accessible to our experience. We have to start, therefore, with where we are, with what is accessible to us within the limited horizon of our experience, namely, this material cosmos that is our present home, including ourselves. From the study of this universe, insofar as it is open to our experience, we shall first derive the general properties, laws, and principles governing all the beings of our experience as a community of many different, changing, and finite (limited) beings. From this we shall be able (1) to discern a very small number of absolutely universal principles applying to all real beings as such, in any possible universe, because otherwise they would be simply unintelligible; (2) to argue from the necessary conditions of intelligibility of our own changing and finite cosmos to an Ultimate Source or Cause, beyond our experience, of all limited beings whatsoever—the philosophical description of what we call "God."

The philosophical ascent of the human mind to this Ultimate Reality belongs intrinsically to the project of metaphysics, as the final capstone of the intelligibility, unity, and meaningfulness of the whole universe of real being. But because of its importance and complexity, it is often treated as a separate treatise of its own, called "philosophy of God," "natural theology," or the like. This makes sense in itself, but because the majority of students do not get the chance to take such a

separate course, we have included the essentials of such a natural conclusion to metaphysics in this text.

II. DISTINCTION OF METAPHYSICS FROM RELIGION AND THEOLOGY

Although the scope of inquiry of metaphysics is universal, embracing all
being, its method of investigation is strictly philosophical, i.e., drawing
on the resources of natural reason alone as applied to our common
human experience, without taking either its data or its conclusions
from any higher source of wisdom transcending the human, such as divine revelation and its theological explication. Should the metaphysician as a personal thinker, however, judge these to be authentic, they
should be respected; and occasionally they can be sources of new illumi-
nation on the deeper meaning of the natural order itself, so as to stimulate natural reason to look more deeply into our human experience to
discern what it may have overlooked before. This is to respect the great
guiding principle of medieval Christian thinkers, who were both theologians and philosophers, namely, that God has spoken to us in two great
books: the Book of Nature, where created things speak to us directly,
and the Book of Revelation, where God himself reveals to us his own
inner nature and his free gifts and special plans for humanity. These
two books, both written by the same Author, cannot contradict each
other; if there is an apparent contradiction, either one side or the other,
natural reason or theological interpretation of the revelation, has made
an error, and each possibility must be reexamined more carefully.

Metaphysics also differs from religion, in that the former is a purely
intellectual or *speculative* quest for wisdom about the meaning of the
universe, whereas the latter involves a response of the heart and *practical*
commitment of the whole person to live according to the plan of, and
seek union with, what one takes to be Ultimate Reality.

III. INCOMPLETENESS OF ALL METAPHYSICAL EXPRESSION

Metaphysics done by human beings is necessarily tied in its expression
to limited human concepts and linguistic frameworks, which are themselves rooted in the intellectual and cultural development of the societies out of which they grew. But these are never complete, totally adequate, or the only possible ways of describing or explaining the

inexhaustible richness of reality. Hence, although metaphysicians can indeed discover universal metaphysical truths transcending all times and cultures, the conceptual-linguistic expression of what they have discovered will always have to resign itself to being incomplete, falling short of the fullness of the real, in a word, *perspectival*, seen from within the resources of thinking, speaking, imagining, and feeling of the metaphysician's own culture in its situation in human history. Hence no definitive, exhaustively adequate *expression* of metaphysics for all times and cultures is humanly possible. But metaphysicians are not locked into their own cultures and languages; they can learn from each other, especially in an age of universal communication like our own, and develop more sensitive and sophisticated conceptual and linguistic tools as they go along if they have the humility to learn from others.

A metaphysics, therefore, done by human beings like ourselves must be humble. But what it can give us, if we go about it carefully and systematically, is a deeper understanding and appreciation of the universe in its unity-in-diversity and its meaningfulness. And to be fully human it is good for us to make the effort to expand our minds to the ultimate horizon of being; the effort itself is deeply enriching, rewarding, and consciousness-expanding.

IV. Objections against the Legitimacy of Metaphysics

Many modern, and especially contemporary, philosophers deny the legitimacy of metaphysics, either because for them it is not a meaningful inquiry at all, since it has no distinctive subject matter, or because it is not possible for human minds to achieve it. Let us look at some of the most common objections.

1. No distinctive subject matter. Every distinct branch of knowledge must study some particular class of things, with some observable trait that sets them off from other things, like physics, biology, psychology, theology, etc. Metaphysics claims to study all things at once. But being is no distinguishing trait, since all have it; it is empty conceptually and tells us nothing in particular. I can't point to it and say, "Here is being, and there is not."

Response. Metaphysics does not have a distinctive *subject matter,* since it treats of all beings, but it does have a distinctive *point of view* from which it studies them. It considers in them only their most fundamental attribute of being itself and the properties and laws which they have in common with all beings, or all changing and finite beings, as these beings exist in the community of other existent beings, acting and interacting with each other to form the universe in which we are all plunged.

This fundamental dimension of being itself, of the actual existence of what they are studying, is taken for granted by all other branches of knowledge, which then go on to study *what* it is and *how* it works. But just because something is taken for granted does not mean that it is unimportant. This is just what metaphysics, and it alone, aims to do: to draw into the explicit light of reflection what all other human inquiry takes for granted or leaves implicit—the foundation of actual existence upon which all else is built and without which all subject matter vanishes into the darkness of nonbeing, of what is *not.* Martin Heidegger, the great contemporary German metaphysician—not himself a Thomist at all— complained that the whole of Western metaphysics, from Plato on, lapsed into a "forgetfulness of being," not of *what* things are, their essences, but of the radical fact *that* they *are* at all, standing out from nothingness and shining forth to us.

One of the few exceptions is the "existential metaphysics" of St. Thomas Aquinas (1225–74), which Heidegger never came to know in any depth and to which we are now going to introduce you. This "radical" (in its original sense of going to the roots = *radices* in Latin) investigation is something that needs doing at least once in your intellectual life. This is your chance now. But it cannot be done by any method of empirical observation or scientific method based on quantitative measuring techniques formulated in mathematical terms, but only by its own proper method of reflective analysis and insight into the necessary conditions of intelligibility of being as such, and finally coming to grips with the most fundamental question of all: "How come there is a real universe at all?"

2. *We, as parts of the Whole, cannot comprehend the Whole.* Some philosophers say that it is impossible for human beings to do metaphysics, because each one of us is only a small finite part of the whole of reality and it is impossible for the part to comprehend the whole of which it is a part. To do so it would have to step out of the whole or be the maker of it like God. Since this is impossible, we must be content to take the universe of reality as a whole for granted and direct our attention to what the parts are like inside it and how they operate and fit together. Hence, questions about reality as a whole, about existence as such, e.g.,

"How come there is a universe at all?" are either meaningless, or, as some are willing to admit, meaningful in themselves and enriching to think about as ultimate mysteries, but incapable of any human answer. (See, for example, Milton Munitz, *The Mystery of Existence,* New York, 1965. So, too, Bertrand Russell, when pushed back to this point by Father Frederick Copleston in their famous BBC debate, answered impatiently, "The universe just is, that's all. Explanation starts from there.")

Response. But this is precisely the wonder and paradox of the spiritual intellect we all possess. Because it is by nature ordered to being as such as its proper object, it is open to the entire horizon of being without restriction, and so can think about it as a whole and about our own place in it, can encompass it in a certain sense in its own thought—not in detail, of course, but in its broad outlines—which other non-intelligent beings in the universe cannot do. Hence, by the very fact that we can raise the question about being as a whole, the human person is not just a part of the universe but a whole, within the Whole. Every person endowed with intelligence is thus, at least implicitly, a point of view on the whole universe. This is an essential part of our dignity as images of God. This course is aimed at making this implicit capacity in all of us explicitly conscious and reflective. It is appropriate, therefore, to begin our study by stirring up that sense of wonder at what Heidegger has called "the wonder of all wonders, that anything exists at all."

3. Objections to metaphysics from modern restrictive theories of knowledge. The largest number of objectors to the possibility of metaphysics come from modern philosophers since Hume and Kant, based on epistemological limitations on the scope of our human knowledge. These can be divided into three very general categories: *empiricism, Kantianism,* including its more recent Neo-Kantian versions, and *relativism* in all its various forms (historical, etc.).

Empiricism. This type of thinking denies we can know anything that is not derived directly from some sense experience (strict empiricism of the Humean type—David Hume, 1711–76), or at least anything reaching beyond the range of our human experience in the widest sense. Thus we are never justified in arguing by intellectual inference from something within our experience to some cause or ground transcending our experience, such as God, a spiritual soul that is the root of our acts of intelligence, metaphysical co-principles that are constitutive—but not experienceable—components of every finite and changing being, such as essence/existence, matter/form, substance, potentiality, etc.

Response.   One central flaw in all such theories of knowing is that they are in principle unable to do justice to the very subject or self that is asking the questions, since this is at the root of every conscious sense experience and quest for understanding, but not out in front of our senses as an external object to be sensed by them. In a word, the inner world vanishes in its very attempt to understand the outer world. The empiricist way of thinking also cripples the age-old natural longing of the human mind to understand, make sense of, its direct experience in terms of deeper causes not directly accessible to us. The human mind cannot be satisfied to operate only within this straightjacket of an arbitrarily restrictive epistemology.

Kantianism.   Stemming from Immanuel Kant (1724–1804), who maintained we can never know reality in itself, "things-in-themselves" (which he called *noumena,* that which would be knowable by a perfect, creative mind—*nous*), but only things as they affect us, appear to us (*phenomena*) within our consciousness. Things in the real world do act upon us, but what they reveal of themselves is only a "sense manifold, or jumble of sense images without intelligible order, form, structure. We are the ones who impose form and order and intelligibility on the content of our sense experience, drawing on the a priori forms of intelligibility—plus the a priori sense forms of space and time—which are innate in all human minds. This is the "Copernican revolution" of which Kant was so proud: it is not the world that informs us, molds our minds to conform to it; it is our minds which impose intelligibility—forms, structures, order, etc.—on the world. It is we who are makers of the world *as intelligible.* Hence we do not think the world as it is, as everyone took for granted before Kant, but the world is as we cannot help but think it. It follows that any possibility of doing metaphysics—the study of real being with its intrinsic properties, laws, etc.—is cut off at the root for us human beings, who are locked without escape within the walls of our own minds. We can indeed show that the human mind naturally tends to think of God as the unifying cause of this world, but this gives us no right at all to affirm this as objectively true in the real world outside of our thought. Thus both philosophical theism as well as atheism are cut off at the root, and the way is left open for the inner experience of the moral imperative and subjective religious experience.

In later forms of *Neo-Kantianism,* we still impose intelligibility on the world from within our own a priori's; but these a priori forms are no longer universal and unchanging for all human minds; they are a priori's of culture and of language imprinted in us by the society in which we are brought up; they are neither universal for all humans nor unchanging down the ages, but variable and mutable as history goes on. Various relativisms of culture and history result.

Response.   One of the central flaws in Kant's theory of knowledge is that he has blown up the bridge of action by which real beings manifest their natures to our cognitive receiving sets. He admits that things in themselves act on us, on our senses; but he insists that such action reveals nothing intelligible about these beings, nothing about their natures in themselves, only an unordered, unstructured sense manifold that we have to order and structure from within ourselves. But action that is completely indeterminate, that reveals nothing meaningful about the agent from which it comes, is incoherent, not really action at all.

The whole key to a realist epistemology like that of St. Thomas is that action is the "self-revelation of being," that it reveals a being as *this kind of actor* on me, which is equivalent to saying it really exists and has this kind of *nature* = an abiding center of acting and being acted on. This does not deliver a complete knowledge of the being acting, but it does deliver an authentic knowledge of the real world as a community of interacting agents—which is after all what we need to know most about the world so that we may learn how to cope with it and its effects on us as well as our effects upon it. This is a modest but effective *relational realism,* not the unrealistic ideal of the only thing Kant will accept as genuine knowledge of real beings, i.e., knowledge of them as they are in themselves *independent of any action on us*—which he admits can only be attained by a perfect creative knower. He will allow no medium between the two extremes: either perfect knowledge with no mediation of action, or no knowledge of the real at all.

Furthermore, he has no explanation at all, and can in principle have none, of the miraculous fit between the structures we have imposed on the world, apparently independently of anything in the world, and the way the world responds to our practical action on it based on the predictions thought up by our minds—successfully coping with the challenges of nature, technology, etc. Nor can he explain—in fact he never tries—how we can know other human beings as just as real as ourselves and successfully exchange information with them in interpersonal dialogue. For if it is really I that am structuring your being and the messages you seem to be sending in to me through my senses, then it follows that you are also structuring me and my messages—which cancels out into incoherence: both can't be true at once. No, we are open to truth-grounding communication about themselves from the real active beings that surround us, across the bridge of their self-expressive, self-revealing action. That is what it means to have a mind open to being.

Relativism. Our human knowledge can never be universal and objectively true, but is always relative to, bound within, the a priori frameworks of culture and language of the particular culture out of which it arose, in its particular time in history; and these vary from society to society and from one period of history to another. Since there can be no culture- or history-transcending knowledge, neither can there be any metaphysical knowledge of real being with any claim to universally valid, objective truth.

Response. We cannot respond in detail here to all the various modes of relativism afloat in our world today. One general point is enough. We must indeed take into account the partially differing modes of thinking and self-expression of different cultures. Yet we can transcend our own culture enough to do that, as is shown by the fact that we can translate more or less accurately from one language to another, between all the major languages in the world.

And once any theory of knowledge makes the claim to effectively block any access to time- and place-transcending objective truth, it immediately turns back upon itself and self-destructs, like a snake devouring its own tail. For the only significance and relevance of such a theory, if it is not to be merely trivial or a game, is that it tells us what is actually the case, what is true, about *all* human claims to knowledge, in all places and times through history. If not, its message is really trivial: knowledge in Paris, or New York, in the 80s, is relative to their culture, but not in Chicago in the 90s. Yet the very attempt to make the stronger claim stick immediately contradicts the very theory it is affirming. Any attempt to block effectively our access to objective knowledge of the real automatically blows up in the face of the one making the claim and becomes either trivial or a game, which we can choose not to play.

Conclusion.   It seems that all those who deny the possibility of metaphysics are implicitly committed to some metaphysical positions: (1) To
deny metaphysics as the study of being they must start with a metaphysical stance in looking over the entire field of human knowing and
its relation to reality; in a sense they start off as fellow metaphysicians,
as Bradley, the English metaphysician, has acutely observed. (2) If they
refuse to do metaphysics, they must all take for granted their own existence, that of other human beings, and the whole horizon of experience which are their data—the given—to be explained. These basic
data must all be left *unexamined,* since they have banned even raising the
radical question: How come *there is* a universe to be studied at all? If you
can't escape presupposing a metaphysics of some kin, why not admit it,
and try to follow wherever it leads?

To sum up our discussion of objections against the possibility of a
valid human metaphysics of real being, it turns out that all of them rest
in the last analysis on some form of arbitrarily restrictive theory of
knowledge. It is interesting to note that in ancient and medieval philosophy it was metaphysics that dominated epistemology, whereas in
modern philosophy since Descartes it is epistemology that has dominated and controlled what metaphysics is allowed to say, if anything.
With all these arbitrary roadblocks out of the way, we are now free to
pursue with critical alertness the deeply challenging and deeply enriching enterprise of asking ultimate questions about the intelligibility
and meaning of the universe of real beings, which is our home. A
warning is in order, however: since the metaphysical quest will lead us
to confront some of the profoundest problems of the origin and
meaning of the universe, and therefore of the meaning of your life, a
basic moral attitude is required to pursue the quest authentically. It is
the self-discipline of fidelity to the call of truth, wherever it leads, and a
willingness to change my own life if necessary to be in harmony with
what I have discovered from the Book of Nature.

V. The Ultimate Root of All Metaphysical Inquiry:
The Drive to Know and the Intelligibility of Being

*1. Radical dynamism of the human spirit toward all being as true and
good.*   At the root of all intellectual inquiry, including the metaphysical
quest, is the radical dynamism of the human mind toward the fullness

of being as true, what Bernard Lonergan (the contemporary Jesuit philosopher-theologian) calls "the unrestricted drive of the mind to know being, that is, all that there is to know about all that there is." Its horizon of inquiry is nothing less than the totality of being, of what truly is. This radical dynamism, both longing and capacity, without which we would never be drawn to know anything, is inborn within us, defining our nature as human and not merely animal.

Complementary to the drive of the mind to know in the human spirit is the *drive of the will* toward the fullness of being as good, as to be appreciated, loved, enjoyed, as bringing us happiness. In a sense it is even deeper than the drive to know, for, as St. Thomas says, unless knowledge itself appeared to us as something good to possess, we would not be moved to desire and actively seek it. Truth itself is one of the ultimate goods. From the first moments of our human existence we are living out implicitly, though not yet consciously, these two basic drives. Philosophy, especially metaphysics, helps us to raise them into explicit, reflective consciousness and understand their role in our lives. Since our present concern is metaphysics, the search for the truth about being, we shall restrict our inquiry principally to the drive to know.

2. *How does one discover the presence of this dynamism?*   We do so by reflecting on our basic human experience of knowing and willing and its implications. When we first come to know—or love—some particular finite being, we are satisfied with it for a while, exploring it and savoring its goodness. But as soon as we reach its limits, discover its finitude, that it is not the fullness of being and goodness, our minds and wills immediately rebound beyond, seeking for some further being to know and enjoy. And the same process continues indefinitely as long as the object of our knowledge (being as knowable) and goodness (being as good, desirable) remain limited, incomplete, less than the totality of all truth and goodness. We keep rebounding spontaneously as soon as we hit the limits of partial truth or goodness. We can observe the same dynamism at work in our effort to understand any one particular being or event. As long as our inquiry leaves something incomplete, unexplained, presupposed, we tend spontaneously to push further until we get it all clear, out in the open, fully understood. This insatiable curiosity, this wanting to know all that there is to know, is a defining characteristic of human beings, as distinguished from all non-intelligent beings below them.

As I sit back now and reflect on this experience of repeated rebounding beyond every limited truth and goodness, I can sum it up and draw the conclusion: my mind is by its nature oriented toward the totality of being as knowable, as its final goal which alone can satisfy its drive to know. Similarly, my will is oriented towards the fullness of being as good, as the final goal that alone can satisfy my longing for happiness.

3. *The intelligibility of being.*   The unrestricted drive to know gives rise to metaphysics, i.e., the search for the ultimate intelligibility of all being. But if this drive to know on the part of the human knower is not matched by a correlative openness or aptitude of all being to be known, in a word, the *intelligibility of being* in itself, then the drive to know becomes a monstrous living absurdity, a cruel illusion, a deep natural longing that is part of our being, defines us as human, yet is in principle unfulfillable, a radical frustration built into the very nature of things.

But this radical scepticism neither makes good sense in itself nor is an acceptable reading of the common experience of humankind. If it were, then the scope of our knowledge would be drastically reduced to nothing but the immediate empirical observation of what is. Any attempt to *explain* what we observe in terms of not immediately observable causes or any other conditioning factors, on the grounds that otherwise the things or events observed would be unintelligible by themselves, would be ruled out ahead of time as futile. Thus, all problem-solving in the real order, even of the simplest practical problems, would be ruled out in principle, since the very search for a solution beyond what is immediately observable presupposes the implicit acceptance of the principle of the intelligibility of being. Nor can we avoid the difficulty if we say that just some areas of being are intelligible, for example, material, quantitatively measurable being, and not others. First of all, we have no way of knowing this ahead of time; we would have to know already the whole domain of being in order to know which parts are intelligible, which are not—obviously impossible, as we begin our exploration. Thus there is no way of knowing ahead of time whether the particular domain we are investigating right now might not be precisely one of the areas of being that is unintelligible! So too, all human attempts at problem-solving, whether in metaphysics or any domain whatever, presuppose in practice the implicit commitment to the principle of intelligibility of all being. For unless you take for granted, at least implicitly, that the problem in front of you waiting to be solved—always a problem in some way of the incomplete intelligibility of the data before you—is in principle soluble and therefore intelligible, there is no use in even starting to search for a solution.

But it would be impossible for any human being actually to live that way, without attempting to solve any problems. And it runs counter to the whole actual experience of our human race. The whole extraordinary history of human development in coping with nature, meeting and solving its challenges by the use of creative science, technology, etc., bears witness to the success of our common commitment to the intelligibility in principle of all of nature—including implicitly all of being. In a word, the real world of nature answers back our commitment to its intelligibility by saying equivalently, "Yes, I am open to being understood by mind; I do not give up my secrets easily to human intelligence, but if approached properly and with patience and cooperation I am open to being understood by mind on all the levels of my being. It may take a long time; but come and try. I'm ready and waiting."

It is true that our success at problem-solving has always been partial down through the ages. And it is true that it is impossible for us to *prove* ahead of time that all being is intelligible, as we start the philosophical or scientific quest, since no one of us can ever know being in its totality in this life. But if the parts of being have been shown to be intelligible one after the other down through time, why not the whole? All the positive evidence invites us in this direction, since there is no clear evidence shown to us in history of the contrary, that is, of anything which has been clearly shown to be definitively *unintelligible.* By this I mean not just a mystery, something not yet understood by us, but something that shows itself as positively contrary to intelligence, intrinsically absurd, in principle resisting all access to intelligibility of any kind.

Thus, in order to live our human lives effectively at all we are called to make a kind of *commitment in hope,* an act of *natural faith,* so to speak, in the radical intelligibility in principle of all real being, without arbitrary qualification or a priori limitation. As Einstein, the great physicist, once remarked, "All science of a high order presupposes a kind of act of faith in the intelligibility of nature. And the wonder of all wonders is that in fact nature has shown itself to be intelligible."

The first great conclusion of our metaphysical inquiry: mind and being are correlative to each other, made for each other, open by nature to each other, as the two great complementary poles of the universe. Can we surmise that perhaps the fundamental role or mission of mind in the

midst of being is to bring the whole of being into the light of consciousness, as far as we can, speak out its meaning—be the "spokesman of
being," as Heidegger put it—and refer it back with gratitude to the
hidden Source from which it came to us as gift? We cannot indeed
master this primordial correlation of mind with being by our own
limited minds, since we are not the author of it; but we can accept grate-
fully the already established situation we are born into as human beings
whose very nature is defined as endowed with the unrestricted drive to
know all being; and we can respond to the call to follow it out wherever
it leads. It is part of our dignity as humans to respond to this challenge—and opportunity. So we have to live humbly with the paradox
that, on the one hand, we cannot prove with any absolute certitude
ahead of time the principle of the intelligibility of being; but on the
other, we cannot carry on our human lives without committing ourselves to it in principle. For if we attempt to deny it explicitly in our
thoughts or words and still carry on our human living by solving problems which implicitly presuppose its validity, we find ourselves in what
philosophers call a "lived contradiction": what we deny in our words we
presuppose in our actual living. Though you cannot be forced *logically*
to accept the principle of the intelligibility of being, why not go along
with the pull of your nature and open your mind to the invitation of
being itself? There are no good reasons against it and many good ones
for it. As Jacques Maritain, the French Thomist, has put it beautifully,
"There is a nuptial relationship between mind and being."

VI. The Method of Metaphysics

Although it is hard to pin down one fixed method for all metaphysicians, especially for the creative discovery phase, it seems to me that
Thomistic metaphysics unfolds roughly along two lines of inquiry:

1. Descriptive. The discovery and description of the basic attributes common to all beings, the basic general kinds or categories of
being, and the basic data about the universe of our experience which
give rise to the central problems of metaphysics calling for a solution.

2. Explanatory. The search for the ultimate laws, constitutive principles, and explanatory causes of the beings of our experience when
they are shown to lack intelligibility in some way when taken by themselves alone. In a word, it is the passage from what we can observe in our

experience to what lies beyond our direct experience but is necessary to posit in order to save the intelligibility of the latter, lest it sink into the darkness of absurdity or unintelligibility. Most contemporary analytic philosophers are willing to allow the validity of the first phase, *descriptive metaphysics,* but not the second phase, *explanatory metaphysics,* because this lies beyond any empirical testing or confirmation either by science or phenomenology. An obvious example is an argument for the existence of God as ultimate cause needed to render intelligible the existence of our finite, changing world. This attitude is a hangover of the empiricist attitude of mind stemming from Hume and Kant, which still hangs on in many subtle ways in modern philosophy, an echo also of the excessive reverence for science as the only valid way of reaching truth.

VII. Two Great Guiding Principles of Metaphysical Inquiry

1. The Principle of Non-Contradiction: The Static Intelligibility of Being

This principle, often called simply the "principle of contradiction," lays down the basic law of intelligibility governing all being whatsoever and all discourse about anything whatsoever. Its classic formulation, coming down to us from Aristotle as probably its first explicit defender, is: "Nothing (i.e., no real being) can both be and not be at the same time and under the same aspect." The principle also holds for all meaningful language: "No proposition can be both asserted and denied at the same time and under the same aspect," under pain of becoming meaningless, although one can, of course, say the words.

If one denies this principle, all meaning, truth, and intelligibility would immediately be destroyed. In the order of thought and language, any assertion would immediately turn into its opposite and all meaningful communication would be rendered impossible. Any being could also be asserted as non-being, any *this* as *not-this,* and so on. Nothing would hold firm in language or even thought about being. In fact, it is impossible to think this position meaningfully even for a moment, without it immediately disappearing into its opposite. One would have to say or think nothing at all, become "like a vegetable," as Aristotle puts it. The positive expression of the principle, called the *Principle of Identity:* A is A, and not not-A, points to the self-stability of being as standing out

against nothingness as long as it is; in the order of thought and language, it points to the stability of meaning and truth that holds out
while being asserted, resisting collapse into its opposite.

It is clearly impossible to *prove* such a principle in terms of anything
else more fundamental, since all meaningful assertions already presuppose it or would collapse into their opposite. Hence it is an ultimate
primary principle of all use of intelligence or discourse, grasped immediately and intuitively by anyone who understands the terms.

Role of the principle in intellectual inquiry.   It is not the starting point
of any argument, in the sense that one can deduce anything else from
it. It is purely static, "A is A, A is not not-A." It serves rather (in its negative form) as a kind of watch-dog principle that comes into action
whenever someone violates it in a discussion and ends up with a self-
contradiction. The principle immediately flashes "red," so to speak, and
signals "Argument invalid; go back and check." Although one cannot
deduce anything new from it, it is an immediate refutation of any argument or discourse that ends up in a contradiction.

2. *Principle of Sufficient Reason: The Dynamic Intelligibility of Being*

Just as the Principle of Non-Contradiction is the static first principle of
all being and thought, so the Principle of Sufficient Reason is the
dynamic one, enabling the mind to pass from one being to another in
the search to make sense out of it, to preserve it from falling into unintelligibility. All advance in thought to infer the existence of some new
being from what we already know depends on this principle. The ancient and medieval thinkers, including St. Thomas, did not formulate
the principle in these explicit terms, but simply included it under the
general affirmation of the intelligibility of being (being as "true"), or
formulated it more precisely for particular kinds of inference, e.g.,
"Every being that begins to exist (or is finite, or participated, or
changing, etc.) requires a cause." But many modern Thomists welcome
the explicit formulation we have given above, as I do, because of its convenience as the most all-inclusive expression of the dynamic intelligibility of being as distinct from the static principle, and one that all
realist metaphysicians use constantly, whether they describe it this way
or not. Yet many still refuse, like Gilson, the great historian of Thomism,
for fear it will be confused with the rationalist interpretation of it by
Leibniz. This need not be.

The principle can be formulated thus: "Every being has the *suffi-cient reason* for its existence (i.e., the adequate ground or basis in exis-tence for its intelligibility) either in itself or in another." If the being contains this sufficient reason in itself, then it is a self-sufficient being. If not, then it must have its sufficient reason in some other real being, which is called its *cause,* on which the being in question depends as its *effect.* This narrowing of the principle to one of its alternatives yields the most general formulation of the *Principle of Causality:* "Any being that does not contain the sufficient reason for its own existence within itself requires a cause" (i.e., some other real being on which it de-pends, either in whole or in part, for its actual presence in existence as it is). Again, being and intelligibility are linked inseparably together. This is the fundamental grounding principle for all explanatory meta-physics, indeed for all explanation in any field, scientific or practical life (e.g., "Why did the lights go out?")

Note that this Principle of Sufficient Reason is not *reducible* to or *de-ducible* from the Principle of Non-Contradiction, though many have tried to do so—in vain, to my mind. For example, if one asserts, relying on the Principle of Sufficient Reason, "No being can come into exis-tence without a cause," it is not a contradiction to deny this; a contradic-tion would give you only "Being *is* non-being." But to assert that "Being cannot *come from* non-being" is a step beyond contradiction into the dynamic relationship of intelligibility between beings. To deny this would not land you into formal contradiction, but it would lead you into a situation of radical unintelligibility, not making sense. For if nothing at all is required for something new to come into existence, then any-thing at all can happen at any time with no explanation needed or able to be provided—and this is quite contrary to our whole experience. It takes effort to make things happen.

This principle cannot be deduced or proved from anything more basic before we actually use it successfully; and it can take time—together with some intellectual maturity and experience—to get in-sight into its validity. But once it lights up in our intelligence, its validity becomes inescapably cogent, under pain of falling into sterile absurdity. To deny it, or cast doubt on it seriously—and not just in words, which some philosophers irresponsibly do—is to cut the nerve of any human attempt to solve any problem, or explain any situation, where the solu-tion is not immediately evident from simple observation of the data presenting itself to us. It would be impossible to live rationally or even to sustain human life for long in the often puzzling and dangerous world we inhabit, where we have to understand it or be destroyed by it. And, in fact, the consistent success of the human race in applying it down the ages, with no case of a clearly shown violation of it, is a powerful reason in its favor, with no contrary good evidence or reason against it. The only *reasonable* human thing to do is to commit oneself to it in hope and follow it as far as it can take us, accepting it as a gift of our human nature, dropped without our planning it in the middle of this vast horizon of being that lies open before us, actively communicating itself to us and mutely inviting us to explore it as intelligible, as meaningful.

The principle must be used very cautiously and responsibly, however, to get reliable results. It does not mean that there are not or cannot be *mysteries,* things which I or even the human race as a whole on this earth cannot yet understand, whose sufficient reason we cannot yet crack. Nor can I impose any answer that appeals to me just in order to get rid of the mystery. It means only that being in itself is intrinsically intelligible, open to being intelligibly known in some way (perhaps only by mystical experience or revelation granted from above), i.e., guaranteed to be not radically unintelligible, definitively contrary to, excluding in principle all intelligibility.

To apply the principle properly we must follow this procedure. (1) First we must show clearly why a given being, or event, or set of data to be understood does *not* contain within itself the sufficient reason for its own existence as it is, but rather, if taken by itself alone, positively excludes any adequate sufficient reason of its own, is irremediably unintelligible by itself alone. Then, (2) we can proceed to affirm that it *must* have its sufficient reason in some other being or set of beings. Then, (3) we go about seeking for the appropriate identification of its explanatory cause(s). And we do so either by hypothesis and empirical testing (the scientific way) or by showing that all alternative solutions save one are either contradictory or unintelligible (the philosophical way, and in particular the metaphysical way). If the philosopher cannot show that all solutions but one are impossible, he must at least try to show that his solution is more fruitful and illuminating than any other and why the others are deficient.

Some metaphysicians claim it is never possible to exclude other metaphysical systems or visions of the whole, hence not possible to reach any metaphysical truth, only more or less high probability. Hence metaphysical systems belong more to the order of esthetics, of beauty, like works of art, than of genuine knowledge or explanation. There is a kernel of truth in this, just as there is in simplicity and beauty as indications in science of which is the most fruitful hypothesis, the one most likely to be valid. Still, I think, with St. Thomas and many others, that one can quite often achieve genuine metaphysical truths that exclude the opposite, though sometimes not. And there is one decisive difference between a work of art and a metaphysical explanation. Works of art do not compete with each other; one can never exclude another as the only possible work of beauty on a given subject—that does not make sense. But metaphysical systems do. They always try to show why in some way there is no other reasonable alternative solution to this problem or way of seeing the world, or at least that theirs is the most illuminating and fruitful one, whereas the other competitors are all significantly deficient in some way. In a word, metaphysical systems compete; works of art do not.

Without further discussion, let us proceed to carry out our metaphysical inquiry into the actual structure of the intelligibility and meaningfulness of being, beginning with the reality immediately accessible to us in our human experience of this world. The best way, after all, to show that a realist metaphysics is possible and worth doing is not to argue about it ahead of time and refute objections to it, but to go ahead and actually do it as competently as possible. Let's go! And let me suggest, metaphorically speaking, that you will need two pieces of equipment for the metaphysical journey: first, a diving suit—to enable you to plunge to the inner depths of being to uncover its most basic properties and structure; and secondly, a pair of wings—to enable you to soar above the multiplicity of beings and discern how they all fit together as a meaningful whole in the all-embracing community of being.

QUESTIONS FOR REVIEW AND DISCUSSION

1. What is the purpose of the philosophical enterprise as a whole, and of metaphysics within it?

2. What is its starting point? How does God fit in?

3. What is the difference between metaphysics and religion in their approach to reality? What two books has God given us to read about reality? Why do both need to be read?

4. Why must a human metaphysics always remain humble?

5. What is the point of the following objections against the possibility of doing metaphysics and the response to each?

(a) No distinct subject matter; (b) we as parts of the universe cannot grasp the whole; (c) empiricism; (d) Kant and Kantianism; (e) relativism.

6. What is the root within us of all metaphysical inquiry, the dynamo of our whole life of the mind? The evidence for it?

7. Why must this drive to know demand the complementary principle of the intelligibility of being? All being? Evidence? Can this be proved ahead of time?

8. What is the method of metaphysics? (a) Descriptive? (b) Explanatory?

9. Explain the two basic principles or laws on which all metaphysics is built? Can the second be reduced to the first?

CHAPTER TWO

The Discovery and Meaning of Being

Since metaphysics is the study of *being as such*, our first task is to unpack the meaning of this basic term "being," the most fundamental attribute of all real things, in terms of which metaphysics discovers its subject matter and defines its distinctive point of view.

I. Meaning of the Term

In its primary existential meaning, "being" is a noun derived from the verb "to be." Thus, *a being = that which is*, or exists, is real, as in the existential propositions: "This is"; "That is"; "There is a snake in the cellar"; or "This wine is good." St. Thomas distinguishes another secondary non-existential meaning of "is," wherein it functions merely as a *copula* to join together a subject and a predicate without committing itself to the reality of either: "X is Y." It is used chiefly in defining the meaning of terms, e.g., "A bachelor is (means) an unmarried man"; "A square is a closed geometric figure with four equal sides"; "A mermaid is a mythical figure that is half woman, half fish"; or "Hamlet is a character in Shakespeare's play, *Hamlet*." Since the object of metaphysics is real being, we shall be concerned here only with the primary existential meaning. The term "being" used without an article usually means either (1) all that is, or the totality of the real, or (2) precisely that in a thing which makes it to be a being, e.g., "the being of a thing." For clarity we focus on *a being*.

Note in the above definition, *that which is,* the two irreducible yet inseparable aspects: the *is* of actual existence and the *that which,* the subject which exists or has existence. This latter is called technically the *essence* or *what* of a thing. We shall see later the profound implications of this duality of essence/existence within a being, which opens out into two distinct questions that can be asked of anything: *Is* it? and *What* is it? Most Western philosophers tend to focus more in their philosophical systems on the *what* it is. St. Thomas probes deeper to focus on the *is* aspect as the ground of all else and the center of his whole system. That is why the interpretation of St. Thomas presented here is called "existential Thomism."

What does "is" mean?   It is so fundamental that it is impossible to define it by anything clearer, or by setting it off as a class within a wider class, as is done in ordinary definitions, for outside of it there is nothing. We all already know implicitly what it means, because we know how to use it meaningfully, though it is not always easy to spell it out explicitly further. Metaphysics tries to do this. One way is to call up paraphrases, for example: "exists," or—perhaps more evocative—"presents itself": a being is that which is actually *present* in some way, *presents itself* as standing out from the darkness of non-being into the light of being. (Somehow being and light, non-being and darkness seem to belong together.)

Reflective awareness of being.   In ordinary life the term and what it signifies are so all-pervasive that we become used to it, take it for granted, lose our explicit awareness and appreciation of its richness and wonder; we fall into what Heidegger calls "the forgetfulness of being." We get so wrapped up in *what* things are and *how* we can use them that we let drop out of consciousness the basic wonder, "the wonder of all wonders, that anything *is* at all." As the poet Shelley put it long before Heidegger, "The mist of familiarity obscures from us the wonder of our being." The metaphysician must recover this fresh explicit awareness of being itself, the be*ing* of beings, instead of being absorbed in *what* they are, as being "thises" and "thats." This explicit reflective insight into being as such is what makes the Thomistic metaphysician. How does he come to it?

II. The Discovery of Being

Two main paths toward evoking the explicit awareness of the "is" of being are: (1) Exploring *downward* into any individual being to uncover the most basic level of its *act of existence* by which it is present in the real world, by which it *is*. This is the most fundamental of all attributes, which all others presuppose and build upon. All other attributes talk *about* the subject as already given. The *is* posits it radically as *present* to be talked about at all, posits the whole subject with all its attributes at once, to be unfolded bit by bit in subsequent knowledge. Its actual existence is the deepest level in any being.

(2) Expanding *outward,* following the drive of my mind to know all that there is, I notice that this most basic attribute in each being is also that which it has in common with all other beings, the ultimate bond of community of all real beings, forming the universe of reality, the community of existents, present to each other. Once I have reached this all-embracing horizon of being as the totality of the real, outside of which there is only the absolute darkness and emptiness of non-being, I can think of it as a whole, as a *universe,* the ultimate community of all existents, and ask ultimate questions about it, "How come the universe exists at all?", "What is its ultimate source and meaning, the meaning of my life in it?", etc. We are now deep into metaphysics, the only philosophical discipline that can ask such questions. This ultimate horizon of inquiry can only be expressed by some all-embracing term like "being," "the real," "reality," or the like.

But *note* that all metaphysical systems do not have such an explicit term. Some have an implicit equivalent, like "all." But for some philosophers, who are certainly thinking like metaphysicians, such as Plato, Plotinus, the "negative theology" philosophers (God is beyond being), and especially many oriental philosophies (the Ultimate is Non-being or the Void), the "Ultimate Reality" lies beyond the whole domain of being in mystery, which can only be pointed to in silence or spoken of indirectly through metaphors, not grasped by our limited human concepts. One reason for this is that for all of them "being" means limited *essence* or *form,* and so—quite rightly—the Ultimate escapes such limits. St. Thomas escapes this dilemma, since for him the fundamental component of being is the act of existence itself, which lies beyond all limiting essences and forms, pervading them all but irreducible to any one of them. Hence he can speak of God as pure Subsisting Act of Existence that *is,* but is beyond all limiting essences or forms, all *whats.*

Personal awakening to the wonder of being.   To be a good metaphysician, at least in the Thomistic tradition, one must move beyond the merely abstract understanding of the meaning of being toward an existential "awakening" to experience what actual existence means in the concrete for the whole person—mind, heart, imagination, feeling, all together. In the light of this intuitive experience one can then take reflective possession of its meaning, generalize it to the whole realm of actual existents, and develop it into the fully explicit metaphysical understanding of being as *that which is*. Various personal experiences have been found apt for leading us to such an existential awakening to what it means to be. (This is an an exercise in Descriptive Metaphysics; see ch. 1.) Examples are:

1. The threat of loss of one's own existence or that of a loved one: realization of existence through contrast with its absence.
2. An intense love experience: the wonder and delight that so and so is truly real.
3. Experience of an intense hope, longing, at last realized: "At last it's real, not just a dream."
4. The contemplative wonder of a child, a poet, an artist, or a scientist at the beauty and order of the universe, and, even deeper, at its presence at all. Einstein often expressed this.
5. A profound religious experience of gratitude for creation as gift (Jews, Christians, Moslems in the revelation of creation tradition, and, mysteriously, Buddhists).
6. The experience of radical boredom, despair, existential anxiety, total loss of meaning or significance of the universe as a whole and of my life in it: this puts existence itself in question by awareness of our radical contingency, precariousness, as poised over nothingness, "surrounded" by nothingness, e.g., Heidegger, for whom the awareness of being is inseparable from the awareness of nothingness, *Das Nichts*.

Cf. Gabriel Marcel, *The Mystery of Being* (Chicago: Gateway, 1960), vol. I, ch. 10; II, ch. 3; Diogenes Allen, "Two Experiences of Existence: Jean Paul Sartre and Iris Murdoch," *Internat. Phil. Quart.* 14 (1974), 181–87; Frederick Sontag, *Existentialist Prolegomena to a Future Metaphysics* (Chicago: Univ. of Chicago Press, 1969); Stanford Pritchard, "Metaphysics and the Metaphysical Experience," *Internat. Phil. Quart.* 6 (1966), 214–29; Sidney Hook, *The Quest for Being* (New York: Dell, 1963): defends a modern anti-metaphysical stance: "being" is an empty term.

III. Intellect and Being as Correlative

In thus searching for the meaning of being, the metaphysician becomes aware that being is the ultimate objective correlative of the drive of the mind to know, co-extensive with its scope, that which defines it as intellect. Intellect is radically *for* being, oriented toward it by a natural, innate affinity, aptitude, or "connaturality" for being.

The necessary corollary of this—the other side of the correlation—is that being itself is *for* intelligence. Its ultimate meaning and fulfillment require that it be brought into the light of consciousness, that it be *unveiled* i.e., revealed (= remove the veil: *revelatum*) to mind. This unveiling of being to mind is *truth*, expressed beautifully by the Greek word for truth (*aletheia* = the unveiled). Thus, the fundamental intellectual vocation of every mind-endowed being, and hence of human beings as the only intellectual beings we know of in our material cosmos, is to *unveil* being, bring it into the light of consciousness and speak it out in a *logos,* or meaningful word. As Heidegger has put it, "Man is the spokesman of Being," planted in the midst of it *(Dasein)* to listen to it with reverence and speak out its name and meaning truthfully. Thus, a human being can be defined as the being called to raise the question about being and accept his responsibility for listening to it with reverence and speaking out its meaning in a recreative human *logos.*

Being as inexhaustible mystery: The veiled-unveiled. By the term "being" the human mind expresses all that there is, but indistinctly, indeterminately. And we can never know any real being exhaustively, at least in this life. Hence being for us is always half light, half shadow or mystery, the known-unknown. And our whole intellectual vocation is to draw being gradually, by individual and communal effort, from preconscious obscurity into fuller and fuller light, into *logos.* This task can be completed only—if at all—by being lifted up to share the total vision of the ultimate Source of all being—God, which Christians believe is the ultimate destiny of all humans.

IV. Primary Division of Being: Real and Mental

"Being" means that which is, or is present, in some way. But as soon as we press it hard for clarity and apply it to all the things we know, in the mind and outside of it, it breaks up into two basic irreducible orders: *real* and *mental* being. They are defined by contrast with each other:

Real Being = that which is present by its own intrinsic act of existence outside of an idea, i.e., is present not just as being thought about, but on its own, so to speak. It is what exists, in the strong sense of the term, and is the ordinary meaning of being unless otherwise specified. It has two main modes: (1) a *complete* being, or substance, which can be said simply to be as a whole entity subsisting in itself and not as a part of any other being; and (2) any *part* or attribute of a real being which cannot be said to be in itself, on its own, but only to be in another, e.g., "He is a *kind* man."

Mental Being = that which is present *not* by its own act of existence but only within an idea, i.e., as being-thought-about. "Its being," St. Thomas says, "is its to-be-thought-about" by a real mind. *Main Divisions:* (1) *past and future* as such, which were and will be, but are not; (2) content of *dreams;* (3) *abstractions,* which are drawn from the real but as abstract exist only in the mind, e.g., man, life, etc. (4) *mental constructs,* which can never exist outside the mind but help us to think about the real: mathematical entities (numbers, circles, squares, etc.), logical relations, negations (blindness, nothingness) (which are really only convenient summaries of longer "not-propositions"), hypotheses for testing, plans for action, etc.

Priority of real being.   Since mental being cannot be present save by being thought about by a real mind and can only be understood by reference to the mind thinking it, it is radically *secondary, dependent, parasitic on real being,* which is primary. Real beings (real minds) can generate ideas; ideas of themselves cannot generate real beings. All mental beings are in some way derived from and refer back to the order of real being. They are present in real minds, but they are not themselves the "really real," as Plato thought they had to be in order to ground eternal truths and values. (Later Platonists in his Academy, however, realized fairly quickly that they could not leave ideas just floating independently by themselves, and located them in a divine Mind eternally thinking them.)

Note.   The recognition of this distinction between real and mental being is the first crucial step in the *ordering of our experience* to render it intelligible. To be able to tell the difference between the two is the fundamental mark of sanity, just as to confuse them is the mark of insanity, e.g., to confuse hallucinations with reality, possibilities with actualities.

Ideals are important, indeed essential, to guide our lives as goals-*to-be-realized,* to be *made real,* but are not themselves the realization of these goals. Otherwise, daydreaming would be enough to make our fondest dreams come true.

Criterion of real being vs. mental being. We all in fact—if we are sane—do distinguish fairly easily most of the time between real and mental beings in our ordinary lives. But just *how* do we do this? What *criterion* do we use, at least implicitly? This is not that easy to articulate. But every metaphysician must come to grips with this question. It is crucial for determining how the rest of his system will develop. It seems to me, following St. Thomas—and the whole metaphysical system laid out in this book is built around it—that the only adequate criterion for discerning the presence of real being, one that is both necessary and sufficient and that we all use in practice, whether we recognize it or not, is that of *action.* What is real is what can act on its own, express itself in action, is the center and source of its own characteristic action. I know *myself as real* because I am aware of myself as acting—thinking, deliberating, desiring). I know *other beings as real* because I am aware of their acting on me, actively responding to me, invading me and determining me in ways I cannot control just by thinking about it but must submit to and cope with. Real beings *make a difference* in the real world. Ideas, images, etc., on the other hand, cannot act on their own; I control them by thinking about them, rejecting them, changing them as I will. The child thus quickly learns to distinguish between its images, dreams and real things.

Real beings, in their actions on me and mine on them, have real consequences which I have to cope with or get hurt; ideas do not, unless I act on them.

V. Being as Self-Revealing through Action:
Every Being Is Active

This is an important step forward in our understanding of what it means to be real, and one of the essential keys to the whole thought of St. Thomas, yet one that is not always clearly recognized or appreciated by other metaphysicians. It is through action, and only through *action,* that real beings manifest or "unveil" their being, their presence, to each other and to me. All the beings that make up the world of my experience thus reveal themselves as not just present, standing out of nothingness, but *actively presenting* themselves to others and vice versa by interacting with each other. Meditating on this leads us to the metaphysical conclusion that it is the very nature of real being, existential being, to pour over into action that is *self-revealing* and *self-communicative.* In a word, existential being is intrinsically *dynamic,* not static.

I reach this insight in two steps: (1) By *observation* I notice that this is going on at all the levels of the beings of the world open to my experience: on the inorganic level all the elements are giving off bursts of energy, influencing each other, combining with each other, etc.; on the plant and animal level all living things interact with each other and reproduce themselves to add new members to the community of existents—life is by nature expansive; on the human level it is natural, a built-in drive within us, to interact and share with each other by communication, working with each other, and at the highest level by affectionate, caring love, which is then productive of new members of the community of existents.

2) By *metaphysical reflection* I come to realize that this is not just a brute fact but an intrinsic property belonging to the very nature of every real being as such, if it is to count at all in the community of existents. For let us suppose (a metaphysical thought experiment) that there were a real existing being that had no action at all. First of all, no other being could know it (unless it had created it), since it is only by some action that it could manifest or reveal its presence and nature; secondly, it would make no difference whatever to any other being, since it is totally unmanifested, locked in its own being and could not even react to anything done to it. And if it had no action within itself, it would not make a difference even to itself. It would thus be *indistinguishable from nothingness.* In a word, it might just as well not be. If all beings were such, there could not be a *universe* at all ("universe" comes from the Latin *universum* = turned toward unity). To have a universe, a community of real existents, its members would have to communicate with each other, be linked together somehow and all communication requires some kind of action. A non-acting, non-communicating being is for all practical purposes (in the order of intelligibility, value, action, or making any difference at all) *equivalent* to no being at all. To be *real* is to *make a difference.*

Note that we are not saying that "real being" is logically identical in meaning with "action," but only that action flows over naturally from real being precisely as existent, is an intrinsic *property* of every real being. As the common medieval adage expressed it, *agere sequitur esse*. As St. Thomas expresses it with technical precision: existence is the *first act* of a real being, action its *second act*, flowing immediately from the first. Aristotle himself saw this long ago when he defined a real nature as "an abiding center of acting and being acted on."

Objection. Could there not be at least one being that could be totally self-sufficient in being and perfection that could exist without communicating with anything other than itself?

Response. Yes, there could be one, and only one such totally self-sufficient perfect being, which would be free to create or not create anything else (= God). But in fact this being has poured over in action to create this universe in which we live. If it hadn't, we would not be here to ask the question. And if we were here without the action of this being it would be totally inaccessible and irrelevant to us anyway. The presence of such totally static, inert, isolated beings in the real order, that made no difference to anything, would be totally pointless, and certainly could not be the work of a wise creative God. And so we live in a universe where all the real beings that count, that make a difference, are dynamically active ones, that pour over through self-manifesting, self-communicating action to connect up with other real beings, and form a community of interacting existents we call a "universe."

Note that this expansive dynamism of the act of existence implies a certain ontological "generosity," as Jacques Maritain does not hesitate to call it, within every real being. For the real beings of our universe go out of themselves in action for two reasons: one, because they are *poor*, in that as limited and imperfect they are seeking completion of themselves from other beings; two, because they are *rich*, in that they actually exist and so possess some degree of actual perfection and have an intrinsic tendency to share this in some way with others. Why this should, in fact, be so is, or should indeed be, a source of wonder for the metaphysician. Without it, of course, there would be no universe. But it seems the ultimate reason is that it is the very nature of God himself to be self-communicative love, and since all other real beings are in some way images, participations of the divine goodness, they all bear the mark within them, according to the nature of each, of this divine attribute.

Marvelous to contemplate, it seems that we must say that *to be is to be generous,* in some way! The depths of being as actually existing, as St. Thomas sees them, are indeed full of wonder. Let us look at a few texts in which he expresses this.

1. From the very fact that something exists in act, it is active. *Summa contra Gentes,* Bk. I, ch. 43.

2. Active power follows upon being in act, for anything acts in consequence of being in act. Ibid., II, ch. 7.

3. It is the nature of every actuality to communicate itself insofar as it is possible. *De Potentia,* q. 2, a. 1.

4. It follows upon the superabundance proper to perfection as such that the perfection which something has it can communicate to another. *Sum. c. Gent.,* III, ch. 69. Communication follows upon the very meaning (*ratio*) of actuality. *In I Sent.,* d. 4, q. 4, a. 4.

5. Each and every thing abounds in the power of acting just insofar as it exists in act. *De Pot.,* q. 2, art. 2.

6. Each and every thing shows forth that it exists for the sake of its operation; indeed, operation is the ultimate perfection of each thing. *Sum. c. Gen.,* III, ch. 113.

Conclusion on the Meaning of Being

"Being" in its strong primary sense as real being means *that which is,* i.e., actually exists in the real order, is *present* as standing out of nothingness with its own act of existence outside of an idea. It *actively presents itself to* other real beings by its characteristic self-manifesting, self-communicating action on them, and in return receives their action on it, thus becoming a member in the interconnected community of real existents we call the *universe.*

Cf. Norris Clarke, S.J., *Person and Being* (Milwaukee: Marquette Univ. Press, 1993), ch. I: Being as Dynamic Act.

VI. ACTION AS THE KEY TO OUR KNOWLEDGE OF REAL BEINGS

Just as action is the link that joins together real beings to form an interconnected universe, so it is the link that connects up our minds and whole cognitive apparatus with the world of real beings outside of us.

Since we did not make things ourselves, all knowledge of the real for us must pass across the bridge of action as the primary *self-manifestation* of real being. I know the *existence* of real beings by the fact that they act: *myself* by my own actions, within myself and on the other world; *other real beings* by their action on me, and on each other as observed by me. I know the *nature* or essence of other real beings as *this kind of actor* on me and on others, *that kind of actor,* etc. Thus I do not know the hidden natures of things as they are in themselves apart from their action on me, as Kant insisted on as the only authentic knowledge of real things, and so unattainable. But I do know them as they really do manifest their existence and their natures by their real action on me. Action is precisely the self-revelation of being. Action that is indeterminate, that reveals nothing about the nature from which it proceeds, is not action at all. Hence, all action is necessarily essence-structured action.

This knowledge of being through action is a genuine realism, but a modest, never complete one that can best be called a *relational realism.* What it delivers is how the real world is related to us and we to it. But these relations are quite real, what really *is the case,* verifying the requirement for *truth* = the conformity of mind to reality. And after all, isn't what we really want to know most about things not their inner natures as hidden in themselves, but how we can count on them to act habitually toward us and other beings, what difference they make to us? Our knowledge both of ourselves and of other real beings is thus a knowledge of beings as *agents.*

This knowledge for us human beings, though realistic, conformed to the world as a network of interacting centers, is none the less always necessarily *incomplete,* imperfect, partially perspectival, developing, at least in this life, and for two reasons: (1) No action of any finite being, especially a material being, can fully express its nature in a *single act,* but must reveal it progressively through many actions, and never totally or exhaustively to us. (2) Our own cognitive receiving set, in particular, our five external sense channels, has its own *built-in limits,* or range of receptivity, beyond which it cannot pick up what is perhaps there, but not accessible to us, not revelatory to us, e.g., the spectrum of light waves and sound waves that we cannot pick up with our eyes and ears. We humans, therefore, must resign ourselves to a mode of knowledge that is genuinely expressive of the real, of what is, but is humble, incomplete, beginning perspectivally from a given point in space and time, and always developing. Despite all these limitations on the completeness of our knowledge, there is still an immense amount that we do know about reality, together with its implications for intelligibility and can know further in a constantly expanding penetration into the inexhaustible fullness of being.

VII. The Person as the Best Model for Understanding Being

The object of metaphysics is the understanding of what it means to be for all beings. Still, the method and the results will differ somewhat according to what method of approach and primary model of being one takes to guide one's inquiry. Ancient philosophers tended to look on the world from an impersonal, *objective* viewpoint, as a kind of spectacle spread out before them, outside of them, so to speak, for them to study. Aristotle's own preferred point of reference tended to be, not the inorganic world of what we would call physics, but the living world of biological organisms tending toward their fulfillment, though with Plato and Aristotle *human nature*—what is common to all humans, not the uniqueness of the individual person—became more and more the center of focus. In medieval philosophy the centrality of the person came more and more to the fore, especially through the detailed study of human morality, the virtues, etc. But the medieval approach still tended to focus more on what is common to all human beings, rather than on the uniqueness of the individual person, the "I."

In modern philosophy, with Descartes, the focus of attention shifts dramatically toward the *subject* and the subjective side of being, as seen and experienced from within, not just as an object in front of us to be captured by abstract universal concepts. In fact, the whole history of philosophy, including metaphysics, in the West can be seen as the slow emergence of the subject over the object as the center of focus and intelligibility. Finally, the priority shifted so much toward the subject that the objective aspect of being and the world outside of the human subject turned into predominantly the product of our own human thought—with Kant and the German idealists, Fichte, Hegel, etc., and various contemporary forms of anti-realism and relativism. The drift in the wider culture toward the radical self-centeredness of the autonomous individual—in the individualist liberal tradition of John Locke, etc. that we see all around us today in various unhealthy forms—echoes the same drift in metaphysics. (Is it the philosophy that leads the culture, or the culture the philosophy, or is the influence reciprocal??)

This modern highlighting of the subject, the autonomous, self-conscious "I," has resulted in rich phenomenological descriptions in contemporary philosophy of the inner life of the person as experienced and lived from within, which the medievals left undeveloped or took for granted (though Augustine did give an early model of how to do it). But the balance has swung too far toward the subjective as opposed to the objective to allow a properly balanced comprehensive metaphysical vision of reality as an intelligible whole. To take the person as the center of reference and fullest model of what it means to be is the best corrective for this, it seems to me. However, it is not just the subjective individualist dimension of the person but also its objective dimension as part of the wider human community, not just an "I" but an "I" also embedded in a "We," and beyond that in the wider community of our whole earth as an environmental whole, and still further in the all-embracing community of all real beings. The subjective and objective dimensions of being should come together in a harmonious balanced whole in the human person, a being with both an *inside* (not fully objectifiable in universal concepts) and an *outside* (more amenable to such analysis). Hence it seems wisest to try and understand the fundamental metaphysical concepts and attributes of being as first experienced from within by ourselves then applied by analogy to other beings both below and above us.

Cf. Peter Bertocci, "The Person as Key Metaphysical Principle," *Phil. and Phenomenological Research* 17 (1956), 207–25; Joseph de Finance, S.J., "Being and Subjectivity," *Cross Currents* 6 (1956), 163–78; Norris Clarke, S.J., "Self as Source of Meaning in Metaphysics," *Rev. of Metaphysics* 21 (1967–68), 597–614; Johannes Lotz, S.J., "Person and Ontology," *Phil. Today* 7 (1963), 279–97.

VIII. The Most Fruitful Starting Point for Contemporary Thomistic Metaphysics: The "We Are" of Interpersonal Dialogue

Problem.   Our above unfolding of the meaning of being as active presence presupposes that our human minds are actually able to get in contact with real being, to know it positively and faithfully in both its existence and its nature, even though incompletely, as seen from our

limited human perspective. Ancient and medieval philosophers, for the
most part, took this for granted as evidently given by our success in
dealing with the real world, and, for medieval thinkers—Christian,
Jewish, and Moslem—as belonging to the very nature of human intelligence as a gift from God, who has created the world through wisdom
and made it intelligible through and through. Creation by a wise and
loving God both of nature and of our own minds guarantees both the
intelligibility of the universe and the basic ability of our minds to know
it. See the fine chapter in Josef Pieper, "The Negative Element in the
Philosophy of St. Thomas Aquinas: Creation as the Hidden Key," ch. 2
of *The Silence of St. Thomas* (Chicago: Regnery, 1965).

In modern philosophy, beginning with Descartes, however, the
strong separation (not just distinction) between faith and reason and
the scepticism about sense knowledge, influenced by the new mathematical physics, brought about an epistemological crisis of uncertainty
and doubt about the power of the human mind to know reality as it
is—the famous "problem of the gap" between mind and being and how
to bridge it, if possible at all. After centuries of alternation between the
extremes of overconfident *rationalism* (Descartes, Leibniz, Spinoza)
and reductionist *empiricism,* trusting only sense knowledge (Hume), the
dominant synthesis became that of the *agnostic rationalism* of Immanuel
Kant (d. 1804). According to him, it is impossible for the *human* mind
to know the real world as it is in itself: the world does not inform us,
mold our minds to conform to it. Rather, we positively impose our own
a priori unifying forms of both sense and intellect on the raw, in itself
unintelligible manifold of sense experience that flows into us from the
outside world and is all we can know of the real, since we cannot reach
beyond what appears in our own minds (*phenomena*) to reach things-in-
themselves (*noumena,* the real world). Hence we do not know the world
of reality as it really *is;* we "know" it only as our human minds cannot
help but structure it in terms of the built-in a priori structures of our
own minds, mysteriously common and unchanging among all human
beings—though there was no way Kant could really prove this without
knowing real minds as they are!

Despite later *Neo-Kantian* modifications of the original position of
Kant himself (the built-in a priori forms common to all human minds
now turn into a priori linguistic and cultural forms that evolve through
time and differ from culture to culture = various forms of historical
relativism), some form of Kantian scepticism as to the ability of the

mind to know the real still lingers on in most modern thinking, with its tendency to imprison the human mind in its own subjective thinking. "We are world-makers through language," as many contemporary philosophers put it today.

This atmosphere tends to be hostile or sceptical with respect to any attempt to do a genuine metaphysics or philosophy of real being, such as realist metaphysicians like St. Thomas and Thomists like myself claim to be doing. But this, to my mind, is a sterile cop-out, and cannot for long satisfy the innate, unrestricted drive of the human mind to know all being—all that there is to know about all that there is. As the great modern Thomist, Jacques Maritain, has put it beautifully, "There is a nuptial relationship between mind and reality" that longs to be consummated.

Solution.   What is needed, to reassure the self-doubting contemporary mind of the natural affinity of the mind for the real and of the possibility of a metaphysics of real being, is a starting point of metaphysics that involves a direct existential encounter with the real so luminous or self-revealing that it is not open to practical (I do not say logical) personal doubt or uncertainty. It must also be one that reveals at the same time that we actually know both the existence and, to a significant degree, the essence (or nature) of some real being other than ourselves. The most fruitful (though I do not claim the only effective) such starting point seems to me the privileged case of the "We are" manifested in *human interpersonal dialogue*. The peculiar power of this experience—in contrast to the "I think, therefore I am" of the solitary Cartesian thinker, isolated from the rest of the world and faced with the problem of how to connect up with it—is that it plunges us immediately into a world of active reality shared by others just as real as myself, with whom I can actively communicate, and whose natures are revealed in the same experience.

Unfolding the experience.   When I engage in a sincere dialogue face to face with another person, using a common language that neither of us has made up, and succeed in communicating intelligibly with my dialogue partner—sending, receiving, responding to messages we both understand, though received from outside us through our senses and not under our conrol—the following implications emerge clearly:

1. I am in the presence of *another real being* just as real as myself, but *distinct* from me. It does not make sense to believe that I am projecting or constituting the reality of the other and its message; for if that were

the case, then it would be equally true of the other partner, and each would be making up the reality and message of the other—which is absurd!

2. We exist in a *common field of existence* enveloping but transcending us both: reality is both one and many.

3. By the very fact that we successfully communicate and are conscious of it, I know a great deal about the basic *nature* (= kind of being) of each one of us: we are intelligently communicating (thinking, talking) beings, using bodies for communication, i.e., *embodied minds*, thus different from all the other non-communicating beings coming into my consciousness. Kant and all others like him presuppose all the above in their actual living, but have no grounds in their philosophy for explaining *how* it is possible to know this, nor do they even try.

To know all this with evidence that cannot be practically doubted without falling into a "lived contradiction," i.e., denying in theory and words what one is in fact living out successfully, is to know that my mind has the real capacity to know—incompletely though it may be—both the existence and nature of beings in the real world in interaction with me. All the rest of our knowledge opens out from this starting point. This is enough to launch a realistic metaphysics of being and follow where it leads. One advantage of this approach is that it plunges us immediately into real being as a *community* of distinct but intercommunicating centers giving and receiving from each other across the bridge of self-expressive action. In a word, it reveals to us that *to be is to be together, actively present* to each other. All real beings are doing this all the time. But it lights up with special clarity in the case of a fully conscious dialogue between two free persons.

Cf. Norris Clarke, "The 'We Are' of Interpersonal Dialogue as the Starting Point of Metaphysics," *Modern Schoolman* 59 (1992), 357–68; reprinted in *Explorations in Metaphysics* (Univ. of Notre Dame Press, 1994), ch. 2.

QUESTIONS FOR REVIEW AND DISCUSSION

1. What is the meaning of "a being"? What are its two distinct but inseparable elements?

2. How can we reach explicit reflective awareness of the "is" in being? Do all metaphysical systems agree on this focus on actual existence as the central core of all real beings?

3. What is meant by the "vocation of human beings" as endowed with intellect arising from the relation of intellect to being? In what sense can being still remain a "mystery" for us?

4. Explain the difference between "real being" and "mental being"? Examples of each? What is the key criterion for our distinguishing between the two?

5. Explain the fundamental importance of action as the self-manifestation of being if we are to have a "universe"? Could there be at least one completely inactive being?

6. Finite (all limited, created) real beings go out of themselves to relate themselves to others through action for two reasons: what are they? Does it make sense to speak, as Maritain does, of "the intrinsic generosity of being"?

7. In the philosophical vision of St. Thomas, action is the key to a realist epistemology, or theory of knowledge. Why? Why can it then be called a "relational realism"? Why does it also follow from this vantage point that all our human knowledge of real beings (at least in this life) must be incomplete, imperfect?

8. Why in this book do we take the person as the best model for what it means to be a real being? Compare briefly the ancient, medieval, and modern approaches to the philosophical study of being.

9. What is the point of choosing interpersonal dialogue as the preferred starting point for a metaphysical study of being? Why it is especially effective in refuting Kant's attempt to block access to any realist theory of knowledge or metaphysics?

CHAPTER THREE

Special Characteristics of Our Idea of Being as Transcendental and Analogous

Before we proceed in our search for the universal laws and principles governing all beings, we must pause for a moment to take stock of our "tools." Because of the universal reach of this inquiry across all kinds and levels of reality, we have to make use of special conceptual "tools," i.e., metaphysical concepts that are flexible enough to stretch widely and still retain their meaning. The purpose of this chapter is to examine the special properties of these metaphysical tools that enable them to fulfill their role, which is significantly different from that of the more precise concepts used in other sciences and in ordinary life—though in fact ordinary language makes use of both. If the nature of these conceptual tools is not clearly understood, serious misunderstandings can arise in the process of doing metaphysics, to which the history of philosophy testifies abundantly. The two most significant properties of the idea of being and other metaphysical concepts are designated as transcendental and analogous. A small number of very broad metaphysical terms like being are transcendental; all are analogous.

I. TRANSCENDENTAL

As applied to the idea of being, this means that the latter concept must be *all-inclusive*, both in its *comprehension* (i.e., the content included in its meaning) and in its *extension* (the range of subjects to which it can be applied). Thus being signifies all that is, in everything that is, i.e., everything that is real in any way. Outside of this lies only "nothing" or nothingness, non-being. For this reason, the concept of being is called "transcendental" (from the Latin *transcendere* = to climb over), that is, transcending or leaping over all divisions, categories, and distinctions between and within beings, pervading them all. It excludes only non-being. This is its purpose as a concept, to be the *ultimate all-inclusive term,* to express the ultimate horizon of reality itself and everything within it. It is through such an idea that we are able to embrace intellectually and express to ourselves the whole of reality. It took a long time for most cultures to develop an explicit term to express such a vast perspective, and some, perhaps less metaphysically inclined, seem still to be lacking it (there is a big dispute, in fact, as to whether the Chinese language contains an explicit term to express this).

As a result of this all-inclusive content, the idea of *being* is paradoxically both the *poorest* and the *richest* of all ideas: the poorest and emptiest in its explicit content, since it mentions nothing particular or determinate about anything, save its sheer presence; yet it is also the richest in implicit content, since it signifies implicitly and indeterminately all that there is, omitting nothing from the tiniest particle of matter to the infinite fullness of God.

How Is This Concept Formed?   As a result of its unique all-inclusive character, it cannot be formed by the ordinary process of concept-formation by *abstraction* through which other more limited concepts are formed. That process proceeds by abstracting (selecting) some aspect or aspects of a being and omitting the rest. Thus *human being* selects out only human nature in general and omits sex differences, color, age, race, etc. But the notion of *being* cannot leave anything out, for the aspect it focuses on, being itself, includes everything real in the thing, not only what it has in common with other beings, but also all its distinctive differences, since all are real. Hence it is formed by a special process of "abstraction," which modern Thomists, following the lead of St. Thomas in one key text, prefer to call a *judgment of separation,* since it requires a series of judgments of existence as its basis: First, "This is,"

"That is," etc. Then, the "is" is separated out from all its particular modes or subjects as not restricted to any but transcending all. Then, the verbal form "is" is condensed into a noun, *that which is,* which highlights *explicitly* the *is* and mentions that it is always connected with some *what* or *that which,* but leaves the latter indeterminate, unspecified. Thus, "a being" for St. Thomas means *that which is:* the *that which* signifying the essence or mode of being, the *is* signifying the act of existence or presence in the real order (the *esse* or *to be* of beings, as Aquinas prefers to put it). The idea of *being* is thus unique in being the only concept that explicitly contains the verb *is* as part of its meaning. For most other Western philosophers, *being* signifies only the *thing* or *something that can exist* but may not yet be actually existing—thus for Plato *being* is the eternal intelligible idea or essence; for Aristotle it is the individual essence or substance, presumed to be existing, but not specified as such, etc.

Hence for St. Thomas the judgment of existence, and the noun *being* condensed out of it, are the most basic and primary modes of knowledge we have for speaking about the real; all other concepts and judgments presuppose them and build upon them, for if these are absent, there is nothing there to talk about. (Note the difference from *mental beings,* which have no real being of their own but are concepts constructed by us, whose only "being" or presence is their being-thought-about by us, or by some real intelligence.)

II. ANALOGOUS

It follows necessarily from the above property of *all-inclusiveness* that the idea of *being* must also be what is called an *analogous* as opposed to a *univocal* concept, i.e., it must be a flexible or "stretch" concept, not limited in its application to one rigidly fixed and narrowly predetermined meaning, restricted to one or a few kinds of being only. Since not only the concept of *being* but all the basic concepts we use in metaphysics have to be thus flexible to extend across the whole spectrum of being, it is crucial that metaphysicians understand what is meant by the *analogy* of ideas and verbal terms. Ignorance or confusion on this point has often led to disastrous conclusions later on in metaphysics, such as the danger of anthropomorphism in speaking about God in terms that apply properly only to humans. The use of analogy is also indispensable in dealing with any field that tries to bring together and compare different kinds of being that share common properties, including especially poetry and other imaginative literature. Although many different disciplines make use of analogy, it is left to metaphysics to do a general study of what analogy means, why it is needed, and how it works.

Classification of Terms According to Flexibility of Meaning

A. *Univocal* = when the same term is applied to several different subjects or instances according to *exactly the same meaning* in each case: e.g., concepts of specific, well-determined kinds of things, such as man, woman, elephant, hydrogen atom, tree, automobile, computer, etc. It is designed to be a precise and hence rigid concept, with clearly determined limits. It answers the need for precision in human thinking in any field. The sciences are especially careful to define their terms precisely in this way, wherever possible.

B. *Equivocal* = the other extreme, when the same term is applied to several different subjects according to a *completely different meaning* in each case, so that only the verbal sound or written sign remains the same, with no common conceptual content or meaning: e.g., "He fell into a *well;* he is not feeling *well*." "He put his money into a *bank* near the *bank* of a river." This is simply a linguistic accident, of no further significance, except that that we must avoid using equivocal terms in an argument, which would render it invalid: e.g., "A syllogism (a form of logical argument) with four terms is invalid. But President Roosevelt had four terms. Therefore, President Roosevelt is an invalid syllogism."

C. *Analogous* = a term which lies between the univocal and the equivocal, i.e., it occurs when the same term is applied to several different subjects according to a meaning that is *partly the same, partly different* in each case, e.g., "*strength* of muscles, *strength* of an argument, *strength* of will." The role of such terms (and the ideas behind them) is to be "bridge terms," enabling us to draw together and compare things that are different in kind yet somehow similar; to explore an obscure or newly discovered area in terms of what is already known and familiar; to make metaphors, illuminating one thing by comparison with another; to represent what is beyond our direct or ordinary experience, principally the inner and spiritual world, God, etc.; and to span large areas of experience, even the whole universe, in a single synoptic idea, such as being, action, power, goodness, knowledge, life, love, etc. These are all *flexible* or *stretch concepts* which shift their meaning more or less with different applications, taking on the contours of each yet always holding on to some bond of similarity strong enough to warrant unifying all the various applications under a common idea or meaning, expressed by the same linguistic term. Thus "strength of muscles" is not exactly like "strength of will," but enough like it to warrant the same description. It should be evident why analogous concepts are indispensable tools for metaphysical thinking, which must range over the whole spectrum of real beings to discern what is common to all.

III. Types of Analogy

A. Extrinsic Attribution.   This type is found when the same term is predicated of several different subjects in such a way that it is applied according to its proper, literal meaning *only to one among them* (the "primary analogate") and to the others (the "secondary analogates"), not because of any intrinsic similarity between them, but only because of some *relation to the primary analogate,* usually a relation of cause, effect, belonging to, or the like. Thus: "This man is *healthy;* this food is *healthy.*" "Health" here is predicated in its proper or literal meaning only of the man, but extended "by extrinsic attribution" (i.e., attributed to it for some extrinsic reason) to the food, which is not itself healthy (it is dead) but is called "healthy" because it is related to the man's health as cause to effect: it brings about his health. Or: "His color is *unhealthy*" because it manifests or is the effect of his lack of health. So also: "She is an *American;* she drives an *American* car." Only the woman is properly an American citizen; her car is called "American" only because it is *made by* Americans, or *in* America, not because it itself is an American citizen. This type of analogy is merely a convenient shorthand of language and has no further philosophical significance, except that it does show up in some philosophical theories—seriously defective because of this, St. Thomas says—which hold that God is so totally different from creatures that only God can be said to be truly *being,* whereas creatures are only called "beings" by extrinsic attribution because they *come from God* as his effects.

   B. Analogy of Proportionality.   This type is found when a term is predicated of several subjects in order to express some *proportional similarity* between them: e.g., "A worm *knows;* a human being *knows;* God *knows.*" Note that the similarity expressed is not directly between two essences or natures as such, which in themselves are just different, but between their respective *activities,* what they *do,* as somehow truly similar, while at the same time these natures are quite different in how they exercise this activity. Careful reflection on the principal examples of analogy of proportionality lead us to this important conclusion, not sufficiently recognized explicitly by metaphysicians, it seems to me:

General Principle: Action is the primary bond of similarity between different kinds of being and thus is the ontological ground justifying the application of the same analogous term to them. The analogous term thus signifies a similar type of activity going on in each, but carried out by each agent-subject in *its own distinctive way,* according to the structure and capacities proper to its own essence or nature. Hence the meaning of the analogous term is partly the same, partly different in each application, shifting internally to fit the distinctive mode of exercising the activity proper to each subject, or analogate, but without breaking the bond of authentic similarity justifying expression by one and the same meaningful term. The structure of this type of analogy is called *proportionality,* because it can be expressed as in the form of a "proportion" (borrowed from mathematics, where it originated). Thus: "Subject A in relation to its operation is similar to subject B in relation to its operation." Hence, unlike the analogy of extrinsic attribution described above, an analogy of proportionality is always rooted in some intrinsic similarity. However, this intrinsic proportional similarity between different subjects can be expressed by two different modes of analogous predication:

1. Proportionality Expressed by Metaphor (also called "Improper" or "Non-literal"). This type of predication occurs when the intrinsic similarity between two things is expressed by a term that in its proper and literal meaning applies to only one of the analogates (= the beings compared and named by the same word) and to the others only by metaphor. *Metaphor* is the literary device of identifying one term of a comparison with the other for rhetorical vividness and dramatic effect: e.g., "Watch out for him; he's a fox, a snake in the grass." Or: "I am the light of the world; he who follows me does not walk in darkness" (words of Jesus). The purpose of the metaphor is to express a genuine similarity in ways of acting between the two different kinds of being—man and fox—in a vivid and striking way by a transference of names that is not literally true: a man is not literally a fox, but like it in the cleverness of his operations. But because of the underlying intrinsic similarity grounding it, a metaphorical analogy can always be reduced to a more literal mode of expression, called a *simile* ("This man is like a fox in his cleverness"), but one that is much less vivid and striking, hence less suited for poetic and literary effect.

Role of Metaphor. Metaphor is the very stuff of which poetry is made, and one of its principal functions is to express and illuminate inner psychic or spiritual realities by analogy with material ones—the inner through the outer—and vice versa. It presupposes the recognition, implicit or explicit, of a profound *affinity*, a mutual similarity and power of reciprocal imaging, between all levels of being in the universe, in particular between spirit and matter, the human soul and nature. Thus one can speak meaningfully of "a smiling field," or "a stormy face." The ultimate ground of this mysterious inner bond of similitude running through all levels of being and rooted in the radical similarity of all real beings as real, as sharing in existence, is one of the principal tasks of the metaphysician to investigate.

Thus metaphysics and poetry—and indeed all art—nourished as they are by metaphor, are mutually illuminating. The whole world of symbolism and the symbolic imagination depends on this hidden bond of affinity between all beings. As Caroline Spurgeon, the literary critic, puts it insightfully:

> Metaphor is a subject of such deep import that it calls for an abler pen than mine to deal adequately with it. But I believe that analogy—likeness between dissimilar things, which is the fact underlying the possibility and reality of metaphor—holds within itself the very secret of the universe. (*Shakespeare's Imagery and What It Tells us*, New York: Macmillan, 1936, p. 7).

And, similarly, Stephen Brown expresses the matter thus:

> The metaphorical mode of intelligence is founded on analogies and correspondences . . . between matter and mind. Imagery is a witness to the harmony between mind and matter, to the unity of all creation, and thus to the oneness of its author." (*The World of Imagery*, London: K. Paul, Trench, Trubner & Co., 1927, pp. 17–18)

Cf. Robert Boyle, "The Nature of Metaphor," *Modern Schoolman* 21 (1954), 257–80; Michael Slattery, "Metaphor and Metaphysics," *Philosophical Studies,* Maynooth 5 (1955), 89–99; Philip Wheelwright, *The Burning Fountain* (Bloomington: Indiana Univ. Press, 1954); Francis Fergusson, *Idea of a Theater* (Princeton: Princeton Univ. Press, 1949), where he makes explicit use of the Thomistic analogy of proper proportionality to show how the central theme of a great play echoes analogously in all of its subplots.

2. *Analogy of Proper Proportionality.* This type of analogous predication occurs when the intrinsic similarity between analogates is expressed by a term that is applied to all the analogates in its proper and literal meaning, but with a proportional difference as found in each: e.g., "A mouse *knows;* a human being *knows;* an angel *knows;* God *knows.*" All of these subjects are truly and properly said to "know"; yet their ways of knowing are irreducibly different, based on their diverse natures.

Problem. How is it possible for the same term (word and idea) to thus signify similarity with difference? The reason is that it signifies not just a simple quality or essence but a *dyadic structure* in all the beings compared, thus:

> Subject A in its own way—performing the act of knowing; Subject B in its own way—performing the act of knowing; Subject C in its own way—performing the act of knowing; etc.

The similarity lies on the side of the type of activity (knowing) common to all; the difference, on the side of the different ways the diverse subjects exercise this same kind of activity, according to their respective natures.

Note. This does *not* mean that the analogous concept breaks down into two aspects, one exactly the same, the other totally different. Then it would break up into two concepts, one univocal, the other equivocal, and would no longer be a single analogous concept. Rather, the similarity and difference pervade the whole being of the analogates at once. Each of the analogates in exercising its action is through and through both similar and different with respect to the others. Hence the analogous concept expressing this must be at once similar and different in all its predications. Note, too, that such similarity and difference in the analogous concept do not show up when the concept is considered in isolation by itself, but only when joined with a particular subject in a *judgment* or similar relation, thus: knowledge-in-God, knowledge-in-humans, knowledge-in-dogs.

Analogy of Proper Proportionality as Key to Metaphysical Thinking. This type of analogy, as the only one in which the same attributes can be asserted with literal truth of all its analogates, is an indispensable tool for all serious thinking in philosophy, especially metaphysics, and in many other fields as well. It would not be of much help in trying to understand God to assert that he is only metaphorically good, intelligent, loving, etc.—fine for poetry and liturgical celebration, but not enough for metaphysical or theological analysis.

Systematic Imprecision of Analogous Concepts. Some philosophers are uncomfortable with analogous concepts because it is not easy to pin down their meaning with exact precision, as can be done in science. But this is precisely what should be the case if they are to do their job. One important consequence of the flexibility and wide scope of analogous concepts is that it is very difficult, if not impossible, to state exactly what is the meaning of a concept and its precise limits. The concepts of *being, action, unity,* for example, are *open-ended* at both the top and the bottom. One gets to understand the meaning of such terms not by clear definitions, which spell out the whole range of their contents with clear limits, but rather by *running up and down a spectrum of typical examples* and grasping in a *synthetic insight* what is common to them all. Such concepts always retain a certain vagueness and indeterminacy, so that we know what they mean when we actually use them in a given case, but not precisely what is their meaning in abstraction from all instances. Some philosophers aptly call them "systematically vague concepts" and defend them as indispensable for thinking meaningfully about the universe as a whole. But because philosophers by temperament like to think with as much precision as possible, there is always the danger that, instead of holding the meaning of an analogous concept stretched open to its full capacity, one tries to force it into artificial clarity, pin it down too much, and end up identifying it with only a few of its typical instances and excluding other possible meaningful applications. Thus *being* can be understood as signifying only *material being, knowledge* only *human rational knowledge,* etc. It is an essential skill of a good metaphysician to learn to think analogically if he is to think properly about being or any of its properties or laws, extending as they do across the whole range of real being with all its similarities and diversities.

IV. ANALOGY AS APPLIED TO THE CONCEPT OF BEING

If any metaphysical concept is going to be analogous in the full and proper sense of analogy (= the analogy of proper proportionality), it must certainly be that of *being,* since it is the broadest in scope of all concepts, signifying the fundamental bond of unity underlying all other unities and differences between all real beings, and so cannot be univocal. And surely to say that something "is, is real," cannot be just a metaphor, for it underlies all proper non-metaphorical analogies, without which all language and thought would dissolve into metaphor and finally become unintelligible. For metaphor means "like something else," and there is nothing else that being can be like that is not being, since outside of it there is only non-being. Hence, *being* must be analogous according to the only kind of proper and literally true type of analogy, that of proper proportionality.

But here a problem arises. Earlier we concluded that to express a genuine proportional similarity between real beings an analogous concept must signify a *duality structure,* i.e., some kind of similar action or activity exercised diversely by the various subjects of which the term is predicated. But how can a term like *being* express an activity? It seems to express only the single simple attribute of presence. But that is just the point of the Thomistic notion of being, not found in other "essentialist" interpretations: *being* expresses not just a simple what or essence, but precisely a *proportion: that which is = that which* (some particular subject or *what,* some essence or nature) as *exercising the act of be-ing,* not as a static state, but as an act of standing out from nothing and actively presenting itself to the community of real beings. St. Thomas does not hesitate to call it the *virtus essendi,* or power of being, terming the act of existence (the *esse* or to-be of things) the *first act* of a being, and the action which flows from it, its *second act.* But this same act of active self-presentation is presented or acted out in a distinctively different manner according to the particular essence or nature of each, from the tiniest sub-atomic particle lasting only a fraction of a second to the infinite eternal fullness of God.

Thus the Thomistic notion of *being,* when unpacked fully, signifies precisely a *proportional similarity,* the ultimate one, namely, (1) some particular essence or nature, some *what,* as subject; (2) owning and exercising the act of existence; (3) each in its own distinctive way. Or, to condense the proportion into a more convenient duality: a real being = (1) a particular nature or essence, in its own distinctive way, (2) exercising the act of existence or active self-presentation common to all real existents. The difference in each case derives from the first side of the proportion, that of essence; the similarity from the second, or act of existing (standing out of nothing), though both the sameness and the difference permeate the entire being in an indissoluble union—*this-being.*

The Analogy of Being vs. the Univocity of Being. Some metaphysicians in St. Thomas's own time, e.g., *Duns Scotus* (d. 1308), and *William of Ockham* (d. 1347), with their followers to this day, defended the univocity of the concept of being against Thomas. Both were leaders in the strong development of logic at the end of the Middle Ages (anticipating many of the developments of modern symbolic logic), and logicians tend to be uncomfortable with flexible ideas, "systematically vague concepts" like the Thomistic analogy of proper proportionality, especially as applied to being in God and creatures. And since their metaphysics were "essentialist," i.e., focussed on being *as essence* (not including the act of existence as part of its content), it was hard for them to see how the concept of *being* could be applied to different essences without breaking up into several distinct concepts ceasing to have the same meaning at all, hence useless as a valid term in any syllogism or other logical argument, where all the terms must remain strictly fixed in the same meaning. Therefore, to retain any unity at all, *being* always had to be a univocal concept, even applied to God and creatures with their immense diversity as finite and infinite. But they had to pay a heavy price for this apparent logical clarity: they had to make the concept of *being* so extremely abstract as to empty it of practically all content and make it merely an empty linguistic marker *standing for* both God and creatures but, as Ockham explicitly admitted, expressing *nothing common* at all between God and creatures! The result was to render God considerably more remote and inaccessible to human reason than St. Thomas's God, with important repercussions for the philosophy, theology, and finally spirituality of the late Middle Ages.

V. APPLICATION TO GOD

This is the most crucial test of analogy and its most fruitful achievement: its extension to language about God, allowing us to talk positively about

God without falling into anthropomorphism. Here is where essentialist types of metaphysics run into trouble, as Thomists see it. For if one holds that "being" signifies only essence, and since the essence of God is infinitely distant from the finite essences of creatures, then it seems one has only three options, none of them attractive: (1) if one insists that the notion of being is *univocal,* it gets so emptied of content as to tell us almost nothing; or (2) one draws the divine essence down into too close a likeness of the limited essences of creatures, thus falling into *anthropomorphism* (the "idolatry of human concepts," as many Jewish thinkers claim); or (3) one opts for the so-called "*negative theology*" in one of its many forms, that is, one can say nothing positive about God but speak of him only through *negations:* God is "above being, non-being, non-personal or above personal, non-knowing, non-material, non-finite," etc., the Mystery beyond all human words and ideas that can only be pointed to in silence or in metaphor. This is the path followed by *Buddhism* (consistently) and *Advaita (Non-dualist) Vedanta* in Hinduism (less consistently) in the East; and in the West by the *Neoplatonic tradition* (who allow only "One" and "Good" to be predicated positively of the Ultimate Reality), followed with various qualifications by various Christian thinkers like *Pseudo-Dionysius, Meister Eckhart, Nicholas of Cusa,* etc.; and the great medieval Jewish thinker, *Moses Maimonides* (d. 1204). Maimonides states very clearly the total inaccessibility of God to our concepts and words: "Those who are familiar with the meaning of similarity will certainly understand that the term Existence . . . Wisdom, Power, Will and Life are applied to God and other things with perfect equivocity. . . . There is in no way or sense anything common to the attributes predicated of God and ourselves: they have only the same names and nothing else is common to them" (*Guide of the Perplexed,* London: Routledge 1958, I. 56, p. 79). This famous book still inspires many Jewish thinkers today, e.g. Martin Buber, *I and Thou* (Edinburgh: Clark, 1958, p. 80): "God is the Being . . . that may properly only be addressed, not expressed." But despite their theories it remains extremely difficult, if not impossible, for most religious thinkers, especially in the West, to stick consistently to their purely negative rule for speaking about God; positive notions keep creeping in, in prayer, worship, etc.

Karl Barth, the famous Swiss Lutheran theologian, also denies any analogy between the language about God taught us about God by Christian revelation and that drawn by natural reason from our experience of this world. Original sin has so darkened our natural reason to the things of God that the supernatural knowledge of God given us by Christian revelation bursts in on us as a total gift from above, bringing with it the very power to understand this new divine language, accessible only to those who have divinely given faith. Hence any attempt to bridge the gap between God and ourselves by natural reason (philosophy) will be either helpless or idolatrous: "I regard the analogy of being as an invention of Anti-Christ, and think that because of it one cannot become a Catholic" (*Doctrine of the Word*, Edinburgh, 1936, p. x). Later, however, he softened his position, after his colleagues pointed out to him that he, too, was constantly using analogy implicitly, and must do so to speak any human language at all. God speaks to us through our already existing human language, transforming it but building on it.

Thomistic Analogy Applied to God. Here lies the advantage of St. Thomas's analogy of proper proportionality applied to his existential notion of *being* in speaking about God: it can avoid all the above impasses and inconsistencies, because it transcends their (at least implicit) essentialist modes of thinking about being and so contains a *proportion* within it that allows for internal flexibility of similarity and difference within each application. For the Thomistic notion of *being* as *that which is* (an essence exercising the act of existence in its own particular way) focuses explicitly on the similarity of the act of existence in all real beings—not on their essences or forms, save as modes-of-existing; hence, it does not require that in applying the notion of being to God we must know or specify the mode of existing of the divine essence, *what God is like*. We affirm only *that* God exists, is actively present in his own distinctive infinite way, but not *how* he exists, what his essence is like in itself, which is totally hidden from us. Hence, we can leave the essence of God intact, without drawing it down to our own level (anthropomorphism) yet affirm something supremely positive about its "owner" that links it with the entire community of all other real existents, God's creatures. Thus, God becomes accessible to our human minds as the fullness of existence, yet transcending all the particular modes of existing that we know from our own this-worldly experience.

The same analysis holds true of all the other positive attributes that can be truly and properly affirmed of God, such as activity, unity, power, wisdom, goodness, love, etc. They are all predicated according to the analogy of proper proportionality, i.e., they signify some activity (in the

broadest sense) that is similar in God and creatures but without specifying the mode of performing the action proper to the particular subject, whether God or creature.

Role of Analogy in Theology. The analogy of proper proportionality
plays an extremely important role in theology, wherein all the attributes
asserted of God must be understood analogously to avoid the two extremes of *agnosticism,* on the one hand (= there is nothing at all we can
say meaningfully about God, nothing at all similar between God and
creatures), and naive *anthropomorphism,* on the other (= drawing God
down to our human level, too much like us). Some try to straddle the
issue, claiming that we can speak of God positively, but only in *metaphorical* terms. Too many Christian theologians today are insensitive or
confused on this point, often speaking about God as though all our language about God is basically metaphorical, which means not literally
true. They seem unaware of the decisive difference between predication by *metaphor* and by the *analogy of proper proportionality.* Thus, in her
otherwise valuable book on the Christian doctrine of the Trinity of Persons in God, Catherine LaCugna makes this statement: "The systematic
theologian needs to keep in mind that every concept [when applied to
God], whether it be 'substance', or 'relation', is fundamentally metaphorical" (*God for Us: The Trinity and Christian Life,* San Francisco:
Harper-Collins, 1991, p. 359). But if every theological concept is only
metaphorically true of God, then nothing is ever literally and properly
true of him, not even "wise," "loving," "personal," "one," even "being"
itself. But this would be disastrous for taking seriously any traditional
creed or formula of belief. Luckily, however, the majority of religiously
educated believers intuitively recognize the difference between metaphorical statements from Scripture, such as, "God turned his back on
his people," and literally true analogous ones, such as, "God loves his
people." A simple test for distinguishing between metaphorical and
properly analogous statements about God is the following: With respect
to a metaphorical predication, such as "God holds us in his arms," one
can both affirm it (the truth behind the metaphor) and deny it as not
literally true (God has no arms because no body). With respect to a
properly analogous predication, such as "God loves us," one cannot
deny it but must affirm it as true, according to God's unique mode of
loving proper to him. In fact, the analogical statement is the necessary
foundation for the truth behind this or any metaphorical statement.

Note on St. Thomas. I have presented above what seems to me the most adequate systematic analysis of the Thomistic theory of analogy as actually used by St. Thomas throughout his philosophy and theology—and widely agreed upon in its main lines by most—probably not all—contemporary Thomistic scholars. It is well known, however, that St. Thomas himself never worked out a single comprehensive, systematic theory of the analogy he was constantly using very skillfully. This is probably because he was trying to stick as closely as possible to Aristotle, frequently using examples drawn directly from the latter, such as the relation of health to food, substance to accident. But these remain mostly within the structure of the analogy of extrinsic attribution and do not do justice at all to his own much richer notion of proper proportionality as expressing the *intrinsic similarity in difference* of all real beings to each other and to God, their source. This similarity in difference is the *participation structure* of all finite beings as participating intrinsically, in various finite ways, in the infinite fullness of perfection of God himself as the Creative Source of all being—a metaphysical structure quite lacking in Aristotle himself, with his radical rejection of all Platonism, especially the latter's doctrine of participation.

Then, after trying out and quietly rejecting several different conceptual models of analogy as applied to God and creatures, St. Thomas seems to have settled finally on what contemporary Thomists describe quite aptly as the *analogy of participation:* this combines in one complex model both the analogous structure of proper proportionality (intrinsic similarity between all the analogates) plus the analogy of attribution (the relation of causal participation of many different analogates to a common source). In a word, the analogous term (thought and word) gives linguistic expression to an objective *metaphysical structure of participation:* many real beings possessing in various limited ways a common attribute, received from a common source, which possesses the same attribute in unlimited fullness. Beings themselves are not analogous: they just *are,* objectively similar and diverse. But our human thought and language mirror in our human consciousness this objective participation situation by the tool of analogy, with its peculiar ability to hold together in a single flexible term—being, activity, knowledge, goodness, love, etc.—both the similarity and difference we have discovered in things themselves.

Cf. St. Thomas, *Summa contra Gentes,* I, ch. 32; *Summa Theologiae,* I, q. 13, a. 5; George Klubertanz, S.J., *St. Thomas and Analogy* (Chicago:

Loyola Univ. Press, 1960), which collects all the texts and synthesizes them under the term *analogy of participation,* as explained above; W. Norris Clarke, S.J., "Analogy and the Meaningfulness of Language about God," ch. 7 in my *Explorations in Metaphysics* (Univ. of Notre Dame Press, 1994).

CONCLUSION

Let us look back on what we have achieved in this chapter. By examining the concept of *being* as a paradigm case, we have uncovered the special analogical character that is proper to all the great metaphysical concepts and linguistic terms that we will need as tools to describe the fundamental properties and laws governing all the different kinds and levels of real beings in all their diversity, yet similarity, across the entire vast range of reality, from the tiniest subatomic particle with its momentary puff of existence all the way up to God with his infinite and eternal fullness of perfection. The *analogy of proper proportionality* is the key structure behind any proper and literally true analogous predication of any one attribute to many different subjects possessing diverse essences. Such terms always express the proportion of some subject, carrying out an activity common to many, each in its own distinctive way. Thus, all analogous concepts are terms expressing *activity* of some kind, in the broadest sense (or its complementary opposite—being acted upon, or some relation thereto). This must be kept in mind as we use all the metaphysical concepts we uncover during the rest of our inquiry, as we try to gain a deeper understanding of what it means to be and to be related to other beings in the vast community of existents.

All these conceptual tools must be analogous in character to be able to stretch across the entire spectrum of reality. Only thus can we sum up the entire real world and hold it together as a meaningful whole in our finite minds, using a finite language. No one can be a competent metaphysician, it seems to me—certainly not a Thomistic one—unless he can learn to think analogically. Both the grandeur and the limitations of the human mind shine forth here, with its God-given mission to speak out (be "the spokesman of being," as Heidegger puts it tersely) the magnificent richness and diversity of our vast universe of real being, together with its Creative Source, using a finite language. The Dalai Lama expressed the same thought with his typical simplicity and depth (speaking at the Interfaith Meeting in Assisi): "The universe has no voice, and the universe needs to speak. We are the voice of the universe." It can be done, but one must learn how—and analogy is one of the indispensable tools.

QUESTIONS FOR REVIEW AND DISCUSSION

1. What is the point of stopping to discuss the special characteristics of the concepts we use in metaphysics?

2. What does it mean that a concept is a "transcendental" one? Why is *being* such? Why is it said to be at once the "poorest" and the "richest" of all concepts?

3. Most ordinary concepts we use are formed by abstracting a common essence and omitting particular details. Why is it that being cannot be thus formed? How then is it formed?

4. How do the three types of concepts differ from each other: univocal, equivocal, analogous? Why is it necessary that the main concepts used in metaphysics be analogous?

5. *Analogy of Attribution:* What does this mean? Examples? Does it express any intrinsic similarity between the prime analogate and the secondary analogates? Why do we use it?

6. *Analogy of Proportionality:* Meaning? Examples?

7. What is the basis in reality for all uses of analogy of proportionality?

8. What is happening in an analogy of *Metaphorical or Improper Proportionality?* Examples? Why is it not literally true? What is the purpose of using it then?

9. *Analogy of Proper Proportionality:* Meaning? Examples? Explain how such an analogous term can be at once literally true of all its analogates, yet shifting somewhat in meaning for each, i.e., how it can be so flexible, as a univocal cannot.

10. Does an analogous concept contain two parts, one of which expresses just the similarity, the other just the diversity?

11. *Analogy Applied to Being:* How does this work, since being seems to be such a simple concept and not expressing any common action, as other proper proportionality concepts do?

12. *Analogy Applied to God:* How does it avoid falling into anthropomorphism (making God too much like humans) on the one hand, or mere metaphor on the other?

13. Why is William of Ockham forced to hold that the concept of *being* applies univocally to both God and creatures, whereas St. Thomas is not?

14. How does St. Thomas ground the real similarity between God and creatures, making possible a proper analogy between them?

CHAPTER FOUR

Unity as Transcendental Property of Being

New Question. Equipped now with the flexible tools of analogous concepts to carry out our metaphysical search, we are ready to pursue further our inquiry into what it means to be. We have already seen in chapter 2 that to be a real being means to be actively present to the community of other real existents. *Self-communicating, self-expressive action* is, therefore, the first transcendental property of real being as such that we have discovered. By *transcendental property of being* is meant an attribute that can be truly predicated of every real being, precisely insofar as it is a real existent. But activity is the outer face of being, so to speak, the way it expresses itself to others. We are now drawn to look more deeply into the inner structure of every being to see what constitutes it as such, so that without it nothing can qualify as real. What first reveals itself to our reflection is the property of *unity*. Every being, to be a being, must be internally *one*, must cohere together to form an undivided whole, or it cannot be at all. So absolutely central is this attribute that it is agreed upon by metaphysicians of every tradition, whatever else they may disagree on.

I. The Meaning of Unity as a Property of Being

The unity we are talking about here is not numerical unity, that is, "one" as the first in a number series, but something intrinsic within every being, called *ontological unity*. It is difficult to define it positively, since it is so fundamental that anything else already implies it to be intelligible at all. We have to fall back on paraphrases and negative descriptions that point to the positive content, thus: ontological unity as a property of being signifies the inner cohesion of something by which it constitutes an undivided whole. As St. Thomas defines it tersely: *one* = that which is undivided in itself and divided from every other. It coheres together within itself as a single undivided whole, but is distinct in its being from every other being: it is itself, but is not any other being. This is true even of God, even though he contains the qualitative fullness of all perfection. Anything else is *pantheism* = all is God.

Order of Discovery of the Explicit Concept. According to St. Thomas, although the notion of unity is presupposed implicitly in the notion of a being, we discover the concept explicitly by moving through the following steps: (1) First I know *this* being; (2) then *that* being; (3) then this being *is not* that being, is separate or divided off from that one; (4) then each one, though divided off from every other, remains undivided in itself. Thus every real being is *undivided in itself and divided from every other.* To be is to cohere internally as an undivided whole, distinct or divided from every other.

Note carefully that "undivided" does not mean "indivisible," but only that which is at present *actually undivided,* though it may be *potentially divisible* into parts. Thus a biological organism is an actually undivided whole as long as it is alive, but can easily be broken up into parts, at which point it ceases to be a single being and breaks down into many beings.

Now for the proof of the above claim: to be is to be one.

II. Every Being, Insofar as It Is a Being, Is One

Argument. Since unity is so primary and fundamental a property, presupposed implicitly by all others, we cannot present a positive proof based on anything else more fundamental. So we have to resort to an indirect or negative form of proof, by showing that the opposite is simply unintelligible or incoherent (= proof by a negative "thought-experiment").

Let us see if we can think of some real being that is not in fact internally unified, not an undivided whole, but is made up of parts that are divided off from each other, not joined together, not cohering together as a unity. In such a case there is no longer any objective ground for calling it *this* being, an "it," but only a multitude of *thises* and *thats*. There is no *something* that exists in the singular. Furthermore, if we examine each of these parts in turn and if to be this part does not require it to be one, then each part immediately breaks down into a multiplicity of further parts, of *thises* and *thats*. Each of these in turn breaks down into many parts, and so on in an endless regress; there is no way of stopping the disintegration until we reach an "infinite dust," so to speak, of pure multiplicity, where nothing holds together to be a distinct something at all. But pure multiplicity with no inner cohesion at all is indistinguishable from pure nothingness, no-thing-ness.

The conclusion is clear: we must stop at the beginning: i.e., wherever we find a real being it must cohere internally as a unity, an undivided whole, or else it will crumble into an endlessly fragmenting dust of pure multiplicity. *To be real is to be one.* (The same rule holds, in fact, even for the world of thought, of mental being: nothing can be thought at all unless it is somehow unified to form a single unit of thought, no matter how artificial or tenuous the bond that holds it together as a single thought-content.)

This indirect proof by the impossibility of the contrary should dispose our minds to a luminous direct insight into the inseparability of unity and being, an insight into the very heart of every being, so to speak. As the great German metaphysician, Leibniz (d. 1716) put it tersely: "I consider as an axiom this self-identical proposition, diversified by emphasis only: 'That which is not truly *one being* is not truly *a being* at all'" (*Correspondence with Arnould*, Lettre XX, Paris, 1957, p. 164).

III. UNITY AS ANALOGOUS ATTRIBUTE

Since unity as a transcendental property of every being must extend across the whole vast spectrum of different levels and kinds of being, adjusting to the similarity in diversity of each, its meaning must be *analogous* in each application, as in the case of being itself (see ch. 3). It will include, therefore, all the modes of unity, from the absolute unity of pure simplicity, found only in God, all the way to the most complex unity composed of many parts, like a human being, for example, whose brain alone (some 13 billion neurons) is the most complex organism we know of in the entire material universe. The number of possible connections between all these neurons is calculated to be larger than the number of all the individual material particles in the known universe. Yet the human being owning this brain is still one being, a single undivided whole.

New Challenge. Identifying unity as an analogous property immediately raises a new problem from the general theory of analogy. In the chapter on analogy it was concluded that every properly analogous concept expresses *some activity* common to the various subjects it is predicated of, but *performed differently* by each according to its specific nature. But how can unity be understood as an *activity?* It seems at first sight to be a purely static state.

The answer to this question can lead us to a more profound understanding of what ontological unity really means. If we reflect more deeply on what unity is actually like in the concrete, at work inside of real existents, it reveals itself, like being itself, as a positive energy by which each being actively coheres within itself holding its parts together—if it has any—in a dynamic, self-unifying act. To be one is not a static state or given, but an active *doing,* an active ongoing *achievement* of each real being, carried on by each according to its own distinctive mode of being.

Modern science has helped us to see how this is true at every level of material being. For example, we now know—which the ancients and medievals did not—that the unity of the atom is not a static given but is held together by a very powerful energy, the so-called "strong force," so powerful that if it is broken apart by splitting the atom an enormous amount of energy is released, the energy powering the atomic bomb that did such vast destruction during World War II. And in every living organism the unifying central form actively holds together the various cells and chemicals, organizing and controlling them to work together for the good of the whole organism. When this central controlling energy grows weaker, through disease or age, the parts break away, return to their own autonomy of being and action, and death results—the disintegration of a living being as a unified whole, as a being. Even in a spiritual being with no physical parts, its unity is not static but a self-cohering activity through self-embracing love. So, too, in the Triune God of Christian revelation, the Holy Spirit is the active divine energy of love that is the bond of unity between Father and Son. And this dynamic act of self-cohesion will be expressed proportionally—similarly but diversely—more strongly or less so, more perfectly or less perfectly, more intensely and interiorly or more weakly and precariously, according to the nature and level of each subject exercising the unifying power of being as act of existence.

Practical Application: The Integration of Human Personality. Here we have an illuminating and very practical application of this general law of all being: to be anything real it is necessary to be one, *integrated.* Our basic ontological unity as a soul-body whole is a gift to us at birth. We can destroy it, but we cannot create it. But the unity of what is called our psychological "personality" is not given us ready-made. It is something we must work at and achieve by our own conscious action. We cannot really be "someone" as a person unless we can achieve at least some modest success at this; and no one can be a genuine person unless he or she is an integrated person. *How does one develop such an integrated personality?* The unity of any ongoing operation lies out in front of it, so to speak, in the form of the goal or end the agent is seeking to achieve. Hence, to become a truly integrated (unified) personality, we must deliberately unify our multiple actions under integrating goals or ends-in-view for each set of activities (like going to college, playing a game, etc.); set up our own scale of priority of goals and values to organize all these projects and subordinate lower goals to higher, more important ones; and finally, if we are really serious, integrate our whole life under one great dominant goal, which St. Thomas advises should be "one great love." In a word, to be a fully developed, integrated personality one's life must take the form of a *journey,* unified by a final destination or goal. To be a good story, a meaningful story, it must be a *unified story.* To achieve anything "real," you must achieve unity. What is the integrating unity of your journey?

Conclusion: At every level of being, from the lowest to the highest, the law of unity holds: *whatever truly is, must be one.*

IV. INTRINSIC AND EXTRINSIC UNITY

It is very important, in order to understand the world we live in, to recognize the difference between these two types of unity, both found in our world, especially the difference between *real beings* and *artifacts* made by us, such as tables, chairs, machines. Many contemporary philosophers are not sensitive enough to this distinction, which leads them into unnecessary metaphysical paradoxes and confusion at times as to just where authentic being is to be found.

A. *Intrinsic (or per se) Unity* = a unity within the very being of a single real being, such that it exists (is actively present) with a single act of existence and acts as a unit, controlling its actions from a single center of action. This is the strong meaning of unity, the *ontological unity* that is proper to every real being, constitutive of its very being, making it truly a single being both in existence and in action. Examples from the principal levels of real being: an atom, a molecule, a plant, an animal, a human being, an angel (pure spirit), God. Every such being, if composed of parts, as are all the beings in our world of experience, is not just the sum of its parts, but exists and acts as a *distinctive whole,* manifesting characteristic properties belonging to the whole as such that are not merely the sum of the properties of the parts by themselves. Thus the hydrogen and oxygen atoms by themselves are highly flammable, but the new composite being formed out of them—the molecule of water (two hydrogen atoms and one oxygen)—has the opposite property of not being flammable at all, but is rather the main agent for extinguishing fires. The only examples of such intrinsic unities are natural beings (beings formed by nature). We humans cannot create new ones by our own powers; we can only bring together beings already existing in nature which by their own innate active properties have the power to combine under the right conditions to constitute new natural unities, new types of real being, such as atoms into molecules according to certain fixed proportions beyond our control. We are only the mediators, not the direct active causes of the production of such new natural beings possessing their own intrinsic unities.

B. *Extrinsic (per accidens) Unity* = a unity not within the very being of a single real being, but rather between two or more distinct real beings, each with its own distinctive act of existence and center of action, but joined together by bonds of relations. Examples of such unifying relations are: (1) *relations of common purpose* or end-in-view to be attained by collaboration of the members, e.g., an army, a bridge club, a football team, a college, a bank, a congress; (2) *relations of common location,* e.g., a herd of cows on this farm, a classroom, a city, a country, a stadium, a forest, a mountain; (3) *relations of common time,* e.g., an hour, a day, a year, etc.; (4) *artifacts,* created principally by human beings but also by many animals, i.e., collections of simpler beings joined together to serve a common purpose imposed by an outside agent for its own ends, but possessing no intrinsic unity of their own as existing and acting wholes, e.g., chairs, tables, machines, bridges, computers, airplanes, bird's nests, anthills, etc.

Most ordinary people and philosophers have no trouble recognizing the difference between intrinsic unities (individual real beings) and extrinsic unities (collections of real beings united by relations) in the case of the first three kinds of extrinsic unities mentioned above, since our language distinguishes clearly between *singular* nouns ("a man," a dog") and *collective nouns* ("an army," "a family"). The real difficulty—and confusion—occurs principally when dealing with artifacts. They are such a constant presence in our lives, especially in city life, and we are so accustomed to using and speaking of them as individual units with names imposed by us, that it is very easy to slip into the habit of treating them on a par with genuine real beings possessing intrinsic unity—and blur the profound ontological difference between them. Linguistic philosophers are especially vulnerable to such confusions, because such artifacts are used as subjects and objects of sentences in the same way as real beings. But such artifacts possess *no intrinsic unity* of their own in either existence or action, no characteristic active properties of the whole in itself apart from the purposes we have imposed on them from without. Thus there is a single center of action in a bird, a plant, a human, which controls their various activities from within, so that these acts are acts of the whole as such; there is no such controlling center, no such activity of the whole as such, in a table, a chair, a ship, a machine. The wood in a ship does its own thing, the metal its own thing, the engine its own motions. The only unity is the unity of order imposed by us on all these independent entities so that the sum of their various actions ends up with a result that serves *our* independent purposes in which the real components have no interest. There is no action of the chair as such, as a unity, but only its combined actions which serve my purpose as something to sit on and support me. This is especially important to remember when dealing with machines, since so many philosophers today are tempted by scientific reductionism: for them, all higher beings, such as living cells, plants, animals, even humans are really only complex collections of the lowest level of being, atoms, etc., or just highly complicated machines. The most ontologically accurate definition of a machine is the terse but brilliant one proposed by the metaphysician Paul Weiss: "a machine is a complex whose parts are extrinsic to each other." This is not true of any real being, any intrinsic unity.

Criteria for Distinguishing Intrinsic from Extrinsic Unity. The basic criterion is always the same: whether the datum we are trying to understand manifests by its action that *it acts as a unit, from a single controlling center of action.* But it is not always easy to discern the difference by mere observation from without, nor by any scientific measuring process. You can't point with your finger to the exact location of the center of unity and action in a body, since it pervades the whole being at once. It can only be discerned by an act of intellectual reflection on the evidence and an interpretative judgment, which may be mistaken.

There is, however, one crucial test that can often—not always—be applied, namely, if parts are removed from the whole being examined, do these continue to act in the same way, exhibit the same properties outside the whole as they did inside? If the former, the unity is *extrinsic;* if the latter, it is *intrinsic.* For example, take an airplane and a bird: if you remove the parts of an airplane, its steel, plastic, wood, cushions, etc., they continue to exhibit the same properties outside as inside and can be put together again in the proper order to reconstitute the plane. Try the same with a bird: remove the head and wings, and they immediately become lifeless, turn into lower chemicals with quite different properties; the bird dies and the dead parts cannot be put together again to reform the living bird. The same with computers, all machines. Similarly, with stones, which not only children but many non-scientific grown-ups even today naively assume to be single real beings. Chip off pieces, and they continue to exhibit the same chemical properties by themselves; but once you reach the level of molecules and break these down into atoms, the active properties of these parts dramatically change into quite different ones. This is a sign that you have reached the highest level of intrinsic unities within the extrinsic unity of the complex we call a stone.

This criterion is a clear one when it can be applied. But it obviously cannot be applied when the members of a large system—even when recognized as intrinsic unities (e.g., humans)—cannot be removed from the system and still survive. Thus, if we are trying to judge whether our whole universe is an intrinsic or extrinsic unity, we cannot remove parts such as ourselves outside the universe as a whole, since the latter is all-inclusive and there is no outside to it. How then do we know the universe is not an intrinsic unity (= pantheism or monism)? The crucial evidence is that then all moral responsibility would be destroyed, since all actions would be controlled by a single higher center of action, and we could no longer control them by our own individual wills, i.e., be free, or have any individual moral responsibility—in a word, we could not be persons, and the evidence against that is too strong to be ignored or denied.

V. Materialist Reductionism

One of the most serious consequences of ignoring or denying this crucial distinction between intrinsic and extrinsic unity is the temptation to embrace the philosophical position called *Reductionism,* which in practice always ends up in a radical *materialism.* This is perhaps the most serious threat today to an adequate philosophical (not to mention cultural and religious) vision of what the world of real being, our universe, is really like. Many scientists, acting as philosophical interpreters of their science, proclaim it, and many philosophers, under the spell of the immense prestige of modern science, tend to accept it as the most probable philosophical explanation of reality. It is an important responsibility of metaphysicians to come squarely to grips with this disastrous flattening out and impoverishing of the rich qualitative diversity of the community of real existents.

Meaning: Reductionism is the doctrine that all the socalled higher levels of being are really *nothing but* more or less complex collections or systems of the lowest level material elements, i.e., atoms, or whatever else science discovers as more fundamental. Thus Carl Sagan, scientist and professed materialist reductionist, has given us a classic statement of the doctrine: "I, Carl Sagan, am nothing but a collection of atoms bearing the name, 'Carl Sagan'." These complex arrangements of the lowest elements can either be the work of nature, independent of human agents—we call these molecules, cells, plants, animals, humans, etc.—or the products of deliberate human agency—we call these artifacts or machines. But the ontological status of all is the same: all socalled beings, no matter how complex, are in reality nothing but collections, aggregates, of the lowest elements, and these, of course, are material. All the qualitative levels of being, the traditional hierarchy of being, are collapsed into the lowest—the "flattened, or nothing-but universe," as some have called it.

Response. The fundamental flaw in this metaphysical view of the universe is that it simply cannot do justice to one fundamental type of evidence that is the basic ground for affirming different qualitative levels of being, namely, the appearance in the real world under appropriate conditions of new compositions of simpler elements which have irreducibly new properties and characteristic activities that are more than the sum of the properties of its simpler components and neither deducible from the latter nor reducible to them. In other words, a *new whole* has appeared, which now has new properties proper to the whole as such, so that this new whole now exercises its own specific causal influence on its parts, organizing them and controlling them to produce new effects not possible to them by themselves or as a mere sum of simpler properties. Characteristic action is the self-manifestation of a real being, manifesting both its actual existence and its nature as a real being. Thus, the intrinsically immaterial activities of the human intellect and will transcend the powers of any nature whose parts are materially extended in space and tied down to it. So, too, for the properties of living compared to non-living entities, animals endowed with sense cognition compared with plants, etc. It is the activities characteristic of the new whole as distinct from the sum of its parts that Reductionism cannot do justice to and so either denies, ignores, or tries to explain away by rhetorical assertion. Characteristic unified action flows from the nature of every real being and is the only reliable manifestation of it to us. Look to the evidence, listen to it! Any philosophical theory that denies, ignores, or cannot cope reasonably with it by that very fact condemns itself as a fatally flawed philosophical explanation.

Basic recurring problem in the relations between philosophy and science. In the analysis of any complex real being that has an intrinsic unity and yet includes a diversity of parts, a balance must be kept between two perspectives: on the one hand, the unity of the whole must be recognized that dominates and organizes the activities of the parts, exercising a positive causal influence downwards on its own parts. This is what philosophical, especially metaphysical analysis, highlights, concerned as it is with the being of the entity in question. We might call this the *whole-to-part* type of analysis. On the other hand, we must not so stress the unity that the real distinctness and diversity of the parts, with the resultant upwards causal influence of the parts on the whole, is wiped out. This is the *part-to-whole* type of analysis, which modern science aims at pursuing as far as possible, trying to explain human psychology in terms of neuroscience, neuroscience in terms of biology, biology in terms of physics, macroscopic physics in terms of quantum physics. Both approaches are needed for the fullness of human understanding; but there will always be a certain tension between them, so we must take care to hold them in balance. Many scientists are now coming to recognize explicitly this two-way flow of causality, especially in living beings: from the bottom up (parts to whole) and from the top down (whole to parts). The second is the one most neglected or overlooked by modern thinkers, heavily influenced by science. Metaphysics tries explicitly to restore this balance.

Postscript

We should be careful as philosophers, attentive to the evidence of the real, not to understand the relations between intrinsic and extrinsic unities (real beings and collections of real beings) in too naive and oversimplified a manner. In reality, the two often join together to form complex, mutually supporting systems or societies. Thus most complex living organisms on our planet, while possessing a center of intrinsic unity and action, are also inhabited by whole colonies of fellow travelling parasites (bacteria, etc.), which have their own intrinsic unities yet have become dependent on the host system for their survival. In fact, the host system itself can become dependent on their services for its own survival or well-being—we cannot digest our food properly without the help of friendly bacteria, which are still not intrinsic parts of our own being, or whose actions we control from within. Thus our world appears to be a vast interlocking system or community of unities of all different kinds, sometimes working for, sometimes against each other. One thing seems to be sure in our world: to be is to be a unit in a community, in a system, or perhaps better, in a system of systems.

Cf. Terence Nichols, "Aquinas's Concept of Substantial Form and Modern Science," *Internat. Phil. Quart.* 36 (1996), 303–18; Ivor Leclerc, "The Problem of the Physical Existent," *Internat. Phil. Quart.* 9 (1969), 40–62; Arthur Koestler and J. Smythies, eds., *Beyond Reductionism* (New York: Macmillan, 1976); Anna Lemkow, *The Wholeness Principle* (Wheaton, Ill.: Quest, 1990).

QUESTIONS FOR REVIEW AND DISCUSSION

1. What is meant by a "transcendental property of being"?

2. What is the difference between "one" as part of a number series and "one" as an ontological property? Is "undivided" the same as "indivisible"?

3. Sum up the argument why every being must be one.

4. How can unity be an analogous property, when it does not seem to signify any action, as do other analogous terms? The answer to this is very significant for understanding the unity of different kinds of beings, including God. Why?

5. How is the psychological unity of a human personality achieved? What is the basic principle at work?

6. What is the difference between intrinsic and extrinsic unity? Examples? What are the criteria for distinguishing them, e.g., an airplane from a bird? Is the universe as a whole an intrinsic or extrinsic unity? How can you tell?

7. What is meant by the method of "Materialist Reductionism" in analyzing the nature of beings in our material world? Why is it such an obstacle to authentic understanding of the being of complex real things? What has its method left out or overlooked in the nature of real beings?

CHAPTER FIVE

Being as One and Many

Participation in Existence through Limiting Essence

INTRODUCTION TO THE PROBLEM

We have already discovered *unity* as an essential property of every real being: it is impossible to *be* at all without being internally one, cohering, unified. This unity does indeed allow for a multiplicity of parts or components within the being, but the unity must dominate if there is to be a being at all. This problem of the *One and the Many,* which we have met here for the first time within the unity of a single composed being, now opens out naturally to the problem of the One and the Many on the vast scale of the entire universe of real beings: how all beings, compared with each other, are at once many and diverse, yet somehow share in the common attribute of actual existence that joins them in one great all-embracing community of existents that we call "the real order," or simply "reality." Thus the totality of the real is somehow *both one and many.* How can this be? How must reality be structured in order to remain at once both many and diverse yet sharing in a common unity?

This *problem of the One and the Many,* as it is called, is the ultimate paradox of being and the deepest and most fundamental problem of all metaphysics, of every intellectual effort to achieve a total, unified vision of all reality. It is a question which all the great thinkers of both East and West have grappled with down the ages. One of the most profound and daring of these attempts to solve the problem—and one whose full implications have not always been caught even by his own disciples—is that proposed by *St. Thomas Aquinas* (1225–1274), as interpreted by the contemporary "existential Thomism" school. What is presented in this chapter is the author's own streamlined version of this central metaphysical vision. But the reader should be warned that not all Thomists, even contemporary ones, go along fully with the radically existential interpretation here presented, which I have chosen because it seems to me the most profound, coherent, and successful of all the attempts of metaphysicians to solve this basic problem (or, put more modestly, to live intellectually at home with the mystery involved, in all its luminous richness, which resists being exhaustively captured in any set of concepts or words.) To cope with this problem, however, we will have to make the effort to expand our horizon of thinking all the way to embrace the whole universe of real being in a kind of *synoptic vision*—not in detail, of course, but in its general lines as a single great community of a vast multiplicity of diverse beings, yet all somehow unified and present to each other by sharing existence. As one philosopher has put it, it is "rising above the fascination of the part to reach toward the vision of the whole." Or, as the great Chinese Taoist mystic, Chuang Tzu (c. 300 B.C.) has expressed it: "Great thinking sees all as One; small thinking breaks down into the many." Complete thinking must think both together.

Presentation of Problem

As soon as I attempt to take a synoptic view of all beings as beings, to compare all beings together under the aspect of their actual existence, I discover that I am obliged to affirm two apparently opposing propositions about each one of these beings. I am compelled to affirm that every single real being, compared to every other, is at once *similar* to every other, because each one is, exists, is real; and yet *dissimilar* to every other, because each one is precisely *this* being and not *that* one. In a word, A is; B is, etc., but A is not B, etc. Both of these basic attributes must be maintained, if I am to do justice to my experience and to the common bond underlying all expressions of my experience, namely, the "is" of judgment, whether the existential "is" asserting existence itself ("This exists") or the attributive "is" applying a real predicate to a real subject ("This is a human being").

One side of the picture, the distinction and diversity of beings, is obvious; but the commonness or unifying bond must also be affirmed. Without this common unifying bond, I could not even assert that the differences are real. For it is a general principle—which we here run into for the first time—that all distinction implies a deeper underlying bond of unity; it is impossible to compare any two diversities except on the basis (at least implicitly presupposed) of something underlying that they have in common—which in the present case would be that they are both present on the same "playing field" of existence in order to be compared to one another. Total diversities, with nothing whatsoever in common between them, are incomparable, in fact unthinkable. (Stop here and meditate a little on this very simple but very deep and pregnant principle of all thought and being, to which oriental thinkers have been especially sensitive.)

Hence *two main problems* confront the metaphysician here: (1) *One of fact:* must we take seriously both the multiplicity and the oneness of beings, or can we affirm only one aspect and deny the other as mere appearance, illusion, or projection of our minds? Some philosophers have attempted the latter, drastic "solution." (2) *One of explanation:* If we take both aspects seriously, how can they both be reconciled, fitted together, without contradiction? What kind of unity is involved? How can both the unity and the diversity be harmonized within each being? This is the challenge now awaiting our solution.

BASIC TYPES OF SOLUTION

Radical Monism.   In its extreme form this solution denies all multiplicity and diversity in being as illusion, to be gotten over by intellectual-spiritual enlightenment. Being is radically one: pure undivided Oneness alone exists, is truly real. Thus, in the beginning of Western thought *Parmenides,* the Presocratic (ca. 444 B.C.), who is probably the only literal radical monist in the West, denies all diversity within being, hence all change, which implies difference before and after. His famous argument, which has challenged metaphysicians ever since, runs thus: Whatever is, is being. Now if A and B are both real, and yet different from each other, they must differ by something real. But then this, too, must be being. Now it is impossible for two things to differ by what they have in common. Two things equal to the same thing, being, are equal to each other. Hence all things must really be one single being. And since real change implies real difference before and after, there can be no real change either. Thus the one great all-encompassing truth is: "It is," or "Being is," and the one great falsehood: "Being is not." All else is an illusion of the senses, to be broken through by enlightened intellect. This seems to be the first doctrine in the West of the conflict between appearance and reality—reality being the object of intellect, appearance and illusion the product of the bodily senses. As you can see, this left a whole set of philosophical puzzles for later Western thinkers to unravel.

In the East, the primary example of this radical Monism is the *Nondualist (Advaita) Vedanta* school of Hinduism (Sankara, eighth century A.D.). According to the *Upanishads* (the written accounts of the meditations of the original great philosopher-mystics), there are two great fundamental truths: (1) "The Brahman (Ultimate Reality) *is* all this and all that" [what appear to be many and diverse things]. (2) "The Brahman is *One* without a second." Hence all multiplicity and finitude, according to Sankara, is illusion, due to the veil of ignorance, *Maya,* though it appears to be real to those still wrapped in the mists of ignorance and not united with the Divine One, the only true reality. How does one explain this illusion? For one in the illusion, veiled by Maya, there is no solution; for one enlightened and united with the Brahman, the problem has disappeared!

But caution: for many of this school, if you push them hard, it seems that "unreal" does not mean totally unreal in our sense of the term, but *not fully real,* with no independent reality of their own compared to the One truly and immutably Real. The Many can be said to "exist," but not to be fully "real." *Example* of radical Advaita Vedanta teaching: Guru is teaching this doctrine in a clearing in the forest, surrounded by his disciples. A wild elephant suddenly charges in, trumpeting madly. Everyone, including the Guru, takes off into nearby trees. When the elephant has gone, they return and gather again. The disciples, puzzled, ask the Guru: "Master, we thought you taught us that all this is illusion. Then what about that elephant? We notice you took off into a tree as quickly as anyone." Guru, smiling benignly, looks around at them and replies: "What elephant?" End of objection (???)!

Mitigated Monism. Under this heading would fit the various forms of so-called *pantheism* (*pan-theos* = all things are God), which does admit real diversity, but only as modes or modifications or "parts" of a single all-embracing Divine Being or substance, not as distinct beings existing in their own right with their own autonomous existence. Thus ancient Greek and Roman *Stoicism* held that the world is one great Living Being, with the material cosmos as its body and God as its soul. In the modern West, *Spinoza* (d. 1677) is the prime exemplar: there is only one authentically Real Being, one substance = God = Infinite Substance; all other "things" are only diverse finite modes or "accidents" of the one Substance. For something to exist fully, in its own right, it must be self-sufficient, hence totally independent, hence infinite, and there can be only one such. *Hegel and some German idealists* may be interpreted as holding a sophisticated version of this: All reality is really the one Absolute Spirit unfolding itself in time and space through progressive finite appearances. The "reality" of these, however, is so qualified as to remain elusive, hard to pin down.

Many oriental philosophies can be roughly fitted in here. Alongside the strict Non-dualist Vedanta described above, there is another, *Bhakti* or devotional tradition far more common among ordinary people, of which the leading exponent is *Ramanuja* (11th century A.D.): the finite world and specially finite persons are real, but not with independent reality, only as modes or "accidents" of the one Divine Reality, in whom their ultimate reality is rooted. But human persons can truly love God as the one Great Lover. Positions like this are often called today "panentheism" (all things are in God) and are also finding exponents in the West, such as *Charles Hartshorne,* the disciple of Whitehead, and Process Philosophy, *Sally McFague,* Protestant theologian, who maintains: "The world is the body of God our Mother."

Radical Pluralism.   Only the plurality and diversity of things are real. There is no underlying real unity or unifying bond among them distinct from their irreducible particularity, not even the unity of one common Source (at least knowable to us). Unifying terms like "being" are mere mental abstractions, mere verbal-conceptual devices made up by our minds to help us conveniently speak about them all together in our limited vocabulary. All *empiricists* could be fitted in here. Nothing can be said to be real unless I can observe it in some distinct sense impression. But I cannot observe or point out "being" as some distinct new property alongside all the other particular properties I observe in things. Hence "being" refers to nothing real; it is a mere verbal or mental construction that deceives philosophers into thinking it refers to some distinct reality. Better to drop it entirely; we can easily get along without it. Thus metaphysics itself is but a myth carried over from the primitive mind, which thinks all words refer to real things. Cf. *Sidney Hook* in his famous essay, "The Quest of Being" (in his book of that title).

Mitigated Pluralism.   They admit a certain unity of being, but only in the sense of a brute minimum fact signifying an objective reference for my true judgments. They are not willing or able to delve any further into what is behind, or the ground, of this objectivity of our knowledge. Once this objective reference is verified (= something *out there,* "outside my thought"), there is no further interest in it for itself; all the philosophical focus is on *what* it is, its *nature or essence,* and *how* it operates, is related to others, not on the "is" of actual existence binding all together. Such philosophies are often termed *essentialist,* because focused on the essences of things, rather than *existentialist,* focused on existence.

Many philosophies go further to assert a certain unity among all beings in that they all derive from a single common Source, God, or the like—an *extrinsic unity* of common origin, not an *intrinsic unity* of real similitude through participation among all beings coming from this common Source. But these too belong to the general class of essentialist metaphysics.

Participation Doctrines.   These more richly complex and synthetic doctrines try to do justice both to the real multiplicity and diversity of beings and also the intrinsic bond of unity among them. This intrinsic unity is usually interpreted as some kind of "participation" in a basic common attribute; but this is interpreted diversely by the different schools. Thus, the long *Platonic tradition* (Plato, Plotinus, Neoplatonists) interpret this common attribute as *unity/goodness,* deriving from the Ultimate Principle = the One/Good. *Being* for them is not ultimate, since it signifies only the system of determinate, finite essences, beyond which is the absolute One, the Good, "beyond all being and essence" (Plato's *Republic,* Book V). For *St. Thomas,* whom we shall be following, the bond of unity comes from diverse participations in the act of existence, the common perfection embracing all levels of being, finite to Infinite, deriving from the Ultimate Source, the pure Subsistent Act of Existence with no limiting essence, which is God. For *Hegel* and others of this school it might be said to be a kind of participation in Absolute Spirit or Consciousness, although the reality of such participations remains elusive and ambiguous. For *Marxists* and other materialists, it might be said that all things are different degrees or modes of matter or material energy, the "lower" evolving into the "higher" under its own power. The influential, recently contemporary metaphysician *Martin Heidegger* is

one of the rare thinkers for whom there is a certain unity of Being, transcending each particular being or entity, yet nonetheless apparently
purely immanent in and dependent on them, with no further transcendent unitary ground or Source existing independently of them.
However, in his later thought Being seems to take on an inscrutable
transcendence of its own as *Es gibt* ("There Is"), intrinsically temporal
in nature.

EXPLANATORY THEORY OF THOMAS AQUINAS (EXISTENTIAL THOMISM): PARTICIPATION IN EXISTENCE THROUGH LIMITING ESSENCE

1. Problem of Fact

Must one take seriously both the *multiplicity/diversity* and the *unity* of
being?

Response.   One must take both seriously, both the Many and the
One in being. Both radical monism and radical pluralism are cop-outs;
they leave out too much of what is undeniable in our human experience, what should not be left out, lest the philosophical explanation eliminate or distort the very data of experience it is supposed to
explain.

The *diversity and multiplicity* cannot be denied as illusory without
contradicting an essential dimension of my experience, more certain
than any theory that tries to explain it away: I experience myself—and
so do most other adult human persons—as a free responsible center
and initiator of action, in interaction with other such independent centers, now agreeing with them, now disagreeing and acting against them,
struggling to develop myself and attain my own happiness, making
friends with others, whom I realize I cannot control; I take responsibility
for my own morally good and evil actions. If all there really is One
being, with all else illusion, then it follows: there is no one to be the *subject* of such illusions—I really do believe I am an agent distinct from
others—or to struggle to overcome it. And all moral responsibility and
moral evil would have to be denied, since the supreme perfect One
cannot without absurdity be accused as responsible for all the obvious
moral evil in the world, nor can such moral evil be simply denied.

Nor can all of us (at least human persons) be merely *parts* of one single real being, for if these parts really compose God's being, then it must be material, finite in many ways, imperfect, dependent on its own parts to exist, and so require a cause which put all its parts together to make one. But an infinite spiritual energy cannot have any finite, especially material parts. Also, more immediately evident, I would have no moral responsibility for either evil or good, since a part is governed by the whole in which it is and not independent in its action: my hand cannot be blamed for stabbing someone to death, or my sexual organs for raping someone. Also genuine, freely given *love* would be impossible for a mere part of a whole. All this is destructive of my whole dignity and responsibility as a moral person and unacceptable as an explanation of what it is to be a person with other real persons in our world.

The unity of being must also be taken seriously as something grounded objectively in the world, not just an empty word having no real reference but only linguistic convenience. The term "being" or "is" expresses what is most fundamental in all my experience, presupposed by everything else I say about the real world, namely, that "I am, and the other people and things I am dealing with *are*." There is a radical, totally objective difference between mere ideas, possibles, figures of my imagination, etc., and *real beings*, which must be expressed by the same word or expression, whatever it is in each language, since it expresses something they are all doing together: being actively present to each other in a common "field" of existence. Total diversity can neither express this common field of mutual presence nor the difference between mere possibility or ideas and reality. It is not the same to affirm *what* something is and *that* it *is*. All this points to the objective fact of a similar state common to all real beings, which we express in English by "being," "is," "exists," "is actively present to other real beings," etc., which we might call the *fact of existence* as an attribute common to all.

Furthermore, this fact or truth about real things must be rooted in some intrinsic property, some real act of presence within the thing itself, which grounds and justifies my judgment about it that "it is, is real." Here we pass from the mere *fact of existence* to the inner *act of existence* grounding it—a crucial passage in understanding which leads us into the Thomistic vision of what it means to *be*, to be an *actual existent*. For this inner act of existence is not reducible to an essence or mode of being, a *what*, nor a mere *static state*, but a *dynamic act of presence* that makes any essence or nature to be real, to present itself actively to other real beings. Unless we cross over this conceptual threshold of under-standing in depth what it means to *be* (as a verb), the whole Thomistic doctrine of the essence/existence composition, all finite beings will re-main incomprehensible or mere empty linguistic formalism. It may take a bit of metaphysical meditation to make this passage in under-standing from the *fact of existence* to the *act of existence* if you have never thought about it before.

2. *Problem of Explanation*

How do these two equally undeniable aspects—the multiplicity/diversity and the unity or community in existence—of all real beings, which seem at first glance to be irreconcilably opposed, fit together harmoniously within each real being, as we have seen they must?

SOLUTION OF ST. THOMAS

First a condensed summary of his conclusion, then the explicit formal argument in which his "synoptic insight" or "metaphysical vision" can be laid out.

   Summary.   Every real being, save perhaps one, must be constituted by a real metaphysical composition or inner structure or complemen-tary polarity of two correlative metaphysical co-principles within the unity of one being: namely, (1) an act of existence, by which it actually exists, is actively present in the universe of real beings; and (2) a limit-ing essence, by which it exists in this or that particular mode or manner of existing, as this or that particular being and not some other.

   Argument.   *Step 1:* Every real being compared to every other (e.g., myself compared to every other being) is both *like* every other being in that it actually "*is*," or *exists,* and *unlike* it in that it is *this* being and not *that* one.

   Step 2.   But this could not be unless every real being—save perhaps one—were made up of an inner metaphysical composition or substruc-ture of two really distinct, i.e., objectively irreducible (not separable), metaphysical co-principles (i.e., roots, or grounds, or sources: "a prin-ciple" is that from which something flows, either in thought or in being): one the *principle of similarity,* the other the *principle of dissimilarity.*

Reason: Similarity and dissimilarity are *opposite* and *irreducible* attributes. But it would be impossible for both to have their sufficient inner ground rooted in one and the same identical principle within each of the beings possessing these opposing attributes. For then a being would be both unlike every other for the identical reason that it is like them. But this does not make sense, is not intelligible. To put it another way: if something *exists* precisely because it is *John Smith,* then everything that exists would have to be John Smith—which is clearly not the case: existence is found in a vast diversity of other instances. Or if John Smith is *John Smith* precisely because he exists, then again everything that existed would have to be John Smith = false. Hence these two attributes must be rooted in two really distinct metaphysical co-principles within every real being—save perhaps one.

Why the exception? Because in any set of beings that possess the same common property, it is enough that all have some distinguishing note or attribute added on, except one, which then becomes distinct from all the others precisely because it possesses the common property in simple purity and fullness, without any composition with a distinguishing principle. Thus, in the set A, A/B, A/C, A/D . . . , all the members possess the common property A, but all are distinct from each other, both like and unlike each other, because of their distinctive co-principles, although one remains simple, thus also unlike all the others. The logic of such sets allows for one and only one possible exception in every set. We do not, however, know whether such a possible exception actually exists in our universe until we have established the existence of God as the one infinite Source of all being—which we have not yet done (see Ch. 14). Aside from this one exception, every new member that enters into the community of real existents must have its own new distinguishing note in addition to the act of existence; otherwise, it will coincide with some other member.

Step 3.   What is the nature of this composition of two distinct co-principles within every real being (save perhaps one)? It cannot be a composition between two complete beings. *Reason:* this would destroy the unity of every real being in question. We have already established that every real being must be intrinsically one as part of the very meaning of what it means to be. But you cannot make one being out of two; this is a contradiction. Hence their distinct reality must be less than that of a complete being or thing, but rather that of two *mutually correlative co-principles* or co-constituents, each incomplete by itself, within the enveloping unity of the one complete being, distinct but inseparable, i.e., one cannot exist alone without the other. A helpful image might be that of the two poles, positive and negative, of an electrical system. One is not the other, but unless the two are there no current will pass between: so no real being, unless both co-principles are present and functioning. This kind of composition or polarity within a real being has been given the technical name in Thomistic metaphysics of a *real metaphysical composition* (i.e., not physical parts, because the two co-principles must interpenetrate). This composition is *real,* between really distinct principles, because they are contraries and irreducible one to the other. But they are less than the strong real distinction between two complete beings, because that would destroy the unity of the real beings that are the data to be explained.

This real metaphysical composition is a very delicate but powerful philosophical tool for analyzing the inner structures of beings without destroying their basic unity, as we shall see when we come across other cases of the One and the Many in being that need explaining. One must always, however, guard against the danger of hardening up the real composition of co-principles, through a heavy-handed logic, to become a composition between two things, which destroys its effectiveness. This happened with later philosophers after St. Thomas, e.g., William of Ockham and his Nominalist disciples.

Step 4. Now we have to *identify* and give appropriate names to these two metaphysical co-principles in terms of the functions they fulfill. (1) The principle of similarity between all beings as existent is aptly called the *act of existence.* (2) The principle of dissimilarity making each being distinct from every other is aptly called the *essence* or particular *nature* of each one, the reason why it is *this* being and not *that* one.

Step 5. The question now arises of exactly how to conceive the relationship of these two co-principles to each other: are they two positive realities added on to each other, or are they related as positive and negative? Which is higher, which lower?

A. *The act of existence* is certainly a positive principle, in fact, the foundation for all else that is positive in a being, if it is to be real. But is *essence* also a positive reality in its own right, added on to the foundation of existence to yield all the different levels of perfection within reality?

Many have tried this path. On this view, existence would be a *minimum* basis, the same in all (the mere brute fact of existence, of standing outside of nothingness); and essences would be new positive perfections added on to the minimum basis of existence to produce higher and lower levels of reality. In a word, *existence + essences,* both real in their own right.

Response. No, this is not possible. Nothing real or positive can be added on to existence from without. For what is added must already be real, have existence within it; otherwise, it is adding on nothing real. Existence envelops absolutely everything in a being that is in any way positive or real; hence, the essences supposedly added on to produce higher reality would already have to be real to add on anything at all. Hence, the act of existence cannot be a minimum level onto which essences are added as further reality. If they are real, existence has already slipped into them; it can never be a minimum.

B. But if existence cannot be a minimum onto which anything else real is added on from the outside—outside of existence there is only nothingness—then the principle of existence must be a *maximum,* an all-encompassing plenitude, with essences serving as limiting, diversifying principles within the fullness of existence itself, diversifying being by limiting it in different ways from within, partially negating the fullness of being by diverse, limited modes of existing. The relation of essence to existence can thus be only one of subtraction, not addition: Existence − essence 1, − essence 2, etc., each of which is a distinct partial negation of the total fullness of existence possible. Essences are thus not something positive added on to a minimum base of existence, but rather intrinsic limiting or restrictive principles particularizing and finitizing each act of existence that is not the total plenitude of pure unrestricted existence, thus allowing for many different real beings, all limited participations, through different essences, in the unlimited fullness of existence itself. The possibility is also left open—which we will later discover must in fact be the case—that there may be *one,* and only one, *unlimited act of existence,* embracing all positive perfection possible within it in a single, infinitely intensive Act (without limiting essence) which, in turn, would have to be the Ultimate Source for all other beings. This would be the philosophical name for God. But we have not yet reached this topmost level of being; we are building up step by step from below. And note well that even if one is not willing to accept the existence of an ultimate reality like God, one would still have to accept

the real composition of essence/existence to render intelligible all the
multiple, diverse participations in the common attribute of existence
that we see all around us and make up what we call the real universe.

Step 6.   There is one last refinement in the understanding of essence as limiting principle: St. Thomas does not understand it as a
purely negative principle, but rather as a determinate capacity which
allows only so much existence (i.e., not a quantitative notion but a qualitative level of intensity in participating in the fullness of active energy
that is existence itself) and no more. It can be thought of, therefore, as
a kind of *receptive capacity* that receives and "holds" existence to this
level—as long as we do not turn it into something independent with a
reality of its own: it is totally correlative to the actuality of existence that
fills it. Thus the cause which brings a new being into existence must "co-
create," as St. Thomas puts it, both the intensive energy, the *virtus
essendi,* or power of being, as he does not hesitate to call it, and its limiting capacity to which the existence is fitted simultaneously together as
forming a single, limited whole being. It is the whole being that is
brought into being by the cause, not the co-principles separately, which
can never exist by themselves. Metaphysical co-principles can exist only
"married," never as single or divorced.

Conclusion

The One and the Many are thus reconciled as constituting together the
world of reality. The first great problem of metaphysics is thus resolved,
but it takes serious philosophical reflection to take in all the implications of this extremely rich and central metaphysical doctrine of St.
Thomas and to hold together the entire solution at once in a single
"synoptic vision" of all real beings as forming a single all-embracing
community of existents. All have not made this effort, it seems, or have
not known how to go about it, so that the doctrine has been open to
many misunderstandings and objections down the ages.

OBJECTIONS AND DIFFICULTIES

This central Thomistic doctrine has been much criticized, misunderstood even in his own time. Here are the main ones:

1. The main difficulty comes from misunderstanding the real metaphysical composition of the co-principles of essence and existence as though they were two beings, two things, each real in its own right, and then somehow stuck together to form a single real being, which, as two things really distinct, remain separable in principle, at least by the power of God. This would clearly be absurd and impossible, since a real essence separated from its existence would be nothing, and a real act of existence with no limiting and distinguishing essence would be nothing in particular or the total fullness of being, God himself, which can be only one. They are not such at all, not two things, but two incomplete, correlative, mutually implicating co-principles, each less than a complete being but rather an inner structure or polarity of opposite constituent principles within the intrinsic unity of the one real being. They are called really distinct only because they each play distinct and irreducible roles within the whole; but they are by nature inseparable—one cannot be without the other.

The objectors almost always share two biases: (1) They have bought into the later, heavy-handed interpretation of real distinction, brought in by *William of Ockham* (d. 1347), whereby the only acceptable criterion is the separability of the principles in question: to be really distinct = to be separable as two things. This criterion of separability for all real distinctions continues on down through Oxford University, where it started, inherited by *Hume* the empiricist (who also studied there) and has persisted throughout most of modern philosophy without further critical reflection. It actually wipes out that whole delicate tool of metaphysical analysis of the inner structure of beings without compromising their intrinsic unity, which is the notion of a real metaphysical composition of co-principles. (2) Secondly, they usually do not take seriously existence as an inner *act* of energy-filled presence that is the source of all perfection in a real being, rather than merely a static state, and hence do not take seriously the participation structure of all existents as diverse participations in this central perfection of existence, which is the key to St. Thomas's powerfully unified vision of reality. You cannot discover the need for the real distinction of essence/existence just by examining a single being by itself; it requires a synoptic vision of the whole of reality as both one and many, a community of diverse existents, to see the point of the argument.

2. The act of existence (best understood as the "activity of existing") which is participated in diversely by many different essences

is not to be understood crudely as the one infinite act of existence of God himself, which is somehow divided up among creatures like pieces of a pie. God has no pieces nor can he lose his infinite fullness by creating more beings. Each particular act of existence is a new one, fresh out of the oven, so to speak, which exists only as correlated with its own particular limiting essence, not first in an unlimited state, then afterwards limited. We are not "parts" of God. But each one is limited, not because it is an act of existence, but because it is correlated with its own limiting essence. Yet all are analogously similar, because they all participate in the common perfection of existence as active presence. They all share in an objective similarity that cannot be denied and needs the same term to express it: _real._

3. Yet it must be admitted that it is not easy to understand, let alone visualize with the imagination—which we always tend spontaneously to do—how a negatively limiting principle of essence can be really distinct from what it limits. First, one must not try to visualize it—the imagination is equipped to visualize only complete beings—not to think out why something *must be*. Second, one must always keep in mind that this distinction between metaphysical co-principles is not one between two real things in their own right, but is the minimum degree of real distinction: *less* than between two complete beings yet *more* than simple identity. The two, to make proper sense, must always be thought together: limited-existence, mode-of-existing. And the limiting principle cannot be identical with the existence it limits, because if so, then wherever anything existed it would have to exist with this same limit—which is clearly not the case, since many different beings simultaneously exist, and one is not the other. So we must hold onto something like a "real distinction" (as signifying the objective irreducibility of component constituents whose functions are opposed to each other), like an inner polarity of opposites neither of which can be present and function without the other.

So to understand properly what is the core of the Thomistic doctrine, what is most important in it, it may be better not to focus on the technical meaning of "real distinction" or "real composition" in themselves, but rather to see the whole universe as diverse limited participations in the all-embracing perfection of actual existence (*esse* = the to be of real beings, the verb form of *ens* or being in Latin). Perhaps the easiest way to represent it intellectually to ourselves is as a case of *sharing*, i.e., when one source shares the fullness that it has with several others who receive it in various limited degrees according to their diverse capacities. Thus, a great mathematician can share his rich mathematical wisdom as a teacher with many students, each of whom will receive it, not in its original fullness but as much as he can assimilate according to his own limited capacity at this point. One must obviously distinguish here between the wisdom communicated, shared, and the different limiting capacities of the various receivers: it must be said to be the same wisdom, but diversely received according to the distinct diverse capacities of the receivers. Thus the best way to think the whole universe of real being as both one and many is from the *point of view of God,* the infinite fullness of pure unlimited existence, and the one ultimate Source of all being, as actively intending and willing to share, to communicate, his own fullness of being with many other limited beings, each according to its own limited degree or capacity (essence), each corresponding to a distinct *idea* or plan in the mind of God for sharing his own unitary fullness with many. The unity of existence in the many participants derives from the unitary fullness of the Source and the single idea, intention, will, to communicate this to many according to different modes or manners of being. *Sharing* is a universal phenomenon in our world and the technical structure of real metaphysical composition within each being seems to be the best available way for our minds to express it in our language, though it does remain the deepest mystery of being that no concepts or language of ours can fully and exhaustively express. Thus the full understanding of what we already have good reasons for affirming, the universal participation structure of essence/existence in all real beings save perhaps one, must wait till we make the final ascent to God as ultimate Source of all being, in chapter 14. St. Thomas himelf seems to have gotten his whole synoptic vision of being all at once as a philosophical-theological whole from meditating on God's revelation of his name to Moses: "I am who am" (Exodus 2).

V. Implications for Understanding Our Universe

1. This key metaphysical doctrine of St. Thomas—reconciling the One and the Many in the universe as diverse participations of all beings in the central perfection of existence through limiting essence—if properly understood, opens up a magnificent synoptic vision that can

easily deepen into a religious or mystical vision of the whole universe of real beings as a single great community of existents, with a deep "kinship" of similarity running through them all, which turns out when fully analyzed to imply that all are in some way *images of God*, their Source, each in its own unique but limited (imperfect) way. "Ah," one poet said when I explained this to him, "then being is the act of belonging!" Right on! No one can ever be totally alone, isolated, alienated in a universe of real beings.

2. This is also a metaphysical grounding for the new *holistic and ecological thinking* that is springing up all around us among thoughtful people in our painfully alienated culture (alienated from nature, from our true selves, from each other, and from God). It nourishes a sense of affinity with all creation, especially our own little planet earth, as fellow sharers in existence (and ultimately images of the same God, Source of all being), and hence promotes a sense of respect and reverence for all real beings as having their own intrinsic value and not merely being instruments, raw material, for own self-centered exploitation.

3. This metaphysical vision of all real beings as diverse limited participations in the one central perfection of the act of existence opens up quite a new perspective for understanding in depth what it means to be—a perspective quite new and apparently unique in the history of Western thought: it shifts the whole center of gravity in the study of real beings from the *essences* and forms, the *what* in things, to their *act of existence* as the central core, the positive "guts," so to speak, of all the positivity and perfection that is in them—the "existential turn," as it has been called. Most of Western philosophical thinking, from Plato and Aristotle on down through modern philosophy to the recent "existentialisms" of our time, have been *essentialist* in this sense, that while they acknowledged the *fact* of existence as a kind of brute fact or minimum static state presupposed for further study, once this is verified or taken for granted, they paid little further attention to it, focusing almost entirely on *what* things are, their *natures*, and *how* they act. In St. Thomas, what was taken by others as the *minimum*, to which all other perfections were added, now becomes the *maximum*, the core and fullness of all perfection in which all the diverse essences share by limited participation, and the ground for all further growth in perfection. *Heidegger* has lamented what he calls "the forgetfulness of Being" in Western thought since Plato—justly so, for the most part, except that St. Thomas is the outstanding exception. (Heidegger did not seem to know this aspect of

Thomas at all, since the awakening to the full implications of existential Thomism did not emerge till around 1939 and after, with Etienne Gilson and others, after Heidegger had done his main work.) The *recent existentialisms* in Europe, however (Jean-Paul Sartre, etc.), in addition to often being anti-theistic, usually go too far in the other direction and lose sight of essence entirely: "Existence precedes essence; we forge our own essences by freedom," as Sartre puts it, where careful metaphysical analysis gets exchanged for psychological attitudes. "Thomistic existentialism" balances carefully *both essence and existence* in its participation metaphysics, which we do not find anywhere among the contemporary phenomenological existentialisms—although there are significant traces of it in the Catholic existentialist *Gabriel Marcel.*

4. Another advantage of looking at all beings from the perspective of the act of existence as the central perfection of all things, diversely participated in by limiting essences, is that it helps to clarify the relations between God as the unique ultimate Source of all being and the world of finite creatures. On the one hand, it is clear how God, as pure Subsistent Act of Existence (*Ipsum Esse Subsistens*) with no limiting essence, transcends all his creatures as composed of existence and limiting essences, and yet, on the other, why there is a deep similarity to God running through all creatures as all participations in the one central perfection of God himself, so that they can all be truly called "images of God." (To get hold of this insight into existence as the central perfection of all real beings, containing all other modes of perfection within its all-encompassing fullness, which is so unique in the history of Western philosophy, it may help to reverse our way of speaking for a while and say, not "This horse exists, a man exists," etc., but rather "Existence here is found in a horsy mode, a human mode, a rose-bushy mode. . . ." Or: "There is an existent here in the horsy mode, the human mode, the rose-bushy mode. . . .") Some key texts of St. Thomas on this point may help:

> That which I call esse (the act of existence, the to-be of things) is that which is most perfect . . . the actuality of all acts and because of this the perfection of all perfections. . . . For nothing can be added on to esse that is extraneous to it, since there is nothing outside of it save non-being. (*De Potentia*, q. 7, art. 2 ad 9)

> Every perfection of any being whatsoever belongs to it according to its act of existence (*suum esse*). For no perfection would belong to a

man from his wisdom unless he actually is wise, and so of all other attributes. Therefore according to the mode in which a thing has existence is its mode of perfection; for according as the act of existence of a thing is contracted to some particular mode of perfection, either greater or lesser, it is said to be more or less perfect. Now if there is something to which belongs the total power of being (*tota virtus essendi*), no perfection that belongs to anything whatever can be lacking to it. And so God, who is identical with his own act of existence, as shown above, possesses his act of existence according to the total power of existence itself. Therefore he can lack no perfection that belongs to any being whatever. (*Sum. contra Gent.*, Bk. I, ch. 28)

5. Finally, the centering of all perfection in the act of existence as act of presence sheds new light on why material being is a lower mode of existence, involving more limitation than finite spiritual beings. Spiritual beings, even though limited in how much existence they contain, have their act of being all together in one intense, concentrated presence, whereas material beings have it dispersed, spread out in space, parts outside of parts (= extension). Hence they are less unified, less fully and intensely present than immaterial beings, less fully real in the sense of intensive quality of presence. No material being, with parts extended outside of parts, is present to its whole self instantaneously, all at once, but only across time, hence is never fully present to itself at any one moment but only across the dispersal of space and time. Thus also the various beings in a material cosmos can never be present to each other fully, all at once, but only imperfectly and successively, across space-time. We can think of them in an *idea* as all present at once; they cannot *be* together all at once in reality. Hence, as not fully present either to themselves or to each other, we can say that they are less fully real, actively present, than spiritual beings like angels and God.

Cf. W. N. Clarke, "Action as the Self-Revelation of Being: A Central Theme in the Thought of St. Thomas," Ch. 3 in *Explorations in Metaphysics.*

QUESTIONS FOR REVIEW AND DISCUSSION

1. Explain the basic problem of the One and the Many.
2. Explain the basic positions of (a) Radical Monism; (b) Mitigated Monism; (c) Radical Pluralism; and (d) Participation doctrines.

St. Thomas's Solution

 3. Why must we take seriously both the one and the many?

 4. *The Argument:*

  a) Basic data of problem? b) Why must there be a real distinction of co-principles in all beings save perhaps one? c) Nature
  of this "real metaphysical composition"? d) How best name
  the components? e) Relation between the two?

 5. *Main Objections:* (a) Misunderstanding of "composition"? (b)
Misunderstanding of participation "in the act of existence"? (c) Misunderstanding of "essence as limit"?

 6. *Key Implications?*

 7. Sit back now and try to get a *synoptic vision* of the whole universe
as both Many yet somehow One: Can you get a feel for this whole vast
universe of real beings as somehow a single great community of actual
existents joined together by the same bond of similarity that is their
sharing, each in its own distinctive way, in the one great central perfection, analogically common to all—*actual existence, co-presence* in some way
to all the others?

CHAPTER SIX

The One and the Many on the Same Level of Being

Form and Matter I

New Problem

In the previous chapter we uncovered the most fundamental structure of reality: the universal participation of all real beings—save perhaps one—in existence through limiting essence, expressed through the real metaphysical composition of essence and existence. This is the first case we have met of the One and the Many within being, and it holds not only for our universe but for all possible universes containing more than one being.

But now, as we pursue our search for the general laws and principles governing our world and examine the universe of our experience more closely, we discover that, in addition to the basic unity and diversity of real beings in the all-inclusive order of existence itself, there are many smaller domains exhibiting the same one/many pattern. For all beings are not totally unique, totally different from each other in the order of their essences (what they are) but are found grouped together to form *classes, groups, kinds* of being—*species,* as they are technically called—where many individuals have in common not only existence, making them members of the all-inclusive community of existents, but also the same specific kind or mode of being. Thus we find the one and the many reappearing in the order of species, i.e., a class or group of individual beings that possess the same specific nature or essence. The essence/existence structure we discovered previously is much too general and non-specific to take care of this new and tighter unity within their essences. It looks as though a new metaphysical substructure or composition is needed. Thus every human being belonging to the species *homo sapiens* is both an individual human being, distinct from every other, yet somehow very much *like* them all, in that it too possesses the same human nature as all the others. And it is the same for all the beings we know in our experience: all the living beings we know are found existing in groups of many others in the same species—animals, fish, insects, plants (except in the unusual case of the last member of a species going into extinction); molecules, atoms, subatomic particles are all found in vast numbers in each species. How can each member of a species be both *like* all the others, in possessing the same specific nature or mode of being, and yet be *unlike* all the others in that it is this unique individual and not any other?

The problem can be summed up thus: How is it possible for many distinct individual beings to share the same specific mode of being or essence, to belong to the same species? What are the ultimate conditions of possibility that can render intelligible these two opposite attributes in the same being? The peculiar difficulty the solution must cope with—not found in the essence/existence case—is that while each member of the species is a new individual being, unique in its own being and hence essentially distinct from every other, none of them can contain any essential qualitative differences from each other, i.e., all must be essentially equal in nature, for otherwise they would constitute a new species or kind of being. A prime example is the Declaration of Independence, the foundation stone of the Constitution of the United States, with its ringing declaration of the basic equality of all human beings: "All men by nature are created equal. . . ." Here you have the many and the one brought together in the same sentence, together with the specific equality of all who possess this nature.

Note. Such a structure is not a necessary one in all possible universes, like the one and the many in the order of existence, since there could well be a universe where each being would be unique in kind—as would be the case if there existed only angels or pure spirits, each of which exhausts and cannot share the perfection of its own species. But we find as a matter of fact this structure of species and individuals all over in our present universe. It is not up to the metaphysician himself to prove this fact; only when this is discovered does his problem of making sense of it arise.

The fact can only be settled by analyzing our experience, with the help of science. It seems obvious in the case of non-living beings: every molecule of water has the identical inner structure, H_2O; likewise every atom of hydrogen, etc. It gets more complicated with living beings because of the overlapping of evolutionary development. But the notion seems indispensable. Look at the grave implications if this is denied in the case of human beings: if every human being is unique in kind, in its qualitative content of perfection, then we are wide open to claims of superior races or individuals, supermen, rule by elite, no democracy, etc. Christ could no longer be said to take on "our human nature," but we would have to ask "which human nature?" Which one would be redeemed?

So it is much wiser for the metaphysician to accept the fact as either certain or the only one plausible, and come to grips with the *problem* it raises, than to stick his head in the sand and cop out. Strange to say, however, only a small number of metaphysicians have tried to come to grips explicitly with this problem, outside of the long Aristotelian, Thomistic, and Scholastic medieval tradition. One of the few metaphysical explanations proposed is the powerful—and controversial—one put forward tersely by *Aristotle* and developed with considerably more refinement by *Thomas* and his followers. Confrontation with modern science, however, has moved me to refine and modify even further the overly terse and simplified account given by Aristotle, and to some extent by St. Thomas, which can easily be misleading to a modern reader. But the doctrine seems to me too significantly illuminating about the nature of reality to be simply let go with nothing to replace it.

I. THOMISTIC SOLUTION (ADAPTED)

Step 1. Wherever there are many beings belonging to the same species or kind of being, each member of this species is at once *like* every other, because it has the same specific nature or essence, and yet *unlike* or distinct from every other, because it is this individual being and not that other one in the same species. Neither the likeness nor the unlikeness, the sameness nor the difference, can be denied without destroying the very data of the problem with which we began.

Step 2. But since this likeness and unlikeness, found together in the same being, are *opposite* and *irreducible* attributes, each must be grounded in an irreducibly—hence really—distinct root or source within the same being. Otherwise each member of the species will be similar to every other by the identical principle that renders it dissimilar, distinct from the others. But this is not intelligible. If what makes Mary Jones to be human is precisely the same as what makes her to be Mary Jones, then every human being would have to be Mary Jones, for whatever is identical with something must always be present wherever the latter is. But this is clearly not the case, since there are many other members in the same human species.

Therefore, there must be, within the essence or nature of every member of a species, a *real metaphysical composition* of *two really distinct but correlative co-principles:* one to ground the *similarity* of a common specific essence; the other to ground the *distinctness* of one individual member from another. As we saw in the case of the essence/existence composition, these two distinct principles cannot be *things,* or complete beings, because this would destroy the unity of each being that we started off with. Hence they must be metaphysical co-principles, distinct but correlative and inseparable. One can't be without the other.

Step. 3. How to identify and describe these two principles? Let us describe them by their functions, the role they play:

1. The Principle of similarity: This is that principle within each member of the species that makes it to be *this kind* of being and not some other kind. It is the intelligible, qualitative pattern or constitutive structure within the being that makes it to be this kind of being. Aristotle first called it the *essential form* of the being, from the analogy of the form of a statue (what it represents) as distinct from the *material* of which it is composed; and the name has stuck ever since. It is not the outer visible form, but the inner intelligible "shape" or *constitutive structure* of the essence (i.e., the mode of existence which receives the act of existence according to the capacity of its essence). This intelligible pattern or essential form is what is common to all the members of the species; it is what we abstract from the individuating traits of each member to form the universal abstract concept of the common natures of things, e.g., man, dog, horse, computer, etc.

Definition of the principle of essential form: it is that in a being which makes it to be this kind of being and not some other.

2. *The Principle of distinction.*   This is the difficult part of the analysis, to find a principle that will distinguish one individual in the species from another, without introducing any essential qualitative difference between them. For this would immediately change the species from the same or qualitatively equal mode of being to another higher or lower one, which would destroy the original data to be explained. Let us proceed by the progressive elimination of solutions that cannot work.

A. It cannot be another essential form or formal qualitative principle in the essential order. For then (1) this would introduce a new qualitative formal note different in each member, which would automatically turn it into another species or kind of being. There is no use appealing here to different accidental or non-essential properties. For these presuppose that we already have two distinct individuals set up to receive these different accidental properties. Thus two human beings cannot be essentially distinguished by one having red hair and the other black, for to have two different colors of hair presupposes that they already have two distinct bodies and two heads. How are we going to distinguish the two basic subjects who can possess the distinct sets of further attributes?

(2) The second reason is that two essential forms operating at the same time within the same essence of one being would destroy the unity of its essence. Since an essential form is that which determines a being to be this kind of being and not that, two essential forms in the same essence at the same time would make it two kinds of being at once. But this is absurd. The nature of a thing can't be both a man and a dog, or a cabbage, at once! True, a higher form can incorporate the operations and properties of lower types of forms. But then to maintain the unity of the nature it must include them as a single synthetic unity, a single unified structure in which the lower subordinate elements lose their full autonomy of being and operation. To be one kind of thing you must have only one fully operating essential form. Hence the principle of distinction between the members cannot be some other principle on the formal qualitative level, a second essential form.

B. Hence we must adopt the only other alternative: the principle of distinction must be a non-formal or non-qualitative one which is able to distinguish two natures without introducing formal qualitative differentiation between them. Since such a principle is the correlative opposite of form—a qualitative notion—Aristotle first called it *matter*, or *primary matter.* How can this do the job of distinguishing without formal differentiation? Precisely because it is the very essence of matter, as quantitatively extended, to be spread out in space, parts outside of parts—one part of a material body can never be in the identical same place as another (by the Pauli exclusion principle in physics); they must be "spread out" to some degree distinct from each other, though of course they can be connected.

This is just what we need to do the job at hand. The identical form, or formal structure, intelligible pattern, can now be reproduced endlessly in different parts of this extended matter, qualitatively unchanged: each new reproduction is distinct from every other precisely because it is *here* and not *there* in the space-time matrix of extended matter. There is no limit to the process as long as the supply of matter holds out: once there is no more matter to be informed, taken over by form, then there can be no more new members in the species. But to be here and not there is not to be a different kind of being, but only to be a different individual of the same kind. Note, too, that the distinction between being located here and there in space, since it is not a formal, qualitative one, cannot be represented in a purely intellectual concept or idea, but must be pointed to with one's finger or other material instrument, or else indicated by a set of physical measurement operations to be carried out practically from a given spatial perspective: e.g., 10 feet west of this tree, 5 feet north, etc.

Notice that this principle of quantitatively extended matter not only serves to distinguish and thus individuate the form of one individual in the species from that of another; it also serves as a limiting principle. It pins down or limits the form so that it can be and operate only here in the material world and not *there.* If I am living in America, I cannot also get all the cultural experiences and benefits of living in China, and vice versa, nor can I travel there instantaneously but only across the dispersal of space-time. Purely spiritual beings, on the contrary, transcend this space-time dispersal and do not have their being pinned down to here and not there in the world of matter. They can be and operate anywhere they wish just by willing it, which we unfortunately cannot do (although there seem to be a few rare cases of miraculous "bi-location" of some saints in two different places at the same time to carry out some crucial mission).

Reciprocal dependence of form and matter.   Since the form of a material being is individuated only by being received in some distinct part of extended matter, it can neither exist as a real individual being nor operate except joined with its correlative matter, or physical body. Its whole function is limited to carrying on through its body those operations characteristic of its species, which always involve cooperation of the body; it cannot perform purely spiritual operations independent of any body; thus an animal, lacking a rational spiritual soul, cannot form purely intellectual ideas or carry on strictly intellectual reasoning and thinking. Such a form, therefore, is a metaphysical co-principle, which cannot be or operate without its material partner as co-principle. Similarly, matter, in its pure state at the lowest level of reality—which Aristotle called primary matter, or pure potentiality—has no form of its own, but is a principle of pure formless "plasticity," receptivity, determinability by form. Though it has no form of its own, it must always be informed by some form—nothing can actually be a real being unless it is something definite and determinate, not indeterminate, i.e., neither this or that or anything else in particular. Hence it can never be on its own as a complete thing or being, but always needs some co-principle of essential form in order to actually *be* something. Like its companion co-principles of essence and existence, it can exist only as married, never as single or divorced.

As a result, pure matter by itself can never be discovered by any scientific analysis, which can only pick up complete real beings in its empirical measurements, never separate out for study its metaphysical co-principles, since, though distinct, they are not physically separable. Later medieval philosophers after St. Thomas slipped into a much heavier, more "reified" ("thingified") conception of primary matter as a real *thing in itself*, hence in principle separable from any essential form, and then went to look for it by scientific methods. Since they could not find it—we have seen above why—they concluded that there was no such thing and rejected the whole Aristotelian-Thomistic theory of form and matter as the inner constitutive structure of all material beings, settling instead for small atomic particles as the ultimate constituents of the material world. This may well be the case from the scientific point of view, but it still leaves unsolved the problem of the one and the many within species, how there can be many equal individuals carrying the same essential specific nature, how in particular there can be many atoms all bearing the identical very precise formal structure—hydrogen, or oxygen, or carbon, etc. For we now know that not all atoms have the same identical formal structure (there are over a hundred in the atomic table). Here is one example of an apparent conflict between philosophy and modern science that should not be a conflict at all; the two methods are operating on different levels of analysis. Each one needs the other for completeness, but neither one can do the job of the other.

ADAPTATION OF THE ABOVE IN THE LIGHT OF MODERN SCIENCE

The above basic structure of essential form / individuating matter seems to me quite sound and indispensable for solving the problem of how to reproduce the identical essential form (also called technically the *substantial form* to distinguish it from merely accidental forms that do not change the essential nature of a being) in many individuals in the same species without affecting their essential equality in perfection, namely, by providing a material principle of spread-out dispersal across space (= a spatially extended "stuff," parts outside of parts, in different parts of which the same form can be reproduced essentially intact). The same form is said to inform different parts of extended matter, yielding a new individual bearer of this form pinned down, so to speak, in a different location from every other member of the species in the underlying space-time matrix that makes up our material world.

But the original terse presentation of the doctrine can be a bit misleading in terms of the complexity of the make-up of material beings as science has revealed to us today. The impression given by Aristotle and some textbook presentations of the doctrine is that every composition of form / matter is between a form exactly identical in every detail to every other in the species, united directly to pure formless primary matter with no intermediary levels. That is too simple a picture. In fact, though there is definitely one major, central organizing form that operates as the one fully autonomous and operative essential form, it organizes and controls lower levels of organized elements—cells, molecules, atoms, subatomic particles. These already have a certain formal structure of their own taken over and controlled by the central form to make them part of a higher whole; they are not purely indeterminate formless matter lacking any formal structure at all. They are rather subordinate levels of formal organization taken over and controlled or used by the higher central form for the goals of the organism as a whole, hence no longer operating autonomously. Thus it can truly be said that there is still only one fully autonomous essential form operating within the nature of the being.

Analogous nature of "matter" as a co-principle.   But this also means that we must expand the notion of *matter* as an essential component of all members of the same species to include not only totally formless matter but any lower component element in a complex material being. Each such element is so plastic and determinable in its very being—not just on a superficial accidental level—that it can be taken over by a higher entity with a more powerful central form and be turned into a subordinate part of the higher being, thus losing its own autonomy of being and action that it had outside of the compound. This seems to be one of the essential distinguishing characteristics of the being of these lower elements, that they have the real capacity, the *ontological openness,* to be taken over by higher forms to become functioning parts of higher unities. Thus subatomic particles have a built-in capacity and readiness to be taken over and become components of the powerful new unity of atoms; so too atoms to be taken over by molecules, molecules by living cells, cells by whole organisms. Once we reach higher levels of being, whole plants, animals, and especially humans no longer have the capacity, the potentiality, to be taken over by any other being and made part of a higher whole. But because these lower elements have this plasticity, this capacity for being informed and determined by a higher form, not just in a superficial accidental way, but reaching deep into their very essential being, they can be analogously called matter too. And this is enough for them to fulfill their function in the basic Aristotelian-Thomistic argument for the need of a metaphysical composition of essential (substantial) form and matter in every member of the same species. It still remains, however, that when we reach the lowest level of subatomic particle with any organization or structure (form) in it at all—and there are large numbers of these with identical structures within higher, more complex natures—there is nothing left to differentiate and individuate them but a co-principle of pure formless matter, pure extended stuff with no form at all of its own, the ultimate primary matter of both Aristotle and St. Thomas. And in the light of Einstein's brilliant discovery of the interchangeability of matter and energy, in his famous formula $E = m \times c^2$, this ultimate material "stuff" may well be not the static, inert kind of "stuff" that Aristotle, Thomas, and all the ancients and medievals—and many moderns before Einstein—took for granted as their images of matter, but rather the reservoir of primal formless material, or spatialized energy, that physicists speak of when they describe the whole material cosmos as a constant process of "transformations of energy." Note the irreducible duality here of *form* and *energy* even within the language of science!

St. Thomas himself already recognized this need for flexibility and analogy in the understanding of matter, in a small work written in answer to this very question, called *De Mixtu Elementorum* (*Opera Philosophica,* ed. Marietti, Rome, p. 155), translated with notes by V. Larkin, "On the Combining of the Elements," in *Isis* 51 (1960), 67–72:

> We must find another way to state how the elements are, on the one hand, genuinely united and, on the other, are not entirely deprived of their nature but remain in the mixture after a special manner. It is the active forces emanating from the substantial forms of the elementary bodies which are conserved in the mixed bodies [a "mixture" was their technical term for a higher unified nature, not just an aggregate]. Consequently, the substantial forms of the elements exist in the mixture not with respect to their full actuality (*non quidem actu*) but with respect to their active power (*virtute:* which some translate as "virtual presence").

Analogy of essential form. Flexibility must also be allowed here as to how tight the unity and exact similarity of one such form with all the others of the same species must be, in the light of the vast complexity of higher living organisms revealed to us by contemporary biology. Small variations in the number of certain constituent elements in certain organs of the body, more or less calcium, fat, etc., or slight variations in the genetic code—already as large in humans as a complete encyclopedia set—slowly shifting in the process of evolution, are not enough to significantly change the dominant essential form into a whole new one. Just where to draw the line between the end of an old species and the beginning of a new one is beyond the power of the metaphysician to decide. It must be left to the observations of science and the careful study of the characteristic operations of the beings in question. For science the line is crossed between two species when the members of one group formerly considered part of the same species can no longer mate sexually with the other members of the old species and have fertile offspring from the union. There seems to be a certain threshold of change beyond which a significant internal reorganization takes place and a new essential form emerges. *Note* that the traditional definition of human nature is: "Man is a rational animal." What is specified is a being with a power of rational thinking joined to an animal body; but it does not specify in any detail just what kind of body this must be or the limits within which it can tolerate changes in detail. Might it not be that it is the essential form, the spiritual soul, of a human being, as a dynamic energy seeking its own fullest self-realization, which moves the body to take advantage of all the opportunities in its environment, changing through the evolution of our earth? Thus rather than block changes in the body the essential form would actually stimulate them.

So an essential form really comes down to that central unifying force in a material being that binds all its elements together into an intrinsic unity of being and action, not a mere aggregate. It functions as the abiding center of characteristic actions substantially similar—though not identical in all small accidental details—to the other members of its group that thus form a distinct species; in other words, an essential form is what makes a being to be a unity-identity-whole of this kind. The need of such a centralized principle of unity and action in living organisms, and even lower complex entities—long banned in modern science since Newton—is now being increasingly recognized in the latest contemporary science as the "principle of holism." The unity of the organism as a whole exercises a positive causal influence on its parts, so that the flow of causal influence is now not just from the bottom, the parts, upwards, but also from the top down, from the whole to the parts. The recognition of this two-way flow of causal influence in a being, upwards from the parts to the whole and downwards from the whole to the parts, is a significant new development in contemporary science, and this principle of holistic unity in an organism as an effective agent is really almost identical in function to St. Thomas's essential form.

Cf. the illuminating article of Terence Nichols, with whom I have worked, "Aquinas's Substantial Form and Modern Science," *Internat. Philo. Quart.* 36 (1996), 305–18. He calls these lower elements with their own inner organization not complete beings but "holons"—an apt term, it seems to me.

PRINCIPAL DIFFICULTIES AND OBJECTIONS

The principal ones come from the application of the form/matter doctrine to human beings.

I. To maintain that all the individuality of a human being derives from matter, from its body alone, seems to demean the dignity of each human being as having a unique personality, spiritual life, etc. To say that only our bodies are unique and our souls and minds just exact copies of each other does not seem to do justice to our experience of the richness of human individuality.

Response. A. It is true that I cannot start my human journey until my soul is infused into a particular human-type body at a particular time and place on this earth in the process of human history. We are radically historical beings, unlike purely spiritual beings who have no such requirements. We cannot enter human history except in a body at a particular time and place, here and now, not there and then. But from the first moment we do enter this history in the body, our stories become strictly unique, more and more so as they progress, because of the unique environment, experiences, and encounters we have due to our particular location in this historical matrix of life in a material world, which is different for each bodily being.

B. The objection forgets that in the matter/form, body/soul metaphysical composition, each component is correlative, adapted to the other. Thus St. Thomas speaks of each soul being "commensurated" or adapted actively by God to its own particular body, therefore different in what it can do, whether better or worse, in this particular body than it might do, or another similar human soul might do, in another body. Thus the soul itself becomes differentiated in itself from every other, not because it is a different kind of soul, but because it is joined with this particular body as its permanent instrument of self-expression.

Just think of the difference in how the soul can operate from being infused into a *female* or a *male* body! The differences are deep, running all through its personality and mode of self-expression, but they are not because it is a different kind of soul, but because the human soul in each case has to operate and express itself through this particular body, which allows some of its many potentialities to develop, others not, or some more than others. Thus a human soul operating in a male body just cannot conceive, bear in its womb, and give birth to a human child, because it has no womb with which to do so.

Look at the grave consequences if one does not accept this position that there is the same essentially equal kind of soul in all human beings, diversified by the body in which it must live and operate, but that, as some hold, each human soul is individuated, distinguished from every other in itself as a soul, not through the body it inhabits. Then it follows

that each female soul must be qualitatively different in itself as soul
from every male one, i.e., one essentially more intelligent, loving, etc.
than the other.

Now we have broken the unity of the human species: men and
women are no longer essentially equal complementary members of the
same human species, bearing essentially the same human nature, but
are qualitatively different kinds of being. Now we are open to a fundamental inequality, inferiority-superiority, of one sex over the other, an
elitism indicating one should govern the other. Is this what we want as
an explanation of what it means to be human? Which *kind* of human?
And since the same reasoning applies, though somewhat less drastically,
to every man compared to every other and every woman compared to
every other, once each has an essentially different kind of soul, or essential form, then a democracy of equals is no longer possible as a form of
social and political organization; the American Constitution is philosophically incoherent, and out goes the *Declaration of Independence:* "All
men by nature are created equal." A great deal rides, therefore, on this
supposedly purely technical philosophical disagreement with no practical repercussions. "Ideas have consequences!"

II. A Theological difficulty for Christian thinkers (as well as for any who
hold the immortality of the soul). If the human soul is individuated only
by being united to a particular material body, then the body dies, is
separated from the soul, and only much later is the soul reunited with
the body in a divine gift of resurrection. It follows that this separated
soul either remains individuated by itself without its body, or all separated souls coalesce together again into a single human soul. Neither of
these is an acceptable solution for a Thomist, and the second not acceptable for any Christian, or believer in personal immortality before
the resurrection of the body.

Response. This is admittedly a more serious problem for a
Thomist. But it rests on a supposition commonly taken for granted by
early and medieval Christian thinkers, including many still today,
namely, that the resurrection "at the last day" will take place "a long
time later" than the death of the body in this life. This supposition no
longer seems to be a theological imperative. Our time is built entirely
on the framework of physical motion of material bodies in our
world—the movement of the sun, moon, stars, the tempo of heartbeats,
the vibration rate of crystals, etc., all physical motions. Outside of this
material world such time makes no sense; hence it cannot be applied

without modification to the world of spirits outside of our time. It might well be that the resurrection of each body takes place immediately after death in another time dimension entirely that cannot be correlated with ours. Hence there need be no "time" in our sense between death in this life and resurrection in another. How could we now measure this other kind of time, or say it was long or short??

Secondly, it may well be—which is my preference, confirmed by the reports of people who have had near-death experiences, as well as by reliable reports of the appearances of "ghosts"—that what we call "death" is only a separation from, a sloughing off of this heavy visible body but retaining some connection with much more subtle high-energy fields that are still material in essence. Thus the soul would always retain some connection with matter; and this would be enough to keep individuating it. These options, not available to St. Thomas in the intellectual world of his time, seem now open to contemporary Thomists and would undercut the objection entirely.

Solution of St. Thomas himself. To be individuated a human soul must start off in a particular material body. But once it has been adapted to this particular body and lived in it and expressed itself in and through it for a time, it is deeply marked within itself as soul both by God's initial "commensuration" and by these unique experiences, and, even when separated from its body life-partner, bears within it a unique set of characteristics and relations to this particular style of living in the body different from any other human. And this is enough to continue to individuate it. But since the whole human person is by nature an *embodied spirit,* the separated soul still naturally longs for its companion body and cannot be fully happy till it regains it again. By itself, he says, it remains the soul of such and such a body, not the full person "John Smith," but the "soul-of-John-Smith." This, I think, is a fairly strong answer by itself, but can be strengthened by the more contemporary adaptations outlined above, which do away with the problem more radically.

There is another aspect to this theological problem that needs specific attention. It is objected that for St. Thomas there is a natural immortality proper to every human soul, and this seems to undercut the Christian belief that immortal life is a free, supernatural gift of God resulting from incorporation through sanctifying grace into the resurrection of Jesus.

Response. (1) The Christian notion of immortal life is not that of sheer survival of the soul by itself, as many of the Greeks held—not a very rich and happy state for them—but a life of elevated participation in God's own divine Trinitarian life, far transcending what is possible for human nature on its own. In a word, it is a higher kind of immortal life.

(2) The natural immortality of the human soul for Thomas means only that of its own nature it is not subject to decay, disintegration into material parts, since it has none, by any natural causes. But the actual continuation of the soul in existence still depends on the constant support of God's causality giving it being, and God could, if he wished, just withdraw this and let the soul not "die," in our sense, but simply fall into nothingness, be annihilated. That itself is a free decision of God that cannot be forced on him by any creature. So the supernatural gratuity of actual immortal life, especially in its enriched Christian state, still remains intact.

IMPLICATIONS OF THE FORM/MATTER DOCTRINE FOR HUMAN CULTURE

Whether or not a philosopher is willing to accept fully this position of St. Thomas in all its technical details as real metaphysical composition, especially as applied to human beings, it remains that everyone must—as she/he does in practice—accept this basic structure of form multiplied by matter as a key principle for understanding the whole process of human culture and technology. It is the key to all mass production, to all reproduction of the same pattern in different materials, without which no shareable technological products would be possible. Consider this book, or any set of notes reproduced in many copies on our contemporary copying machines. The text, or formal message, corresponding to the principle of form, is exactly the same, barring small accidental errors in reproduction on all the copies. Since all are made from the same one original, it would be a miracle if it came out otherwise. Yet each copy is still distinct from, separable from, every other. How? By being reproduced on multiple sheets of blank paper that have no message already on them but are like determinable matter open to be informed by the same printed formal message. And when the supply of fresh unmarked paper gives out, no further reproduction can be done. Every ball point pen, computer, auto, piece of clothing bought in a store, etc. is but one copy of the same basic pattern or form imprinted upon new pieces of plastic raw material. A garment maker can copy the pattern of a new designer dress and reproduce it in many kinds of cheaper "material" that can be cut or molded any way he/she wishes. *Pattern/material* is a fundamental real distinction used everywhere, and is only another way of expressing this primordial composition of form and matter in our material world, without which it is impossible to understand human culture, technology, and civilization. Since animals cannot abstract form from particular matter, they cannot develop technology as we can by our power of producing abstract concepts of common patterns or forms by abstraction from the particularities of individual, quantitatively extended matter. Fortunately for us, the form/matter structure of our material cosmos matches the structure of our human knowing, which operates by abstracting intelligible form from particularized matter—a point missed by so many modern philosophers from the empiricists to Kant and beyond. If there are no form/matter compositions in reality, then we cannot abstract form from matter and so cannot form general or universal concepts which, though abstract, still retain an umbilical cord of direct connection with the real.

In sum, the form/matter distinction is a fundamental structure running all through the material cosmos in which we live, both in the *order of being* and *the order of knowing,* and neither can make full sense without it.

QUESTIONS FOR REVIEW AND DISCUSSION

1. What are the data in our experience of the world that raise a new metaphysical problem about the inner structure of the beings of our experience, and just what is the problem?

2. Must we accept the fact that all human beings in our world belong to the same species? Why not say that every one is an absolutely unique being with a nature essentially different from every other?

3. What is the argument that each member of a species must have an essence composed of form and matter? a) Data? b) Why a duality of principles needed? c) Identification of the principle of similarity, and its role? d) Identification of the principle of distinctness (most difficult part): what kind of properties must it have to fulfill its role and what sort of principle can fulfill these requirements? What is meant by "primary matter"?

4. Can either essential form or primary matter exist by itself or be discovered separately by science? Explain.

5. Modern science reveals that complex material beings, especially living ones, are composed of many levels of lower elements, such as cells, molecules, atoms, electrons and protons, quarks, etc. How do they fit in to the Thomistic form / matter structure, or are they entirely wiped out when a new specific form comes to be and takes over the underlying matter?

6. Objections: 1) Does our human individuality come solely from our bodies? 2) What about the soul after death: how does it retain its individuality without the body?

CHAPTER SEVEN

The World of Change

Act and Potency

INTRODUCTION

In the previous chapters we have uncovered what might be called the two great "static" structures of the universe of real beings: *essence/existence* and *matter/form*—static only in the sense that they describe permanent structures of being, structures of belonging to the two great communities of reality as long as they exist: the all-embracing community of all real existents, and the smaller, tighter communities of members of the same species or kind of being.

But all the beings thus described are highly dynamic in themselves: as soon as they exist they begin to pour over into self-expressive, self-communicating action, acting on other beings and receiving, being acted upon by them, as we saw in Chapter II on the Meaning of Being. "From the very fact that something exists in act," St. Thomas tells us, "it is active." This introduces us to a whole new and fundamental aspect of reality: the world as changing, subject to change of all kinds. This is one of the most obvious features of the entire world of our experience: not only that there are many different beings within it, but that these are constantly undergoing change, either within themselves or as being transformed into different kinds of being. What are the basic laws that govern this dimension of reality as changing, with the metaphysical principles needed to explain it? This leads us into the second main division of metaphysics: *the metaphysics of change.*

I. DIFFERENT ATTITUDES TOWARD CHANGE THROUGH HISTORY

Ancient world.   The ancient world, and the "primitive" world in general, are haunted by the ideal of immutability, symbolized by the (believed) unchanging nature of the heavenly bodies, the sun and the stars, which they believed were made of a different kind of matter, celestial matter, that was unchanged and indestructible save for its endless, unchanging cycles of local motion, contrasted with the constant birth and decay, "generation and corruption," of all things on our lowly earth. The ideal is the immutable; this alone truly is, and all that changes is a falling away from perfection and being, a source of regret and sadness, a threat to true being. Hence the Golden Age, for these ancient cultures, is put in the past in the paradisiac state; and since history is a falling away from this, it has little positive value. "Time," says Aristotle, summing up the more pessimistic side of ancient culture, "is more of a destroyer than a builder, for we are not sure everything will be reborn, but we are sure everything [on this earth] will be destroyed." Hence the divine is the immutable. For Hinduism and Buddhism, too, in the East, the truly Real is the immutable; what is changing, transitory, is not fully real.

Medieval world.   It also maintained the ideal of immutability as the highest and most perfect state of being and considered change as imperfection, the mark of the deficiency of creatures compared to God. St. Augustine defines *being* without qualification as *the immutable.* Hence for him God alone truly *is,* because he is *always what* he is, self-identical, whereas creatures neither are always, nor are they at any one time all that they are: they are not yet what they will be and are no longer what they were, because they are changing. Still, Christianity brings in a whole more optimistic view of our changing world. The human race did indeed fall from Paradise, but through the redemption of Christ the whole human race, and with it the material, are now headed toward a Golden Age in the future, at the end of and beyond this world of time. *Progress* is now built into our world history, but only as a gift of God for those who are faithful to God's call and beyond human history on this planet.

Modern western culture, beginning with the introduction of the new mathematical science, the explosion of technological progress flowing from it, and the enlightenment attitude, has developed quite a new attitude toward change. For many or most today, change has become identified with Progress, built on the belief in the constant progress of science, separated from its religious grounding, and as something radically good; it is better to change than to remain the same. "To change is to grow; to remain the same is to die." Constant growth, novelty, process is the *ideal,* not a deficiency. The principal institutions of our age—business, science, social institutions, the arts—instead of striving for built-in techniques for conserving the *status quo,* strive more for built-in stimuli that promote constant change (e.g., planned obsolescence of autos). (How does the Church fit into this picture?) However, our recent experience of the imminent possibilities of nuclear destruction, ecological disaster, and so forth, all resulting from the unguided power of science and technology, have cooled considerably our uncritical belief in the "myth" of inevitable progress.

Modern philosophy, reflecting this change in cultural attitude, has in many of its representatives—Bergson, Whitehead, Dewey, many empiricists—tended to oppose being and becoming as irreconcilable opposites and to give priority to the latter over the former. As one has put it, "The ancient and medieval worlds were interested in *being,* the static essences of things; the modern world is interested in *becoming,* the change, growth, development of things." In a word, what is central is process, *becoming,* not being.

Our own metaphysical inquiry will lead us, we hope, to a more balanced view of the two as complementary rather than oppositional. Becoming itself flows naturally out of real beings as dynamic centers of action, searching, as finite and incomplete, to fulfill their own being by active exchange with others, both giving and receiving. So our conclusion will be that every change must be a synthesis of permanence and process; there is no such thing as pure process, pure becoming nor, in fact, pure immutable being outside of the one case of God as the infinite fullness of all being.

II. Some Rival Philosophical Views of Change

Heraclitus (fifth century B.C.). All things are in *perpetual flux,* constantly changing into each other. Fire, which is by its very nature perpetual change, is the substance of all things. The only thing permanent is the *Logos,* the unchanging Law governing the cycles of all change. Already criticized by Plato, this doctrine received its first technical philosophical refutation by Aristotle with his doctrine of act and potency.

David Hume (d. 1776). All we can know about the real world is what we receive from it in individual, sense impressions. But as we look inside ourselves, all we can observe is a constant flow of distinct states of consciousness, moods, thoughts, desires, etc. Because they succeed each other so rapidly, we are led to join them together and believe they are bound together by some permanent thing which we call our *self*, our *substance* as opposed to the passing modifications. But such a permanent unchanging self or substance is but a *myth* invented by the metaphysicians. There is only a stream of distinct impressions, only the flow, nothing permanent beneath it.

Henri Bergson (d. 1940). Reality is not even a flow of distinct states, as Hume thought. The flow is still too broken up into distinct pieces. Reality, in fact, is nothing but a continuous flow of becoming, every moment or phase blending into the next like a seamless robe. It is we with our intellects who freeze it or segment it into distinct fixed forms or things, by our abstract concepts. We try to master the flux rationally by freezing it into the immobile, into a succession of still shots like a movie film. In fact, there is nothing but the flow of change, becoming, with nothing permanent or unchanging underneath. Thus Bergson writes:

> Changes are real. But beneath the changes there are no real things which change. Change does not require a support. There is really no such thing as an inert and invariable subject which is moving. (*La Pensée et le mouvant*, 4th ed., Paris: Alcan, 1934, p. 185)

> If change, which is obviously the texture of our experience, is really the elusive entity so many philosophers have described . . . it will certainly be imperative to restore continuity by some artificially constructed bridgework. But this unchangeable substratum of change, utterly indescribable in terms of experience which knows only changes, disappears more surely the more closely we try to approach it. It is equally as elusive as the ghost of change it was commissioned to ensnare and hold fast. (Ibid., pp. 196–97)

> When we say "the child becomes man," we are careful not to plumb too deeply the literal meaning of the phrase. We would find that when we set down the subject "child," the predicate "man" does yet fit him, and when we assert as predicate "man" it no longer applies to the "child" as subject. The reality is the transition from childhood

to old age and it has slipped between our fingers. All we possess are imaginary pauses in the process, "child" and "man". . . . In truth, if language were molded to the shape of reality, we would not say "The child becomes a man," but "There is a changing from child to man." (*L'Évolution créatrice*, 4th ed., Paris: PUF, 1932, p. 338)

Alfred North Whitehead (d. 1940): the founder and principal figure of what is now known as *Process Philosophy*. The reality of our cosmos is one single, vast interconnected system in a constant process of evolution. "Actuality is through and through togetherness." What constitutes this process is a constant succession of ultimate units called "*actual entities*" or "actual occasions," each of which lasts only for a moment (the smallest quantum of its time) and is a self-constituted act of selective synthesis of the whole universe as it impinges on this entity at this moment. As soon as it "concresces" into completion, it "perishes" and hands on its inheritance to the next actual entity following it. All larger entities of our ordinary experience, molecules, plants, animals, humans, are but closely connected "societies" of large numbers of these actual entities, with no single unifying being of which they are all parts, and no single being which perdures through all the processes of change which they constantly undergo. Thus what we call the perduring "self" in a human being is really a succession of actual entities or selves bound together in a continuous process of handing on their inheritances to another successor, thus binding past and future together, not in a *being* but in a closely knit succession of them. *God,* too, although he is unchanging in his "antecedent" nature considered in himself alone, in his "consequent" nature as he interacts with and guides the world process he is *constantly changing* in time with the latter as it changes. This is the God of Process Theology, quite different from the immutable God of traditional Christian philosophy and theology. It is especially strong among Protestant thinkers, but now includes many Catholics.

In a word, process, or becoming, not abiding natures or beings, is the fundamental structure of reality. What we call "things" are their ongoing processes, held together by the unbroken chain of succession, one coming to be out of the other. But process itself is made up of many discretely distinct, tiny entities, "actual occasions" or "actual entities," following each other in ordered sequence, unlike Bergson's seamless flow without discrete entities except as artificially distinguished by our minds.

III. GENERAL LAW GOVERNING ALL CHANGE:
THE ACT/POTENCY COMPOSITION

There are many different kinds of changes that we observe in the world of our experience, proportioned to the kinds of being involved and their relations with each other. They can be summed up under two main types. Some definitions to begin with are:

1. *Change in general.*   In the order of real being, change can be defined as the transition from one real mode of being to another. We are concerned here with changes in the order of real being, not merely in the order of ideas or mental beings; and intrinsic changes, which affect the intrinsic real being of the beings in question, not merely purely extrinsic relations to something else. Thus local motion, which Aristotle and the medievals generally considered as a primary instance of real change in the moving body, requiring the continuous application of some real external cause, has since Newtonian and later modern physics been reconsidered. If the motion is continuous at the same velocity, it is no longer regarded as a real change within the moving body requiring any cause (once launched and neither accelerated nor decelerated) but only a change in extrinsic relations to other real bodies. So we will not use local motion by itself as a datum for our inquiry, though we could use acceleration or deceleration and changing from rest to motion or vice versa as legitimate examples. Two main types of real change are:

2. *Accidental or non-essential change* = A transition from one real mode of being to another remaining within the same identical being, i.e., its essential self-identity remaining intact. *Example:* a man is now hot, now cold; now angry, now happy.

3. *Essential or substantial change* = A transition from one real mode of being to another such that the being at the end of the change is no longer the same being but a different one, either a different individual of the same species or more usually a being of an essentially different kind. In a word, the original being has disappeared and a new one has taken its place. *Example:* a living organism dies, disintegrates into its component chemicals or is consumed by another, becoming part of the other being.

Three problems resulting: I. Is there a general metaphysical law governing all change? What kind of metaphysical composition is needed to fulfill its requirements?

II. What kind of metaphysical composition is needed to explain the special requirements of accidental change?

III. What kind is needed to explain essential change?

This present chapter will deal with *Problem I.*

CHANGE IN GENERAL: ACT AND POTENCY

Problem. What we are looking for is the general structure of all change, whether superficial or profound, i.e., a generalized theory of the ultimate conditions of possibility within a changing being required to render intelligible any change whatsoever.

Questions. Three basic ones emerge in the course of our inquiry: (1) Must there be a principle of continuity as well as difference in every changing being? (2) What is the relation of these two principles to each other? (3) Why is it that changing beings change only along certain lines, within certain limits, and not just any old way, anything into anything? Monkeys do not turn into mathematicians, nor water into iron.

SOLUTION

One of the central insights of Aristotle and one of his most enduring legacies to philosophical history, it is widely admitted, is his general theory of act and potency as a structure underlying and helping to explain all change. It was taken over not only by later Aristotelians, but by Neoplatonists, all medieval philosophers of any consequence, and in some form or other by many modern philosophers. The solution we here propose has its roots in Aristotle, refined and adapted by St. Thomas, and with some further refinements in the light of contemporary discussion.

General theorem. Every being undergoing real change must have within it a real metaphysical composition of two principles, related to each other as act and potency.

ARGUMENT

Step. 1. Every changing being must be different at the end of the change from what it was in the beginning. Otherwise, there would be no

change at all. This follows from the very meaning of change. Hence
a change requires two really distinct different modes of being before
and after. This is obvious and admitted by everyone who admits change
at all. Aristotle, the first to analyze the inner structure of change, called
these terminal modes or states *actualities*—which became simplified
into the technical term *act*—to signify the actual here and now state of
a being, what is actually the case at any one point in the process, before
or after.

Step 2.   What is less obvious and more often denied, there must
also be a principle of underlying continuity or permanence in every
change, something somehow the same, which passes over from one
pole of the change to the other, joining one to the other.

Reason.   If not, we would not have a *transition* from one mode of
being to another at all, but rather two distinct phases completely uncon-
nected with each other: first, the complete annihilation, reduction to
nothingness, of one being (the being at the beginning of the change)
and secondly, the total creation out of nothing of a completely new
being at the end of the change, in a word, the pure extrinsic juxtaposi-
tion of two totally different beings, one after the other, with no intrinsic
relation or connectedness, no transition from one to the other. But in
this case we would have no grounds for saying that there had been any
authentic change at all, that the first being had changed into the other,
or into a different real mode of being than before. There would be no
transition from one mode of being to another, only the pure static succession of two unrelated beings, with no connection between them,
only that one is simply replaced by the other, with neither undergoing
any internal change within itself.

But this is simply not what we mean by change at all and, in addition, is a wildly implausible (though not logically contradictory) explanation or interpretation of what we observe going on in our experience.
Thus when we observe ourselves or another human being first in an
angry mood, then slowly calming down and finally smiling, we would
have to say that at each discernible moment of the change the previous
human being—myself—was totally annihilated, wiped out of existence
without remainder, and then at the next moment totally created out of
nothing again! But I am clearly aware of myself as going through these
phases and remaining the same self all the while. This would be a total
falsehood, an illusion! The meaning of memory or any sense to personal development, to story, would also disappear. So, too, in the lab

when we see water changing into hydrogen and oxygen, it is not really breaking down into hydrogen and oxygen at all, but rather is being totally annihilated without a trace and succeeded by two new entities totally created out of nothing and quite unrelated to it.

But this is simply too much to swallow as a reasonable "explanation" of what I am familiar with in my everyday experience. It is rather the radical denial of it. The only reasonable alternative, therefore, is some principle of continuity, something passing over from one real state of being to the other, holding together the earlier and the later stages without a total rupture of continuity.

Aristotle called this principle *potentiality*—simplified to the technical term *potency*—to indicate that the principle of continuity was a capacity, an aptitude, for receiving the new mode of being

Step. 3. These two principles must be joined together to form a metaphysical composition of two really distinct metaphysical co-principles. *Reason:* (1) The principle of continuity cannot be identical with the two principles of actuality, for the simple reason that the latter come and go, one succeeded by the other, whereas the principle of continuity or permanence must be present underlying or holding each one in turn as long as it is present. What is identical with something must always be present wherever the latter is present; but the principle of continuity is now joined with the first actuality and not the second, then later with the second, not the first. Hence it can be identical in being with neither. They must be really distinct, irreducible to each other. (2) On the other hand, they cannot be two complete beings or things, each in its own right as independent for they go together to make up the one being that we started with as well as one being we finished with. Hence the real composition must be between less than real beings or complete things, i.e., between incomplete correlative metaphysical co-principles, joining together to form one being both at the beginning and at the end of the change.

Stop a moment here to recognize that we have already solved the first problem: Must there be a principle of continuity as well as of difference in every changing being? Yes.

Step. 4. What is the relation between these two co-principles? The principle of continuity cannot be merely juxtaposed extrinsically to each of the changing modes or actualities of the changing being; it is truly modified, affected in the real order by the process—it loses something real it had before and acquires something real that it did not have before. Otherwise, it is not a real change. Hence it must have an in-trinsic natural aptitude or capacity—potentiality—for possessing and being joined in intrinsic unity to each one of its different modes of being, not only the original mode it possessed at the beginning and the new mode it has at the end, but also, if it can still change, to every other one of its possible new modes along the whole gamut of change open to it. At any one point it is actualized, informed, by its present mode, but potentially open to receive all the other modes its nature allows: in more technical language, it is *in act* with respect to its present mode of being, *in potency* with respect to all its future possibilities for change. At any moment in a process of change the being is a synthesis of act and potency—of present actuality and potential openness to future acts—a potency partially actualized by its present act, but still open, in potency, to all further actualizations possible to it according to the nature and limits of its capacity. If the potency of a being is not yet filled up, it re-mains capable of further change. Once its potency is filled up, it can undergo no further change, except perhaps to lose what it has.

In sum, this principle of potentiality is at once an *openness* to the whole range of changes this being can undergo, and a *closedness* to any-thing beyond this range, because of the built-in limit rooted in the ca-pacity itself. Thus the potency of a plant is not that of a dog, nor the po-tency of a dog that of a human being. A cabbage cannot grow into a king, nor a monkey into a mathematician. A man can build an airplane, but he cannot fly with his own body. (Just what the full potentialities of the whole human person, body and spiritual soul, are, however, is not yet known to us, because of the unlimited range of our knowledge and love and our capacity—at least as revealed by Christian revelation—for total personal union with God himself, the infinite fullness of all being. "Man the microcosm": a miniature image of all levels of reality, from matter to spirit!)

Two types of potency: A) *receptive* (or "passive") *potency* = the poten-tiality to receive from without, e.g., energy, food, information, etc. B) *ac-tive potency* = the capacity to act from within, e.g., to talk, to sing, to make things, etc.

Notice the close connection of potency with nature, as "the abiding center of acting and being acted upon": every nature is defined pre-cisely in terms of its properties, which are really its built-in potentialities for acting and being acted on.

Step 5. This last step brings us to the solution of the third problem we listed at the beginning: Why is it that changing beings change only along certain lines, within certain limits, and not just any old way, anything into anything? Precisely because of the kind of potency they possess, which includes both its openness and its closedness, its limits.

III. Wider Implications of the Act-Potency Doctrine

1. Reverse corollary. If any being that changes requires an inner metaphysical composition of two really distinct metaphysical co-principles, act and potency, then it follows that, given a being that lacks such a composition, i.e., a simple or uncomposed being, it is impossible for it to undergo any kind of change = it is *immutable.* Such is the case with the infinite fullness of all being that is God, who can neither lose nor gain in his own intrinsic perfection, but can actively communicate as generously as he wishes to beings outside of himself, his own creatures.

2. Every real being in the universe will be either pure act or some combination of act/potency. It is not possible to have a real being that all by itself is pure potency, nothing but potentiality, since to be at all one must have some degree, however minimum, of actuality. *To be* = to be *actively* present. Thus ultimate pure primary matter, with no form to give it definiteness at all, can never exist as a real being by itself, but only with some act of existence structured through form.

3. Potency knowable only through act. Since potency, in itself as potency, is only the capacity for some actuality, some actual state of perfection, distinct from it, and since only actualities, what is actually there, can be made manifest to us by the action of the being, it follows that potency in itself can never be directly observed or measured by any human observer. It can only be inferred, affirmed, as a necessary condition of possibility for the actualization of this potentiality in the temporal history of the being in question. Potentialities are known only through their corresponding acts, by hindsight, so to speak.

4. Potency inaccessible to empiricists. As a result, no empiricist who believes that all human knowledge is restricted to what can be observed by some sense experience can discover or allow in his philosophical horizon of explanation anything like potency. This seriously limits the

ability of this philosophy to cope with, to render intelligible, an important dimension of our ordinary experience of ourselves and of the material world around us. It can give no adequate sense to the whole set of
meanings expressed in words that are an indispensable part of our vocabulary, e.g., all words signifying "can," "able to," "ability," "aptitude,"
"capacity for," etc. For when I say, "I *can* sing," my meaning is not reducible without remainder to any form of the verb "to be" signifying actuality, past, present, or future, i.e., to "I *am* singing," "I *did* sing," "I *will*
sing again." I might have decided I will never sing again, but in no
way does this signify that I *cannot* sing. And to say, "I have sung before,"
is in no way what I mean when I say, "I can sing now." One saying refers
to an *actuality*, past, present, or future; the other to a *potency*, an ability
I have now.

This is very important for the *meaningfulness of scientific language*,
which lists the *properties* of chemical substances, drugs, etc., by their capacities, their *potentialities*, their "dispositional properties" (a scientific
term roughly equivalent to the philosophical term "potency"). For example, "Sugar is solu*ble* in water"; "Oxygen is easily flamm*able*"; "Aspirin
can irritate the stomach," etc. This does not mean that this sample of
sugar is dissolving in water, ever was, or ever will be. I may burn it up or
break it up in some way so that it will be gone forever, never dissolved in
water. But it still remains true that it is now soluble in water; that is one
of its inherent properties or potentialities now. To deny this, as empiricists must to be consistent, since potentialities can never be empirically
observed, is to render all "property talk" in science meaningless—which
scientists strongly object to, and rightly so.

CONCLUSION

Our metaphysical inquiry into the structure of all change has resulted
in the very significant discovery of a new distinctive level or dimension
of reality that lies between the fullness of complete actual being and the
complete non-reality of nothingness: the dimension of potentiality,
which, although it must be rooted in some actually existing being, is
nonetheless a positive aptitude or capacity in it for a different degree of
reality than it now has, a positive opening to further being but within
certain definite limits and no further. This metaphysical principle
of potency reveals itself as indispensable to making sense out of our
ordinary experience as well as science—the whole dimension of *ability*,

aptitude, capacity, all "can"-language. This is a fascinating case where our ordinary language, to make sense, implies a definite *metaphysical under-pinning,* one which no empiricist type of philosophy can supply, and must, in fact, deny.

There is another application of the notion of potency, which I have found fruitful in helping scientists talk more intelligibly about the strange world of subatomic particles in quantum physics. The *Heisenberg Indeterminacy Principle* postulates that certain attributes of these particles remain indeterminate or potential until we actually experiment on them, when they snap into actuality. This opens up a surprising new per-spective on what it means for the human being to know the material world. No longer can the human observer, at least as a scientist ob-serving the subatomic world, be the detached, disinterested knower making no difference to what he observes. His very act of observation now makes a difference in what he observes: the knower becomes woven into what he knows as a dynamic whole! The world waits for us to complete it!

Serious problem for the physicist! If this world exists even when we are not experimenting on it—as most, except a few idealists among physicists, still hold—how can we possibly talk about it and say what it is like when unobserved? Some—the *Copenhagen School*—conclude we can say nothing about its real properties at all; we can only talk about our experiments on it. But using the notion of potency we can do better: we can describe them as real potentialities of nature ("disposi-tional properties") waiting to be actualized by us. And even though it is there, no potency can be described by itself apart from its actualization. That's its nature! No wonder, then, that the quantum physicist cannot adequately describe the quantum world if he omits his own experi-ments on it as an inseparable part of what he is trying to describe, the "object" of his own science! The real world we live in is one charged with real potentialities of interaction between beings.

Cf., on the role of potency, E. Moore, "Positivism and Potentiality," *Journal of Philosophy* 48 (1951), 472–79.

QUESTIONS FOR REVIEW AND DISCUSSION

1. Describe the different attitudes toward change in the ancient world, the medieval world, the modern world, much of modern philosophy.

2. Identify briefly the theory of change in Heraclitus, Hume, Bergson, Whitehead.

3. What is the aim of the present chapter?

4. Give the definitions of change in general; accidental change; essential or substantial change.

5. Summarize the Argument: Steps 1 through 5.

6. Why is it that the principle of potency in a being explains both its openness and its closedness to future change?

7. Implications: (1) If a being lacks a composition of act and potency, is it still open to change of any kind?

(2) Must every being in the universe have a composition of potency and act? Can there be one that is pure act? One that is pure potency?

(3) Can a potency be observed directly in itself? Why?

(4) Why is potency inaccessible and inadmissible for empiricist philosophers? What serious negative consequences does this have for explaining our ordinary experience as well as contemporary science?

CHAPTER EIGHT

Self-Identity in Change

Substance and Accident

At the beginning of the last chapter on Change in General we distinguished two types of change: *accidental* and *essential* or *substantial*. This was based on the ordinary, common-sense interpretation of reality. But we have not yet established philosophically and critically whether there is such a thing as accidental change, or substantial change. We must first do this, then search for a metaphysical solution to the problems they raise. We are forced into this procedure because so many philosophers, both in the West and in the East, while admitting the human experiences that give rise to these distinct classifications, deny the basic Aristotelian explanations of them in terms of metaphysical compositions of substance/accident and matter/form, and so do not accept the description of them as "accidental" and "substantial." We shall be following the basic insights of Aristotle, with later refinements of St. Thomas and other contemporary sources. This chapter will handle *Accidental Change*, the next Substantial Change.

I. SELF-IDENTITY IN CHANGE: THE PROBLEM

The kind of change we are most familiar with in our experience is change that we judge to take place within the same being, where the same being undergoes various changes of state without destroying the basic identity of the entity going through them. The most obvious example of this is human beings like myself: I pass through many stages of change as I grow from child to adult: changes in size, shape, degrees of strength, things I learn, skills I develop, goals in life I pursue or turn away from to others, changes in character (good or bad), etc. I take responsibility for my past actions: "I did it." And since I remember many of my experiences, my human life takes the form of an unfolding story—which cannot be a story unless it is about the self-identical person, the same "I." So too with many other beings I encounter along the way: other people, animals, plants, samples of water I heat up and cool down, etc.

Two problems. I. Is it the case that there are beings that preserve their self-identity intact through a series of changes? Especially, is this true of human beings like myself to whom it is crucial for preserving my dignity as a morally responsible person, with perduring goals in life, which I can call *my* story?

II. If this is the case, then how can we explain that this is possible, intelligible, in terms of the inner metaphysical structure of such a being? Here we meet another case of the One and Many in being, this time reappearing not by comparison with other beings but by comparison of changing phases within the same being, so that it appears as definitely one, the same being, yet somehow many, in that it is not the same today as yesterday or five years ago. "I (the same 'I') have undergone many changes over my life. In many ways I *am* and *am not* the same person as I was ten years ago." How can this be? How can I be both one and many under different aspects?

Since the solution of this problem is so crucial for human beings, and since the evidence for the solution is more immediately available to us from our own experience than it is for other non-human beings, we shall first explore the solution as found in human beings like myself, then extend it by analogy to other beings where we have good evidence for affirming it.

II. Rival Philosophical Views

David Hume (d. 1776) and *empiricism*. The source of all my knowledge of the real is distinct sense impressions, which follow one another rapidly in a stream of consciousness. But I have no distinct sense impression of anything unchanging within me. When I look inside myself I can find no permanent "self" or "substance" that remains unchanged, only a steady stream of states of consciousness, following rapidly one upon the other. The idea of something perduring unchanged throughout my life is a projection of the philosophical mind, a myth of the metaphysicians. At any one time we are nothing but a bundle of different physical and psychological states, actions. This has been called "the Bundle Theory of Self." There is nothing else underlying the bundle or holding it together. *Bertrand Russell* in our day has called the notion of perduring, underlying substance merely a grammatical convenience. Carl Sagan, contemporary materialist scientist, speaks thus of himself: "I, Carl Sagan, am nothing but a collection of molecules bearing the name, 'Carl Sagan'."

Alfred North Whitehead (d. 1947) and *Process Philosophy.* What actually exist as real beings are the vast number of "actual entities" or "actual occasions," which last only for a moment and are mostly too small to be observed by us (influenced by the atomic theory of physics). The macroscopic objects we call things—plants, animals, humans, chairs, etc.—are really societies or collections of many actual entities bound together by various relations, causal connections etc., existing at any one time. Down through time there is no actual entity that remains the same, unchanged, but only a series of successive entities that we call one being because the series is closely connected by a chain of "inheritance" of properties one from the other. Thus what we call the human "self," the "I," is really only a succession of selves bound together by a common chain of inheritances (memories, e.g.)—in a word, a process of becoming, not a being that changes or perdures through a cycle of change. This theory seems to have been inspired by the modern scientific theory of the ultimate constitution of material things by a multitude of atomic particles—a theory which is then projected into a universal metaphysical explanation of all reality. God becomes the only reality that can be said to endure (in his "primordial nature") as the same being through time, though (in his "consequent nature") he, too, changes in tandem with the ongoing world of process whose direction he guides and from which he receives.

Buddhism. This is the principal Oriental doctrine that explicitly denies any perduring "things" or "selves" of any kind underlying and persisting through the endless chain of "dependent origination" linking all reality together, in our phenomenal (not "fully real," it seems) world, constituted by one vast web of interconnected, constantly shifting relations. The world consists not of distinct (= separable for them) things but of a web of essentially interdependent relations. A is nothing but a relation to B, C . . . ; B is nothing but a relation to A, C. . . . But, since nothing in such a web has "own being" (*sbhava*), to the enlightened mind all this multiplicity drops off as only the surface of reality, as ontological "emptiness" (*sunyatta*). True ultimate reality, *Nirvana*, lies beyond all multiplicity and change, and once we have given up the illusion of separate selves we can merge into union with It = ultimate bliss. *Spiritual path to Enlightenment:* Give up the illusion of a distinct (= separate) self or ego, "I". Since this ego is the root of all particular desires, and since the inevitable frustration of all such desires is the root of suffering and sorrow in this life, then letting go of the individual separate self is the gateway to the end of all suffering and so of entry into ultimate bliss, *Nirvana*. For the *Mahayana Schools* (India, Tibet, China, Japan) *Nirvana* is interpreted as "Pure Mind." For the *Hinayana* or *Theravada Schools* (Southeast Asia), *Nirvana* is totally indescribable, not even as mind, consciousness.

III. Solution: The "I" as Synthesis of Permanence and Process

Step 1. There must be some principle of self-identity through change in each human person. *Reason:* Otherwise, we cannot explain these facts of our experience:

1) Memory: I remember past events, scenes, things, etc., not just as past, but as *mine,* as *my* past experiences of these events, etc., which I recall as having happened to the same me that is remembering them and talking about them now. No "handing on" of the experiences of someone else in the past could explain this; another's experiences are not mine, even though the objective content might be similar. The no-self theory cannot do justice to this common experience of myself-as-remembering-something-in-the-past.

2) Moral responsibility for my past actions: "*I* did this; and *I* am sorry—or *I* am proud—*I* did so. I take responsibility for this past act as *my* act." Otherwise, guilt, sorrow, contrition, even forgiveness of others all become meaningless illusions to be gotten rid of. The whole moral life, which is inseparable from my sense of personal dignity and self-possession, goes down the drain. Such a philosophical theory is not an explanation illuminating our basic human experience. It is an elimination or suppression of the facts to be explained—the ultimate refutation of any philosophical theory.

3) Promises and pledging of fidelity for the future: "*I will* do this; *I promise.*" "I take you as my wife (husband) for richer or poorer . . . until death do us part." "I promise to pay this debt." It makes no sense to promise what some other self will have to do. But fidelity to promises is an essential part of human dignity and moral responsibility.

4) Experience of carrying through a project toward a goal, through time and a series of steps. This is true even of an argument, an inquiry, even the understanding of a single proposition which takes time to unfold verbally, from subject to predicate, until I understand it as a whole. I am conscious that I am exerting effort over time to carry out this project.

In sum, any philosophical theory which denies or renders unintelligible any or all of the above basic human experiences is not an explanation of our experience but a denial or suppression of an integral part of it. *Note* that any theory which denies a perduring observer throughout a series of changes is self-contradictory: if there is no single observer enduring throughout the process, it would be impossible to know that there is such a series at all, since the observer would be passing away himself every moment and there is nothing to recognize the series as a series. In a word, the observer, the only one who can notice there is a change at all, cannot be fitted into the theory purporting to explain change! The data to be explained have themselves disappeared!

Step 2. This principle of self-identity cannot be identical with the various phases of change it goes through. This would imply a contradiction: the various phases by definition are not identical with each other—otherwise no change—and if the subject is identical with each of them, then it is identical and not identical to itself—which is absurd. Hence we must conclude that the perduring subject of the change must transcend all the particular phases of the process, not simply identical with any but perduring through all as their unifying core, as the subject who has the experiences, *for whom* and *in whom* the process takes place. In technical Thomistic terminology, it forms a real metaphysical composition with these changing phases, a composition whose inner content keeps changing, now taking on some new attribute, now losing another. The composition is *real,* because the components are irreducibly non-identical in the being itself; it is *metaphysical,* because the components are not each a complete being or thing in and of itself, but incomplete, correlative, interpenetrating co-principles or co-constituents of one complete being.

Step 3.   How does one identify and aptly name these co-principles? Traditionally, since Aristotle, the principle of self-identity has been called *substance* (from the Latin *sub-stare:* to stand under), that which stands under all its changing phases as their principle of continuity and self-identity. The changing phases that affect the substance have been called *accidents* (from the Latin *accidere:* to happen to), because they happen to the substance but do not constitute or change its essential self-identity. The substance is thus immanent in, involved in, and expressed in its changing accidents, but though united with, never simply identical with, totally immersed in, or exhausted by any one of them. It is both immanent in yet transcending each one of its successive, accidental states and acts. Hence such a change is called an accidental change, because the substance itself does not change essentially or substantially so as to become another being or another kind of being, but only accidentally.

Note: Accident is a technical term, correlative with substance, and does not carry quite the same connotations as the term when used in ordinary language today. Thus it does not mean something unimportant or unintended: to get married, to end up in heaven or hell, are certainly important, but they remain technically "accidents," because they do not turn you into an essentially different person or different being. You can substitute another term, if you wish, such as "non-essential modification." Metaphysically speaking, accident is only a shorthand for non-essential modification.

Warning.   It is very important not to fall into a misinterpretation of substance that is widespread in modern philosophy since John Locke, and still quite prevalent today, especially among empiricists and phenomenologists, namely, that substance means something static, inert, totally unchanging and immutable. This is not at all the case with either the Aristotelian or the Thomistic substance (though it may be with some later versions). *Self-identical* is not the same concept as *unchanging* or immutable. The proper way to express the authentic meaning of self-identity through accidental change is this: "In an accidental change, the substance itself changes, but not substantially or essentially, only accidentally." Thus the subject that changes retains its essential self-identity through the spectrum of accidental change open to it in terms of its natural potencies.

Substance as dynamic.   Far from being static or inert, substance for St. Thomas, interpreted in the light of his fundamental conception of real being as dynamic act of presence ordered naturally to flow over into self-expressive, self-communicative action, is itself a highly dynamic notion. The substance of any being, as a nature (= "a center of acting and being acted upon"), is intrinsically oriented toward expressing and fulfilling itself through its operations and relations of giving-receiving with others. St. Thomas puts it tersely: "Every substance exists for the sake of its operations" (*Sum. Theol.,* I, q. 105, art. 5); "Each and every thing shows forth that it exists for the sake of its operations; indeed, operation is the ultimate perfection of each thing" (*Sum. c. Gentes,* III, ch. 113). You could not find a more dynamic notion than this.

The notion of *self-identity,* too, does not signify something static and self-enclosed, but open and flexible within the limits characteristic of its nature. Thus every living thing maintains its self-identity by active interchange with the outside world, taking in food, air, etc., giving off waste, etc., and turning into itself what it takes in. The human person can adapt to a wide range of temperatures and foods; but expose it to extreme temperatures or the wrong kind of foods and the power of its self-identity will be overcome and disintegrate into some other being or beings. Self-identity is not immutability but the active power of self-maintenance in exchange with others. Thus the best way to maintain psychological self-identity is not by not changing, doing nothing, but by stability of goals, perseveringly pursued.

Substance and Accident as Potency and Act.   In the preceding chapter on Change in General we uncovered the need of some kind of metaphysical composition of permanence and process to explain all change, such that the metaphysical principles are related to each other as *potency* and *act.* We have now discovered *substance* and *accident* as the first primary mode of such change. The analogous application of these basic notions of potency and act to substance and accident now illumines significantly the special relations between the latter. *Substance,* as the principle of continuity and self-identity throughout the whole spectrum of accidental change open to a particular being, becomes the abiding center of the being's "reservoir" of built-in potentiality or natural aptitude, for the whole spectrum of possible changes—actualities—open to it by its nature.

This potentiality, both for receiving and for active self-expression, is both open to all it can do and receive (active and passive potency) and also *closed* by the limits imposed upon it because it is a finite essence, a limited mode of participation in the unlimited fullness of pure existence itself. Thus the final fulfillment or perfection characteristic of a human being will be judged by the actualization as fully as possible of the person's natural potentialities as embodied spirit—potentialities in the order of body (definitely limited) and in the order of spirit (the unlimited openness of intellect and will to the whole of being as true and good; and, finally, to union with God as the ultimate Source and Fullness of all truth, goodness, beauty, and creative love).

Conclusion. We have discovered above the *First Role of Substance,* as the principle of perduring self-identity through accidental, or nonessential change, the necessary metaphysical underpinning of every human life as a *story* with a point to it. No perduring substantial self = no story; no abiding center of natural potentialities = no growth toward fulfillment, *no meaningful story!*

IV. Second Role of Substance

In addition to its role of unity across time and change, substance plays another indispensable role in the existence of a complex being: to be the unifying center of the many different attributes and properties possessed by one being at any one time, simultaneously. Thus at any one moment I can be walking, talking, hot or cold, angry or happy, etc. These attributes are not independent beings or things on their own, but accidents, non-essential notes belonging to the same one person, myself, and I experience them as such. In a word, they are all accidents rooted in the same substance. Their proper mode of being is not to be in-themselves, but to be in-another, i.e., the substance, which does stand in itself, but never without some modifying accident. The substance has the "static" role here of unifying them all *here and now,* not across time. Aristotle is justly proud of being the first one to identify philosophically these two unifying roles of substance.

V. Metaphysical Definition of Substance and Accident

We are now in a position to give a precise definition of them in philosophical terms. We notice that the various accidental or non-essential attributes are not the ultimate subjects of predication, as that which exists and acts, in the full sense of the term. They are always in a substance, belonging to a substance as parts, aspects, properties, etc., not as wholes. On the other hand, the substance itself is not in or part of anything else, but is that which exists and acts in its own right, as the ultimate subject of predication, existence, action. All attributes are predicated of it; it is predicated of nothing else (save in a proposition of pure identity or a tautology) It is that which makes a being stand on its own, as a unity-identity-whole. Hence the following definitions:

Substance = that which is apt to exist in itself and not in another (i.e., not as a part of any other being).

Accident = that which is apt to exist not in itself but only in another. The latter, properly speaking, do not have their own being, but share the being of their substance. Their being is a being-in-a-substance; the substance is a being-in-itself. Thus, in "This is a *man*," *man* indicates a substance in "This man is *kind*," *kind* indicates an accident of this substance.

Corollary. It should be clear, therefore, that wherever there is being there must be substance at its core. For if everything existed only in another, there would be an endless regress with no ultimate foundation and nothing could ever exist at all. To be is either to be a substance, or to be in a substance. It is possible for an uncomposed, unchanging being, like God, to exist by itself as a substance with no accidents. It is not possible for an accident to exist by itself, but only in another.

VI. Extension of the Substance/Accident Structure to Other Levels of Being

We have discovered and analyzed the substance/accident metaphysical composition first as found in human beings like ourselves, because it is most evident there: we are the only beings to which we are luminously present from within by self-consciousness. We can now use this example closest to us as an analogous model for extending this structure to other levels of being outside of the human—in fact we must do so to render their behavior intelligible. We reach this conclusion in 4 steps:

1. In general, wherever there is found a case of real intrinsic identity in being through change, there must be present a substance/accident structure appropriate to the being in question. For without this structure, the data would become unintelligible.

2. *In animals,* especially in the higher ones more familiar to us, there is clearly manifested something similar to our own human self-identity, though not interiorly self-conscious as in us. There is clear evidence of memory, striving to reach goals through a series of acts, etc.

3. *In plants,* something similar seems to manifest itself, in the process of growth, adaptation to accidents along the way, etc., but already with less clarity of distinction from the earth and the environment in which a plant is rooted. Self-identity is there, it seems, but the integration, interiority, and independence of others are less intense and thorough. The distinction of each organism as a unity of being and action, divided off from every other being, is becoming more blurred.

Note that in all material living beings the self-identity is not confined to or manifested by any one part or parts that remain statically unchanged or materially identifiable as self-identical, but in the unity of an inner force that orders, governs, and integrates the unceasing circulation and interchange of elements that is biological life.

Cf. Hans Jonas, "The Biological Foundations of Individuality," *Internat. Phil. Quart.* 8 (1968), 231–51; *The Phenomenon of Life: Toward a Philosophical Biology* (New York: Delta, 1966).

4. *In inanimate being,* below the level of life, there appear to be something like distinct units of action, hence of being, perduring at least through brief cycles of change, e.g., molecules, atoms, electrons, neutrons, because when you break them up, their properties change significantly: oxygen and hydrogen combined into molecules of water extinguish fires; when broken up into the separate atoms each is highly flammable, etc. But it is not always easy for us to distinguish genuine unities from aggregates. And these units are so integrated with and dependent on systems of particles, fields of force, etc. that their self-identity as distinct becomes very blurred for us. The levels of reality exhibit an analogous spectrum of self-identity, from weak to strong, according as the inner force of unity integrating them is stronger or weaker. Is it possible that the whole material world below plants could be one single great substance out of which emerge more or less distinctly different levels of living things and, finally, human beings with self-consciousness and freedom? Some have thought so. This is not contradictory, but seems less plausible than the existence of many distinct substances.

How is substance known? Not by any single sense impression or direct observation now, but by reflective insight into the meaning of a whole series of experiences in my past life, recognized as mine. Beware of the *misleading model of knowing* (Hume) as taking a look at something, a visual model: what you look at must always be outside of, or distinct from, the looker. To know yourself as abiding self, you don't look out at something else but simply pay attention, become aware of your inner activity of looking, trying to understand. Ask yourself, "Who's looking?" You must know yourself as subject, not just object. When trying to discern substance in others you must judge from their actions.

VII. Main Objections

There is a widespread rejection of substance among modern and contemporary philosophers. But most of their objections derive from a misunderstanding of the classical notion of substance passed down from Aristotle and St. Thomas. There are three main distortions of this classical understanding in modern philosophy:

1. The isolated, self-enclosed substance of Descartes: "Substance is that which needs nothing else but itself (and God, if it is a creature) to exist." It is that which exists *by* itself. The classical substance was that which exists *in* itself. Note the highly significant change in the preposition. Whitehead quotes this definition of Descartes and for that reason rejects substance, since "Reality is through and through togetherness."

Response. Substance is naturally oriented toward action, hence toward *relations* of giving-receiving to all around it.

2. The inert, static, unknowable substance of John Locke. It is the underlying substratum needed to support the properties and accidents of a thing, which are all we can know. But it itself is purely inert, static, not self-revealing by its action. This is the principal reason why most modern philosophers reject substance, and for good reasons.

Response. Substance by its very nature is oriented toward self-expressive action. The last thing it is, is static.

3. The separable substance of David Hume and empiricism. If substance were to exist as really distinct from its accidental properties, it would have to be separable from them, since the only criterion for real distinction is separability. But a substance totally denuded of all accidents (e.g., a human being who is neither old nor young, hot nor cold, white nor black, angry nor sad, smart nor ignorant) is absurd, an empty abstraction. Hence there is no such thing as a substance perduring through time distinct from its accidents or attributes. There is only the *bundle of attributes,* with no other thing binding them together.

Response.   Substance is not a separable thing by itself, but a metaphysical co-principle in composition with all its attributes. It can change from one to the other, but cannot be without *some* accidents. Hume's account of looking into himself and not finding any perduring self is self-contradictory; if nothing remained throughout the flow of inner impressions, then there would be no way of knowing that there was a series at all!

In sum, none of the above positions denying substance can explain the basic data of human experience laid out in Step 1 of the Argument: memory, moral responsibility, perseverance, promises. Josef Pieper sums it up well: "If the substance . . . pole of being is dropped out, the unique interiority and privacy of the person are wiped out also, and the person turns out to be an entirely extroverted bundle of relations, with no inner self to share with others" (*The Truth of Things,* reprinted in *Living the Truth,* San Francisco: Ignatius Press, 1989).

APPENDIX: BASIC CATEGORIES OF BEING

In all our human languages many different attributes or predicates can be "predicated of," or applied to any one being. In that respect each being is a One-Many whole. It is one of Aristotle's great achievements that he was the first one to try to reduce this vast multiplicity to the smallest number of basic irreducible types or "categories" of being that can be predicated of any being to describe it, i.e., can be put after the "is" in the proposition, "This being is. . . ." He considered them as categories of both language and being, first revealed in language, which in turn reflects something in reality. Most metaphysicians after him have tried to meet this same challenge, either accepting the list of Aristotle or making additions or subtractions of their own. Here is Aristotle's basic list: 1. *Substance;* then nine accidents: 2. *quantity;* 3. *quality;* 4. *action;* 5. *"passion"* = being acted upon; 6. *relation;* 7. *time;* 8. *place;* 9. *posture of the body* ("standing, sitting, etc."); 10. *clothing worn* ("wearing a hat, brown pants, etc.").

All these are certainly distinct and irreducible categories of *language.* But many think, including myself, that not all of these are intrinsic modes of being but are reducible to various kinds of *relations,* i.e., the last four. Hence the basic irreducible categories of being itself are reducible to: *substance, quantity, quality, action, passion, relation.* The rest can be generated by different relations (e.g., *place* = relations to other bodies). Perhaps attributes indicating time and place are irreducible, depending on your analysis of them; but the last two can be reduced to relations, and certainly the last one, clothes, are not a part of the real being of a person.

System as a New Category of Being

This chart of the basic categories of language and being, invented by Aristotle, has been handed down among philosophers ever since, with only minor changes. It is basically accurate and helpful as it is. But many, including myself, think there should be introduced a new category of being that has become more and more important in the world as we know it today but was not given sufficient attention by Aristotle and his successors, even though there was abundant evidence for it even in their day. They gave the impression that the world of reality was adequately described as a group of individual substances, each with its own set of attributes (accidents), which were grouped together by many sets of relations. But they interpreted these relations as accidents, each adhering in *one* individual substance. Thus friendship was constituted by two relations: one in A toward B; the other in B toward A. But that neglects the reality of order existing between substances, perhaps best expressed by the term *system.*

This is a new mode of unity existing between and binding together individual substances, which is not merely the sum of many different accidental relations but forms a *new unity* with its own properties that is not reducible merely to the sum of all the individual relations, but is a new mode of unity that resides in all the members at once. Such unities of order, or systems, are, for example, families; political and cultural social groups; churches; societies, large and small; ecological systems (the earth, the ocean, smaller land units, river basins, rain forests, etc.); tightly organized animal societies; insect colonies; fields of force in physics (electromagnetic, etc.) in which particles are immersed, etc.

Thus one can say there is a "family spirit," permeating a whole family; a team spirit; a national spirit; a corporation spirit; a school atmosphere and spirit; the equilibrium of an ecological system, even though all the parts are in constant motion, etc. Thus we say naturally, "*This is* an army; *this is* a family; *this is* a university; *this is* a beehive." Since this kind of predicate cannot be reduced to any of the other Aristotelian ones, but is needed to express reality as we experience it, it seems it should have its identity as a distinct category, which we can conveniently call *system*. Even in his own day, Aristotle used language like this and should have been more sensitive to its implications.

What is a system? It is a set of relations forming a new unified order, or "togetherness," being-together (*mit-sein* in German), which has its own set of properties as a system and influences its members accordingly. Metaphysically speaking, as we are doing, it is not as strong a unity as a substance, so has no single characteristic action of the whole as such. But it is a stronger mode of unity than just the sum of many different interactions or relations, and so deserves recognition as a distinctive mode of real being between the autonomous self-existing being of substance and a mere aggregate of external, superficial relations. Hence it belongs to the order of accidents, but is a unique kind of accident that inheres in many subjects at once—a new form of one-in-many—and so deserves a name of its own because of its special properties.

Importance and universality of system. All the real beings we know belong to some kind of order or system, most of them to many different systems on different levels (an ecological system, a family, various social groups, etc.), and depend on them for their survival or well-being. Hence it is a central feature of our universe of real being to be related to others by belonging to a system or systems. Accordingly, although it is accidental to which particular beings and systems we are related, it is an essential characteristic of our natures, both as material and as spiritual beings, that we be related to some other beings and systems of them. Thus we may justly say that both substantiality and relationality are primordial dimensions of reality. In a word, *to-be* implies *to-be-together*.

Relation of the individual to the whole. This varies greatly according to the kind of order and system one belongs to and the nature of the being that belongs. In some systems the system itself as a whole dominates the individuals so strongly that their individuality becomes almost submerged or wiped out, e.g., the ants in an ant colony or bees in a beehive are so powerfully governed by the "psychic field" of the whole that they surrender themselves instinctively and totally to the good of the whole, and will die soon if removed from it, even though they have adequate food, water, etc. The system has almost totally absorbed them; it so dominates them that they can be almost said to compose one being, but not quite.

In human social systems, a balance should be maintained between individuality and service of the whole. Totalitarian systems tend to submerge the individual for the good of the whole. Healthy systems respect and develop the talents of the individual precisely in and through his union with the whole.

Cf. Alburey Castell, *The Self in Philosophy* (New York: Macmillan, 1965); John Macmurray, *The Self as Agent* and *Persons in Relation* (both Atlantic Highlands, N.J.: Humanities, 1991); W. N. Clarke, S.J., "To Be Is to Be Substance-in-Relation," in *Explorations in Metaphysics* (Univ. of Notre Dame Press, 1994), ch. 6; Calvin Schrag, *The Self after Postmodernity* (New Haven: Yale Univ. Press, 1997, reviewed in *Internat. Phil. Quart.* 38 (1998), 101, by W. N. Clarke; M. Lazerowitz, "Substratum," in *Philosophical Analysis*, ed. M. Black (Ithaca, N.Y.: Cornell Univ. Press, 1950), 176–94—strong attack on substance; James Felt, S.J., "Whitehead's Misconception of Substance," *Process Studies* 14 (1985), 224–36; Special Issue on *Substance* in *Proceedings of Amer. Cath. Phil. Assoc.*, 1987—good articles on Aristotle, Thomas, Locke, Hegel; Peter Bertocci, "The Self in Recent Psychology of Personality: A Philosophical Critique," *Phil. Forum* 21 (1963–64), 19–31.

QUESTIONS FOR REVIEW AND DISCUSSION

1. What are the two main problems challenging us with respect to self-identiy in change?

2. Summarize the rival views of Hume, Whitehead, and Buddhism.

3. The Argument: Summarize the three main steps.

4. What has gone wrong in the two principal misunderstandings of substance: a) substance as static; b) self-identity means immutability?

5. What is the connection of act and potency to accident and substance?

6. Explain the second role of the substance/accident composition, in addition to self-identity through change.

7. Give the final metaphysical definitions of substance and accident.

8. How can we extend the structure of substance/accident to other levels of being beyond the human? What are the problems? Cautions?

9. Identify and respond to the three main distortions of the notion of substance in modern philosophy since Descartes.

10. What are the main categories of being for Aristotle? Suggested Thomistic reduction from ten to six, and why?

11. Why should *system* be added as a new, distinct category of being?

CHAPTER NINE

Essential or Substantial Change

Form and Matter II

In our last chapter we carried out a metaphysical analysis of the most common change found in ourselves and the world around us—accidental change, a nonessential change during which the being undergoing the change retains intact its essential self-identity throughout the process. But to reflect adequately on this world as revealed by our experience, we must now turn our attention to the second great type of change it manifests, a much more profound and radical one traditionally called *essential* or *substantial change* in contrast to nonessential or accidental change. Examples of this are constantly forcing themselves upon us, often painfully: the death of a living organism, often one dear to us, like a favorite plant, a pet animal, a living person (relative or friend); the assimilation of food, once living, now consumed and transformed into our own human substance; the breakdown of complex inorganic molecules into their atoms or smaller components (often with a dramatic change of properties); or the synthesis of atoms or smaller molecules into larger ones, with consequent change of properties. For example, the atoms hydrogen and oxygen by themselves are highly flammable, whereas combined to form water they are powerful extinguishers of fire—and there are various other examples in both the living and the non-living world.

Definition of essential change = a transition from one essential mode of real being to another, so that at the end of the change there is

another real being entirely from what was present at the beginning—
either another individual or more often a different kind of being
entirely.

Two Main problems: I. Are there, in fact, such deep changes in
reality, or are all changes merely accidental re-arrangements of already
existing elements, as many Reductionists hold?

II. Granted that such deep essential changes exist in our world,
what metaphysical substructure is necessary to render them intelligible?
We have already seen in Chapter VII that all change (of no matter what
kind) requires in the changing being some kind of metaphysical composition of co-principles that are related to each other as act and potency. One mode of this is the composition of accident and substance.
What kind of metaphysical composition fits the needs of this deeper
change?

I. Problem of Fact

The facts point overwhelmingly to the conclusion that profound
changes, which can only be called essential and not merely accidental,
do in fact occur in our world. The general principle is that if the active
properties of a being change radically after a change, then this is a sign
of a change in its nature. "By their fruits you shall know them."

1) *The death of a living organism* is certainly one: all the higher activities and properties characteristic of the thing when living are now gone;
it reverts to merely chemical ones. If this is not an essential change, a
change of nature, then nothing else is.

2) *The assimilation of food,* now dead, into the living substance of an
organism, to become bone, muscle, sense organs.

3) *The breakdown of a molecular compound into its atomic components,*
e.g., water into H and O, a case in which the characteristic properties
change drastically, in fact, to the opposite. Similar to this is the *synthesis*
of several atoms to form a more complex chemical molecule with different properties, or even a living cell. Since the basic natures or
essences of beings are manifested by their actions, change in the latter
indicates change in the former. There is no other criterion for the distinction of natures.

Note. If someone claims there are no essential changes in the material world, but only aggregates of lower elements undergoing merely accidental changes—this is called Reductionism—then one cannot adequately explain that, at least in living things, as even many scientists now admit, there is a new unitary force in the organism as a whole that exercises positive causal influence downwards on its parts, and this new force, not present before in the elements by themselves, must now be present in order to exercise positive causal influence. This "holistic" principle of unity fulfills precisely the function, under a different name, of St. Thomas's *essential* or *substantial form,* which determines the nature of a being.

Cf. Terence Nichols, "Aquinas's Substantial Form and Modern Science," *Internat. Phil. Quart.,* 36 (1996), 305–18.

II. PROBLEM OF EXPLANATION

We have already shown in chapter VII on Change in General that every change involves a synthesis of permanence and process, i.e., some metaphysical composition within the changing being of co-principles related as potency to act. Otherwise, the change would not be a transition at all but a sheer sequence of two unrelated stages: total *annihilation* of the first being and total *creation* out of nothing of the second being—which does not make good sense. We shall not redo this argument. Our problem that remains is more precisely what kind of intrinsic metaphysical composition is required in a being that undergoes such a profound change as to become a different being entirely. We shall be drawing for our argument on the famous Aristotelian doctrine of form/matter as the necessary underpinning for rendering intelligible all substantial change—one of the central pillars of his whole metaphysical system—with refinements from St. Thomas and further refinements from dialogue with modern science. This central and original doctrine of Aristotle was accepted by almost all schools of thought in the West for a thousand years, then came under heavy fire with the entry of the new mathematical experimental science in the 16th century. The essential metaphysical insight in it seems to us still indispensable philosophically, though it cannot be tested by science.

ARGUMENT

Step 1. What are the changing acts in an essential change?   This step is easy and widely admitted. At the end of an essential change a new essential mode of being is present that was not there before, i.e., a new being is present, no longer the older one there before. Therefore, the act at each end of such a change must be a principle of being that determines each being to be this essential mode of being rather than another; it must be the essential determining principle. Aristotle called this essential or substantial form, since form, as we have seen already in Chapter VI on Form and Matter, signifies the inner determining structure, the unifying intelligible law of a being which makes it to be this kind of being and not some other. In essential form we are dealing with the primary and most basic form in a thing. Essential change, therefore, is the transition from one essential form to another in the same underlying potential subject.

Step 2.   What is the underlying potential subject that passes over from one pole to the other? This is the most difficult part of the solution, since we cannot observe empirically what is going on under the change of forms or how it takes place, but only the actualities resulting. So we must proceed by setting up alternative hypotheses and eliminating those that do not work.

Thus underlying potential subject, which has the potentiality to receive both of the forms in succession, must be *either* (1) *another substantial form* underlying the one that changed, or (2) some *non-formal* or *formless principle* which lacks an essential form of its own but has the potential to receive such a form and be determined by it to become this kind of being. But alternative (1) is impossible; therefore, alternative (2) must be the case.

Reasons.   It cannot be (1) another essential form. For if a being is truly one in essence or nature, this kind of being and not several different kinds at once, then it cannot possess more than one essential form at any one time, since it is precisely the essential form that determines the being to be this kind of being and not that. To have several distinct essential forms at once would destroy the intrinsic unity of the essence and make it several different essences or kinds of being at once, joined merely in an accidental unity of an aggregate or society, but not a being with an intrinsically unified essence or nature, that is, a human being, a dog, a rosebush, etc. It cannot be all at once and still be something. *Conclusion:* Since essential change is a change in essential forms, and since there can be only one essential form at one time in one essence, then the potential subject that passes over cannot be another essential form.

Therefore, it must be (2) some non-formal or formless principle, some real principle but lacking its own essential form (i.e., lacking an autonomous, fully operating form of its own). What could be the positive property of such a principle if not a formal one? Precisely that which is the opposite of form and quality, namely, *quantitative extension in space.* Aristotle first called this *hyle,* and the Romans *matter* (*materia*), as the opposite of form, as that which can receive different forms or shapes, that out of which various kinds of material objects can be formed, now one way, now another. The ultimate non-formal, quantitatively extended "stuff" that underlies and supports all forms in our material world, which has no form of its own but is open to (= a *potency* for) all forms, he called *primary matter,* and also *pure* or *radical* potency.

This is exactly the same principle we discovered in Chapter VI as the correlative metaphysical co-principle of essential form, required to explain how the same essential form can be multiplied in all the individual members of the same species—except that now it is playing a different role, almost the reverse of its previous one. In its previous role, it was the matter which was different in each case while the form remained the same in all the members of the species; in the present case, it is the *matter* which remains the same and the *forms* which replace each other during the essential change.

KEY POINT IN ARGUMENT: THE UNICITY OF ESSENTIAL FORM

Note in the above argument that it is only because there can be only one essential form at one time in one real nature that the principle of continuity through the change must be primary matter. St. Thomas insists on this unity of essential form (he preferred to call it "substantial" to distinguish it from merely accidental forms), in order to ensure the unity of real natures, since unity, as we have seen in Chapter IV, is an absolutely essential property of anything that truly is. Hence this one essential form must reach down through all the layers and structures of the being in question—all the way down to primary matter—to take over all the operations proper to its nature and make it this one kind of being and not a layering of several different kinds of being at once, which would result in only an accidental unity for the whole.

Rival Franciscan School: plurality of substantial forms. This turned into a hot controversy in the 13th century, the Franciscan Masters (St. Bonaventure, Duns Scotus, etc.) holding against St. Thomas that there was a distinct substantial form at work in every composite material being for each level of being in it: a *form of corporeity* to make it this shape of body, a *vegetative form* or soul to give it vegetative life, an *animal form* or soul to give it animal life, and an *intellectual form or soul* to endow it with the immaterial life of intellect and will and make it a human being. *Note* that if one accepts this doctrine, substantial change is easily explained in most cases simply by the replacement of one or more of the top layers of substantial forms in a being; what passes over is one or more of the lower substantial forms already there, without the need of reaching all the way to primary matter as the principle of continuity.

This doctrine did not come from Aristotle but was a legacy from the influential Arabian Neoplatonist *Avicebron* (d. 1070), with his theory that each individual being was made up of a layering of forms participating in the whole hierarchy of Platonic forms, from the lowest specific form to the highest, most universal generic forms like being—all of which were the "really real" for Plato. St. Thomas's objection was that if all of these were actually existing and operative essential forms, then the being possessing them would be many different kinds of being at once and not truly one nature: it would not be a human being all through, but an intellectual soul on top of an animal soul, on top of a vegetative soul, on top of a corporeal form, at once a man, an animal, a plant, and an inanimate body. This would destroy the *intrinsic unity* of such a being.

Although the controversy remained a hot one for a long time, and each side stuck to its own terminology, in practice each side moved closer to the other by various compromises. The *Plurality* school conceded that lower forms were in some way subordinated to the highest dominant form, whereas St. Thomas and the *Unicity* school conceded that in a complex being the lower elements were not entirely wiped out, right down to pure primary matter, but maintained a certain "virtual presence" and corresponding activity under the control of the one dominant form; and once the central form disappeared, the lower elements could then reappear as fully autonomous, essential forms on their own. But while under the power of the one reigning form these lower elements had lost their full autonomy of action and hence of existence, and, therefore, should not be called "essential forms" in the strict technical sense of the terms, since the proper definition of *essential form* had always been "that in a being which makes it to be this kind of being," i.e., possessing this unified essence or nature.

All things considered, I think St. Thomas's is the stronger position, coping better with all the elements of the problem and holding on more firmly to unity as an absolutely primary attribute of all being, even though the Plurality doctrine seems at first glance to be more easily reconcilable with the natural sciences, which insist on the continued presence of the lower elements in higher level compounds.

It should also be noted that even the scientific evidence now gives increasing support to St. Thomas's unicity theory by revealing how lower elements inside a higher complex being do not act just the way they do outside such a being on their own. For example, the electron inside an atom is not localized in a definite position here or there orbiting the nucleus but is smeared all over it at once as a pulsing energy wave; and only when we do an experiment on it does the "wave packet collapse" and the electron appear outside as a particle of determinate, size, location, etc. So, too, when atoms combine into molecules, they open up and share one or more electrons with each other so that there is a new energy flow between them, yielding new properties. So, too, cells within a higher organism develop in quite different ways under orders from the central form, blocking out certain potentialities and actualizing others.

III. A Deeper Inquiry into the Status and "Nature" of Primary Matter

Primary matter is the most difficult and mysterious part of Aquinas's metaphysical doctrine of form and matter for scientists and other philosophers to understand who not used to his kind of depth analysis. Since it can never exist without some form, it can never be directly discovered by any scientific measurement or experiment, which can only contact actualities, never potentialities, and can in principle never isolate metaphysical co-principles from their complementary partners. These can only be argued to philosophically as necessary to save the intelligibility of the data.

Most later philosophers outside the Thomistic School shifted to the much heavier-handed separability criterion for any real distinction and thus gave up the delicate metaphysical tool of analysis that is the Thomistic metaphysical composition of really distinct (irreducible) but inseparable co-principles. They tended to turn matter into a kind of *thing* on its own, with its own actual existence (not just as "married" to some form) and hence in principle discoverable by scientific analysis through quantitative measurement. Since that turned out to be impossible, the whole doctrine of matter without form as that which passed over in a substantial change was rejected in favor of a radically *atomic theory of matter* in which what passed over was the actuality of the atoms themselves, which had been there all the time as atoms. Thus all the higher natures of material beings were wiped out in a radical reductionism so as to become nothing but aggregates of the lowest elements, atoms or whatever. It would seem that the only way to hold on to the intrinsic unity of higher levels of material natures that can change into each other—as is the case in our world—is to posit a principle underlying essential form that is radically potential to be taken over by one higher central form and that can then lose this form and take on another. *Choice:* either radical reductionism wiping out all natures but the lowest, or else the form/matter doctrine expounded above—these seem to be the only realistic alternatives. The first is too high a price to pay.

However, it is very important not to import extra images into the meaning of this principle of matter, but to restrict this to just what is needed by its function in solving the problem of essential change and no more. Thus all that is needed to satisfy the "job description" of this principle is that it be that which lacks any fully autonomous operating essential form of its own but is plastic, determinable, potential to be taken over not just accidentally but deep in its very nature, to become an intrinsic part of a higher being. This intrinsic plasticity, or potentiality at the essential or substantial, not merely accidental, level can be verified either by pure "naked" primary matter, so to speak, or equally by the whole complexus of matter as containing intermediary levels of lower elements in their virtual or submerged state under the power of the central form and potential to be taken over by it or by some other essential form in an essential change. One might say, therefore, that the matter here is the very lower elements themselves, whatever they are, precisely in their dimension of deep potentiality to be taken over by a higher form, in a word, anything less than a fully actual essential form, autonomous in both its existence and operation. Deep down under all lower elements, however, must lie the ultimate primary matter, first, in order to provide the basic property of quantitative extension in space of all material things and, second, to be the principle of continuity when the lowest elements or particles change into each other, as seems to be the case.

What more can be said about this ultimate primary matter?

Aristotle, the medievals and most others until recently seemed to take for granted an image of this principle as a kind of static inert, spread-out "stuff" that had to be energized by form. Contemporary physics, however, since Einstein's brilliant discovery of the convertibility of matter and energy (Energy = the mass x the speed of light squared), now suggests that it might be closer to the mark to conceive the ultimate material dimension of the universe as of itself formless material energy with a built-in tendency to expand into quantitatively extended space. It is a kind of raw energy which of itself has no form but must always be structured by some form, though it can pass rapidly from one to another, and can never be discovered save as it reveals itself through some form (manifested by some definite properties). The total amount of this energy is a fixed constant in the universe (law of conservation of energy), but it can take on a limitless (or at least indefinitely open-ended) number of particular forms. Thus physicists can describe the whole physical universe and its operations as "transformations of energy." Note the two linked but irreducible factors: the forms are forms *of* something distinct, which is *transformed by* successive forms. Radical, spatially extensive energy fits just as well, if not better, all the requirements of the Thomistic primary matter as the ultimate non-formal principle of continuity underlying all forms, a potency at the deepest level to be taken over successively by all forms of material things but identical to none. What is essential to the metaphysical notion of primary matter is a principle of formless, quantitatively extended potentiality, or aptitude to be taken over by successive forms. Whether this be inert "stuff" or formless energy is not determined by the exigencies of the argument itself.

Note on Terminology: The Matter / Form doctrine is frequently called, from its Greek origin, *Hylemorphism* (*hyle* = matter, *morphe* = form).

SYNOPTIC VIEW OF OUR MATERIAL WORLD

Let us look back now to reflect on how the whole material cosmos, which is our present home and the theater of all our experiences in this life, is governed by this fundamental law of form/matter composition as the necessary inner structure—after the still more fundamental one of essence/existence—of all the beings we meet with in our experience. This composition within the essence of all the beings in our world is what makes possible two of the most fundamental features that characterize our world: (1) the multiplication through matter of the same essential form in many different members of the same species—thus allowing societies of equals among human beings, which is not possible in a world of pure spirits (angels); and (2) the involvement of this entire world in a vast process of never-ending change from one essential form to another—"transformations of energy"—which allows an immense proliferation of novelty in new kinds of essential forms and an overall movement of evolution in a general direction upward—slow, groping, tentative, yes, but still mysteriously upward in the long run. Thus our cosmos manifests the character of a vast, restless process, wherein the basic fund of formless material energy is captured now by this form here, now by that there, but never permanently by any, it seems. This underlying pool of energy slips out of control of its present form (under the pressure of the surrounding community of active forms) to be taken over by another, which in turn will yield to another when its appropriate time is over. This is the one great theater in which all our human experience—at least in this life—is played out.

But now the inevitable philosophical—and deeply human—question arises for the reflective person: What is the ultimate meaning of this whole vast interconnected process? We have considerably further to go on our philosophical journey before this question can be adequately answered. Cf. Chapters 14 and 19.

Cf. C. D. Broad, "Some Basic Notions in the Philosophy of St. Thomas," *Philosophy Today* 3 (1959), 199–211—defends matter/ form/ and act/potency as indispensable, but can make no sense of essence/ existence; Ivor Leclerc, "The Problem of the Physical Existent," *Internat. Phil. Quart.* 9 (1969), 40–62; D. Callus, O.P., "The Origins of the Problem of Unity of Form," *Thomist* 24 (1961), 257–85; J. Peters, "Matter and Form in Metaphysics," *New Scholasticism* 31 (1957), 441–83; W. R. Thompson, "The Unity of the Organism," *Modern Schoolman* 24

(1946–7), 126–57; Joseph Bobik, *Aquinas on Form, Matter and the Elements* (Univ. of Notre Dame Press, 1998); Terence Nichols, "Aquinas's Substantial Form and Modern Science," *Internat. Phil. Quart.* 36 (1996), 305–18; *The Concept of Matter,* ed. E. McMullin (Univ. of Notre Dame Press, 1963)—in science and philosophy; William Wallace, O.P., "Thomism and the Quantum Enigma," *Thomist* 61 (1997); Marjorie Grene, *Approaches to a Philosophical Biology* (New York: Basic Books, 1968); Christopher Decaen, "Elemental Virtual Presence in St. Thomas," *Thomist* 64 (2000), 271–300.

QUESTIONS FOR REVIEW AND DISCUSSION

1. What is the definition of essential or substantial change?

2. What are the two main problems calling for solution?

3. What is the solution to the problem of fact?

4. What is the solution to the problem of explanation: Steps 1 and 2?

5. What is the key step needed in the last part of the argument to show why primary matter is required as the underlying principle of continuity? Explain the controversy on this point in the 13th century between St. Thomas and the Aristotelians against the Franciscans and others—which still perdures today. Why does St. Thomas insist there can be only one substantial form in one nature at one time, not many substantial forms, as others held?

6. In the section "A Deeper Inquiry into the Nature of Primary Matter," there are two problems: (1) What is the relation of "primary matter" to the subordinate elements in a complex material being that undergoes substantial change? Does the one essential form wipe out all these subordinate structures right down to pure formless matter? If not, what does primary matter mean here?

(2) What is the "nature" of the pure formless matter underlying all forms in our material universe: inert "stuff" or something more dynamic (inspired by Einstein's covertibility of matter and energy)? Why would the latter satisfy the needs of the basic argument of Aristotle and Aquinas as well as the inert stuff they took for granted matter must be? Which do you think is more plausible in our attempt in this book to do a "creative retrieval" of St. Thomas?

CHAPTER TEN

The Metaphysical Structures of Finite Being

An Interlocking Synthesis

We have now finished the first part of our systematic unfolding of Thomistic Metaphysics: what we might call the *Treatise on the Intrinsic Metaphysical Structure of Finite Beings*. Before moving on, let us look back and take a synoptic view of what we have accomplished. We began with a universe of many real beings. After exploring what is meant by *real being* and its basic property of self-manifestation and self-communication through action, we uncovered the second, equally fundamental property of real being: that every being, in order to be at all, must be intrinsically *one*, self-cohering as a single center of presence and a single center of action.

We then followed the thread of being presenting itself as both *one* and *many* through the various dimensions of being in our universe. The questions raised by this perspective led us to discover the three great metaphysical substructures of all the beings in our experience: *essence/existence, matter/form, and substance/accident*. These three, in endlessly varied combinations, are all that is needed to take care of the fundamental intrinsic properties common to all finite and changing beings. Each being that is both finite and changing (i.e., all the ones in our experience) will possess throughout its span of existence one abiding essence/existence composition—making it to be a member of the community of existents; one abiding matter/form composition—making it to be one member of a species or kind of being; and many different substance/accident compositions as it undergoes its unique history of change in interaction with the rest of the universe. Matter/form in its second role as explanatory structure of essential change is enlisted to render intelligible the more profound changes in the universe where one being breaks down and passes over into a different one entirely.

Synthesis. It is important now to bring together all these inner structures to see how they fit into an interlocking synthesis within the overall abiding unity of each being as a single unified whole. *Analysis* (Greek *ana-luo:* to take apart) must always be followed by *synthesis* (Greek *sun-thesis:* to put together). For none of these compositions, or their constituent metaphysical co-principles, are complete "things" or beings on their own, but only substructures within the overarching unity of the whole being. *Unity* is the beginning and end of all analysis: we begin with a globally grasped but not yet analyzed and articulated whole; if our analysis has been successful, we end with a clearly analyzed and articulated whole, an *understood* whole, but still a whole, a unity, that which is. Let us review them one by one.

I. STATIC STRUCTURES

A. *Essence/Existence.*   This is the first and most basic, the foundation of all the rest, by which each finite being (i.e., every being in the universe except perhaps one) becomes a member of the all-embracing community of real existents by participating in the all-inclusive source of all perfection, the act of actual existence, of active presence, according to the limited mode or degree allowed by its particular essence. This makes possible a universe of more than one being = both *One* and *Many*. The essence as understood here is not just the specific essence making it to be this kind of being, but the whole *individual essence,* containing everything that makes it distinct from other beings (including both matter and form, if both are needed). The essence is like the restrictive channel along which flows and expresses itself the encapsulated energy of the act of existence. As I like to say: "Every finite being is a channeled bundle of energy, the energy of existence."

B. *Form/Matter I.*   This new composition, nested within the above essence-existence one, is located precisely within the essence component. It answers the question of how many different beings can be similar, not only in the widest order of existence itself, but also within the narrower order of the same *specific essence* or *kind of being*, as members of the same species, sharing equally in the same qualitative essential form. To allow many different individuals to share or reproduce the same form without essential qualitative difference, the new principle of *primary matter* was introduced as a principle of quantitative spatial extension that allows reproduction in different parts of this spatially extended or "spread-out stuff," without qualitative or formal differentiation. This makes possible the co-existence at diverse levels of reality of groups of beings of equal ontological value—which is especially significant at the human level for the existence of families and political (democratic) and other societies of equals—something that is not possible in societies of purely spiritual beings.

Note that the basic theme of *participation*, which we first discovered in the essence-existence composition above, occurs here again, in an analogous manner. Above, it was the *essence* that functioned as limited mode of participation in the fullness of existence. Here, it is *matter* that functions as a limiting principle for the qualitative perfection of essential form, pinning the latter down to be present here and now only and not anywhere else in the space-time matrix that defines material being. Purely *spiritual beings* without material bodies are not thus pinned down in space (perhaps not even in our time?) but can be present and operate wherever they wish to be. In beings constituted by form-matter compositions, however, as soon as the essential form begins to inhabit its particular unique bit of matter, the whole begins a *unique history* different from every other, with increasing accidental qualitative differences as they respond individually to the interactions with other individual beings that constitute their history in our space-time extended material universe.

PARTICIPATION ON THE VERTICAL AND HORIZONTAL DIMENSIONS

The *essence/existence composition* explains participation on the vertical or up and down scale of being, making possible a hierarchy of beings higher to lower in qualitative perfection. It is the principle of essential form inside the essence that makes this possible: change the essential form and you change the qualitative level of perfection of the being. On the other hand, the *form/matter composition* allows multiple participations of the same form but now on the horizontal level of the same level of qualitative perfection, since multiplication on the quantitative level does not change the qualitative degree of perfection, but allows all the members of a species to be equal in ontological value and dignity. "All men by nature are created equal" (Declaration of Independence).

Note the *special middle status of form* in this trio of metaphysical co-principles: existence, form, matter. As form looks up to existence, it is a limiting principle on what is above it; as it looks down on matter, it is itself limited by what is below it. The form-matter composition was picked up by Aristotle and many other philosophers, but they did not push deeper to uncover the essence-existence one, which St. Thomas alone seems to have explicitly identified and articulated.

Reverse corollary of the form/matter doctrine. If all multiplication of the same essential form among more than one member of a species requires a composition of matter and form, then it follows that among beings that do not possess matter but only purely qualitative essences, that is, pure forms, there can be only one member of each species. As St. Thomas puts it, each form exhausts the perfection of its own species. Since matter does not limit or restrict the concentrated fullness of perfection and action of its form, the only essential differences it could have from other beings would be qualitative ones, which would immediately change it to be an essentially different species. Thus as Aquinas puts it: "Gabriel [the angel] *is* Gabrielity; but no man exhausts humanity." (Not even Christ, the God-man, as man; the only fullness of Christ as man will come from the final beatitude of the whole human race with Christ as its Head.)

II. THE DYNAMIC STRUCTURES OF BEING AS CHANGING

Act/potency. The general structure of any changing being must be a synthesis of a principle of changing actualities (actual states of being) replacing each other on a foundation of some principle of permanence or continuity = a synthesis of *permanence and process.* The general type of relationship of these two co-principles will be that of an actuality or *act* to a potentiality or *potency,* that is, a principle that has an intrinsic aptitude or natural capacity to receive a spectrum of possible actualities within certain overall limits that define its nature: "What is the *nature* of this being?" Response: "What can it *do* or *become?*" As soon, therefore as a being has exhausted the entire spectrum of its possible actualizations, its history of change is over.

This general structure of change now becomes specified in two basic modes of change:

Accidental change: substance/accident.   Here the changes take place within the enduring self-identity of the same being, constituted by its *substance,* which is in potency to the whole spectrum of its possible non-essential changes of state, called *accidents.* Notice that the substance principle here is not a static thing by itself but a dynamic principle of flexible self-identity, which does itself change throughout a series of non-essential changes, but only *accidentally,* not *substantially* or essentially. It is the principle of substantial or essential self-identity through change, i.e., its history of interactions with the beings in its surrounding world, or environment. Once the impact of these other beings, or of destructive forces within it, becomes so powerful that it can no longer be actively assimilated into the being's own intrinsic unity, then the substance loses control of its own being, collapses as a being on its own, and turns into some other being or beings in a substantial change. The substance is identical in being, though not in name (because of its particular function), with the whole form-matter essence that is composed with the act of existence.

Two roles of substance. 1) As principle of simultaneous unity holding together all the non-essential attributes that a being possesses at any one time: the one possessing the many. 2) As principle of enduring self-identity or unity across time, throughout the being's temporal succession of non-essential changes: the one perduring through the many.

Essential change: form/matter II.   This second form of change, that is also such a characteristic feature of our universe, where the very substantial essence itself of a being is broken down to turn into another being entirely, requires a new structure of act and potency to render it intelligible. Here the acts that replace each other are the essential form of the old being and the essential form of the new being. And since there can be only one fully autonomous operating essential form at any one time in one essence, what passes over as the principle of continuity must be a non-formal principle (i.e., lacking its own essential form in the full sense of the term). This we called *primary matter* as the opposite of form, that which in its very deepest nature is plastic, determinable, with the radical potentiality to be taken over by a higher form to make up the unity of a higher essence. Here the one positive non-formal property of matter, its quantitative extension in space, comes in to fill the bill.

Thus we discover the second great role of the same form/matter composition we discovered earlier in the one/many structure of species. The same principle of matter that earlier was different in each composition of form and matter now becomes that which remains the *same* throughout the change from one essential form to another. The one/many relation is reversed.

III. SYNTHESIS OF ALL THE COMPOSITIONS UNDER ACT AND POTENCY

This synthesis of all the metaphysical compositions into the one overarching structure of act-potency, as different expressions of this same basic relationship, is one of the characteristic distinguishing notes of the Thomistic metaphysical system. This synthesis is not strictly needed in order to understand why each of these compositions is necessary or how it works. But it does add a certain splendor of harmony and a more tightly interlocking unity that delights and gives deeper intellectual satisfaction to the mind. It is also the expression of St. Thomas's peculiar genius: his original synthesis of the two great metaphysical streams of thought before him: the Platonic-Neoplatonic and the Aristotelian.

Aristotle was the first to lay down the act and potency doctrine to explain the order of changing nature, which Plato excluded from the realm of true and certain knowledge—limited to the unchanging world of divine Ideas—and hence only "a likely story." But *potency* was understood by Aristotle exclusively as a capacity for change, not of limitation in a participation structure of the universe, which he rejected as too Platonic. Thus he had no room for an essence-existence composition, in which form itself was a limited participation in the higher ultimate unlimited fullness of existence that was God. Form for him was the ultimate principle of perfection in the universe, while existence was simply taken for granted and given no explicit place within his metaphysical system itself. Remember that for Aristotle the universe had no beginning and no end, and his God, The Prime Mover, was the ultimate source not of the existence but only of the cycles of motion of the universe. The world just *was*, eternally, with no explanation given or possible.

Thus form, as the ultimate principle of perfection, beauty, etc., was always that which limited the indeterminacy, the unfinished, chaotic, disordered character of matter and all potency, transforming it into order, beauty, perfection. *The perfect,* for him as well as for Plato and all the ancient Greek world before Plotinus, was the finished, the finite, the limited, i.e., the formed. The *imperfect* was the unlimited, i.e., the unfinished, the indeterminate, the formless, namely, matter and potency, the not-yet-endowed-with-form. Aristotle sums up this attitude of ancient Greek thought in his saying: "Nature flees the infinite as the unfinished."

Plotinus, the founder of Neoplatonism (d. 270 A.D.), initiated a dramatic new turn in this history. He posited an ultimate principle, the *One and the Good,* beyond the whole realm of distinct, determinate, finite Platonic Ideas as well as Aristotelian forms: an utterly simple, infinite, concentrated fullness of perfection beyond all limitation even of intelligible form, from which flows out the whole universe by necessary emanation in successive descending levels, each constituted by a further limited participation in the perfection above it. The metaphysical structure of the whole universe is thus a vast hierarchy of descending levels of limited participation in the ultimate unlimited fullness of the One or the Good. It is the infinite now that is the ultimate perfection, while finitude falls on the side of imperfection.

The *Greek Fathers* took in this new metaphysics of the structure of the universe and adapted it to fit the Christian vision of creation, wherein God becomes the infinite Source of all being with all creatures as finite participants in this infinite fullness.

St. Thomas, too, like all Christian thinkers after the 4th century, took over the same basic vision. But for him it still remained imperfect, incomplete, because in its Neoplatonic sources *God,* the *Ultimate Good,* was beyond being, which was still understood as finite intelligible essence below the Good. This still left an unresolved duality between the Good and existence: to be the Ultimate Reality and the Source of all that is, the Good itself would have to actually exist, possess actual existence more fully than everything else. Plotinus was unwilling to make this move because he feared this would put a composition of Good plus existence in the utterly simple One, and he would not give up the priority of the Good.

St. Thomas bit the bullet by turning the priority upside down. The one ultimate utterly simple fullness of perfection must be the *Pure Act of Existence* itself, Subsistent Existence itself (*Ipsum Esse Subsistens*), beyond all limiting essence, with the Good as a primary but subordinate attribute expressing the very nature of Being itself. So he took over the general structure of Neoplatonic participation as a technical conceptual tool and poured into it his own original metaphysical vision of existence itself as the ultimate core of all perfection, shared with all creatures by multiple modes of participation through diverse limiting essences. This goes far beyond Aristotle, who had rejected all participation structures as too Platonic, and is also significantly different from Platonic and Neo-platonic metaphysics.

But St. Thomas, who was one of the chief sponsors of a purified Aristotle as a better candidate for expressing Christian thought than the anti-matter Platonism, wanted to include his own new participation metaphysics of essence/existence under the one great all-embracing Aristotelian metaphysical doctrine of *Act and Potency*, which was the distinctive trademark, so to speak, of the whole Aristotelian philosophical system. So he expanded the original Aristotelian meaning of act-potency as an explanation of change alone by redefining potency as any principle that receives and limits an actual perfection to some finite mode, whether this is a structure of change or not. His fundamental theorem of the relationship of potency to act now becomes: "Act is not limited save by reception into some distinct limiting potency." Thus pure act of itself is by nature unlimited, as happens in the pure act of *esse* in God.

This new expanded interpretation of the act-potency structure beyond the realm of change now fits perfectly all the three Thomistic metaphysical compositions: essence-existence, matter-form in both its roles, and substance-accident; it now becomes a general synthetic formula for expressing in analogous applications the entire structure of Thomistic participation metaphysics, both the static and the dynamic compositions. Thus *essence* is to the act of existence as limiting potency to act in the order of qualitative perfection; *matter* is to form as another mode of potency limiting the actuality of form by pinning it down to here and not there in the quantitative order of spatial extension, but also serving as the principle of continuity for the transition from one essential form to another, determining the outside limits of possible change accessible to the beings involved (very wide in this case, but not unlimited); *substance* is to accident as receptive and limiting potency to the whole range of accidental perfections open to successive participation by this particular kind of being.

Thus the whole universe reveals itself as endlessly different proportions or "dosages" of act and potency, extending all the way from Pure Act unmixed with potency at the highest level of being, down through a vast symphony of variations on the basic theme of act and potency by different modes of limited participation in the actuality of perfection—ultimately existence itself—by different modes and degrees of potentiality extending all the way down to the lowest degree of actuality possible—but *not*, note carefully, to a level of pure potency existing with no actuality at all. Pure potency rooted in no actuality at all would drop off the scale of real being into nothingness. Pure act can exist by itself, not pure potency.

In addition to the aesthetic beauty and intellectual satisfaction of such a profoundly unified vision of the universe, St. Thomas saw a special advantage in thus transposing all the metaphysical compositions into the mode of act and potency as a way of overcoming one of the key weaknesses of the Neoplatonic participation structure of the universe. The ultimate individual beings for them seemed to be a layering of many participated higher forms—each more universal than the other—one on top of each other, but without any clear principle of unity binding them all into the unity of a single being, since all the forms were like acts in themselves. In an Aristotelian act-potency composition, however, in any one such composition there can be only one dominant act at one time; every other component must be subordinate as potency to act. As St. Thomas often puts it: "Out of two entities in act it is impossible to make an intrinsic unity (*unum per se*). One has to be act, the other potency." (*Sum. C. Gent.* III, ch. 18)

What St. Thomas has done, therefore, in his synthesis of what seemed to him best in both Aristotle and Neoplatonism, is take from Neoplatonism the basic structure of participation, pour into it the "new wine" of his own doctrine of the act of existence as the core of all perfection, diversely participated by limiting essence (form and matter), and transpose the whole into the Aristotelian relationship of potency to act to ensure the intrinsic unity of all three resulting compositions—existence-essence, form-matter, accident-substance—needed to render intelligible all the ways that reality manifests itself as both one and many.

Synthesis: The whole interlocking system of metaphysical compositions on different levels within a single real being can be summarized thus: All express relationships of act to potency.

$$\left.\begin{array}{c}\text{complete}\\\text{real being}\end{array}\right\} = \left\{\begin{array}{c}\dfrac{accidents}{\text{existing}}\\\text{substance}\end{array}\right. = \left\{\begin{array}{c}\dfrac{existence}{\text{essence}} = \left\{\dfrac{form}{\text{matter}}\right.\end{array}\right\} = \dfrac{Act}{\text{Potency}}$$

A GLOSSARY OF KEY DEFINITIONS

1. *A real being* = that which actually is, is actively present in the community of other real beings, manifesting itself as real by its action.

2. *The act of existence* = that which makes a real being to be actively present in the community of real beings.

3. *Essence* = that which makes a being to be what it is, i.e., this particular being distinct from every other.

4. *Nature* = the same essence considered as abiding center of action from which flow the being's characteristic actions.

5. *Substance* = the same essence considered as that which renders a being apt to exist in itself and not in another—i.e., not as a part of any other being—and which therefore functions as the principle of unity holding together all its various accidental attributes and the abiding principle of its self-identity down through all its accidental changes across time.

6. *Accident* = that which can exist not in itself but only in another, i.e., as modifying some substance as its foundation.

7. *Form* = that which determines a being to be such-and-such in any order, accidental or essential-substantial.

8. *Essential form* = that which determines a being to be this kind of being and not some other. Also called substantial, as opposed to accidental.

9. *Primary matter* = that non-formal principle of quantitative spatial extension that functions as a *potency* receiving the qualitative perfection of form, limiting it to this-location-now in the space-time matrix of the material world, and also serving as the principle of continuity in the transition from one essential form to another in essential change.

10. *Act* = the actuality or actual presence of some positive mode of perfection.

11. *Potency* = any potential subject that receives and limits an act, and is the principle of continuity underlying and determining the limits of the actual changes it can go through.

Cf. W. N. Clarke, "The Limitation of Act by Potency: Aristotelianism or Neoplatonism?" *New Scholasticism* 26 (1952), 167–94; "The Meaning of Participation in St. Thomas," *Proceedings of Amer. Cath. Phil. Assoc.* 26 (1952), 147–57. Both are reprinted in my *Explorations in Metaphysics* (Univ. of Notre Dame Press, 1994), chapters IV and V.

QUESTIONS FOR REVIEW AND DISCUSSION

Much of this chapter is just a condensed review of what has been done before in more detail. But the last part has several new points, which the following questions touch on:

1. Under Form and Matter I, it is pointed out that form, considered in relation now to existence, now to matter, has opposite relations to limitation, whether it functions as a principle that limits or is itself limited. Explain.

2. The doctrine of matter as principle of individuation in a species with many members has a surprising application when applied to pure spirits (angels) who have no matter. How are angels individuated? How many are there in one species?

3. How does act/potency apply to the three metaphysical compositions: essence/existence, form/matter, accident/substance?

4. In the Synthesis section, an historical account is given of how Aquinas made a new synthesis of Neoplatonism, Aristotle, and his own original doctrine of essence/existence. What were the contribution and weakness of Aristotle; of Neoplatonism? How did Thomas correct each?

CHAPTER ELEVEN

Being In Time

What Is Time?

Data.   Time is an all-pervasive dimension of being as we know it in our world. All our lives and all our activities are measured in time-spans: "What time is it?" "How long will this class last?" "How old is she?" "When shall I meet you?" "Time goes so fast; I wish I had more time." Time is an ingredient of all memory, of past, present, and future. We are *beings-in-time.*

Metaphysical Problem.   There is an immense literature on time from the point of view of psychology, biology, physics, literature, theology, etc. We shall focus only on the metaphysical problem of the relation of time to being: *what mode of being is time?* For example, what mode of being is "one hour of time"? Is it real being, mental being, or a combination of both?

Meaning of "Time."   It is a well-known paradox in the history of thought that, whereas everyone knows quite well how to use time-expressions in his or her own language, it is quite difficult to identify and formulate precisely just what time means, what constitutes it, and how to define it. St. Augustine pointed this out dramatically long ago in his *Confessions.* Hence we shall first have to work out its relation to being before we can come up with an adequate definition. What we can begin with is what we all know from our ordinary experience, namely, that time either is, or is somehow inseparably connected with, change or succession of events which occur before and after each other. Is something

161

more needed or not? Is time but another name for change? It is astonishing how many philosophers—trusting too much to their imaginations, I think—have become seriously confused about this, turning time
into a kind of objective being on its own. *Newton* was the main culprit,
but also not a few others following him, such as *Kant,* etc. Our answer to
the above question will be "No." Something more is needed: the unifying *intervention of consciousness.* Time is a synthesis of real and mental
being, founded in reality, existing formally in the mind.

I. What Is the Being of Time?

Method: We shall argue from its necessary conditions to its status
in being:

1. Time implies real succession or Change.   That is, it implies real successive change in some real being or beings. Without real succession of
some kind there is simply no basis for distinguishing "before" and
"after," which are essential ingredients of all our time language. Time is
opposed in its very meaning—the reason why we use the term at all—to
simultaneous, motionless presence. It follows that time is inseparably
dependent on real change, succession, as its foundation. It does not
make sense to treat it, as some have tried to do, as though time were
some entity in its own right prior to change, which then measures all
change and succession, in which all change is immersed as in some
evenly flowing river—the "River of Time" notion. *Newton* is mainly responsible for this view of time as a "river," prior to all material things,
flowing always at the same regular rate, in which all material change is
immersed and by which it is measured, i.e., *Newtonian Absolute Time,*
which Immanuel Kant later turned into a necessary a priori form of
the senses.

Why does this theory collapse under metaphysical analysis? The
"River of Time" conception is really only a bewitching projection of the
imagination, which dissolves as soon as one tries to think it through,
even though some philosophers can be found to defend it even today.
For if time is something real in itself, some real "flow" before all
changing bodies—hence presumably independent of them in its own
being—then what is it the flow *of:* the flow of some other changing material body or bodies, or of some real field? Surely not of some spiritual
being; that would not make sense. The flow can't be real and be just

flow of flow, pure flow of nothing real that is actually changing. Further, how fast does it flow, measured by what? How does one come in contact with it, get into its flow? As soon as one tries to think through these questions, the notion collapses, as not making sense, as substituting a vague, internally incoherent image for an intelligible idea. One first needs some real succession before time can appear at all. Time must be a derivative property built on the foundation of real change.

2. *Real change by itself is not enough to generate time.* Real succession is the necessary foundation for the appearance of time, without which time itself disappears, but it is not yet enough. Why not? If real succession is taken by itself alone, then it is only the present phase of it that here and now actually is; the past has already gone and the future is not yet here. Time does not appear unless the various phases of the succession are compared and recognized as before and after one another. Hence the explicit appearance of time requires the holding together of the successive phases of the change so as to compare them as before and after. But since neither the past nor the future are real now, actually present now, the only way they can be held together for comparison is through some mode of being that can make them present simultaneously. But the only way this can be done is by the *mode of consciousness,* which can make past, present, and future present to each other in the order of mental being, i.e., can make present in the field of consciousness things that are not together in their real being—for consciousness is by nature always a simultaneous field. Thus memory makes present in consciousness now what I clearly recognize in the same consciousness as no longer present in reality.

Hence the very meaning of time as the recognition and comparison of before and after in a change sequence requires that time exist formally as such only in a consciousness, which alone can gather together the successive phases of a real change into a single present unity and compare them as before and after each other. Only what is present in consciousness can be compared with something else in it.

Hence we conclude that time, formally as such, is the unification in some consciousness of the successive phases of a real process of change, recognized as before and after (or successive to) each other. Or, put slightly differently: time is some real process of successive change, held together and recognized as such in the unity of an act of consciousness. It is thus a creative synthesis of real and mental being; its foundation is real being, but it exists formally and explicitly as time only as a mental

being, a being in consciousness—something we humans have produced in creative cooperation with the real world. In brief, one hour of
time cannot exist as a real being outside the mind because all its parts
cannot exist all at once: at any moment all its past ones are gone and the
future ones not yet present. It can be present as a unity only in a conscious mind.

3. *Time as Measured.*   The above Step 2 reveals to us the essence of
time in its status in being as a synthesis of real and mental being. But this
still does not explain how in the language we use about time we constantly measure time, so that we can ask and answer, "What time is it
now?" "When does the train leave?" "How long does this class last?"
"How long did he live?" (Note how naturally we transpose time terms
into space terms: we speak of "length" or "space" of time; the reason is
that we see space as a field of simultaneity, like that of consciousness—
things are together in space, not in time.)

Now the only way to measure something is by comparing it with
some standard of reference. So we measure the motion here by comparing it to some other motion taken as a standard of reference. Thus
we measure the motion in question by how long it takes in terms of
sun-time (motion of the earth around the sun), or moon cycles, or whatever. All such measuring, therefore, requires three components: a
motion to be measured, a standard of measurement, and a measuring
consciousness.

Choice of a Standard.   Theoretically one can choose any motion as
the standard, either public or private, for measuring the time-span of
any change. There cannot be any one objective, absolute measure of
change obligatory in the nature of things. It depends on the *choice* of the
measuring consciousness.

The meaning of time, now expanded into measured time, has become: a real change process, as measured by a unifying conciousness, in
terms of some other change process taken as standard of reference. Any
convenient standard will do.

4. *Public or conventional time.*   For social convenience as living together and interacting in time, any social community must choose some
publicly available, commonly agreed-upon standard of measurement. It
should be as regular, even, and easily observable as possible. The most
natural one for human societies has been for ages the most clearly
visible and regular motion in the universe for us, i.e., sun-time, the
regular daily motion of the earth around the sun (formerly believed to

be the motion of the sun around the earth, but the measurement re-mains the same), combined with the yearly cycles of the seasons. In modern civilized societies this has been broken down, for greater conve-nience—the sun is not always visible—into mathematically identical units of hours, minutes, and seconds on a 24-hour basis of one revolu-tion of the earth per day = clock-time, which in turn is measured for everyone by the master clock at Greenwich, England. We all check our clocks by it (TV stations, etc.).

The scientific community, however, since it was noticed that there are infinitesimal variations and slowings-down in sun-time, now uses for its high-precision purposes the more precise and regular oscillation of crystals, etc. But for ordinary public life, sun-time is still the standard for most human beings.

For special purposes, however, especially among more "primitive" peoples living closer to nature, moon-time and tide-time are also used ("I'll meet you in two moons," or "when the tide comes in"). The stan-dards would obviously be different on some other planet, or solar system, or galaxy. But note that even in our world, in the older, pre-industrial societies still living close to nature, people do indeed use the same sun-time as ourselves, but not divided up into exactly equal mathe-matical units, as we have done by transposing sun-time into our clock-time. These clock units are purely quantitative and impersonal, and do not reflect at all the qualitative psychic affinity of the people with nature and its non-mechanical natural rhythms. For them time is more qualita-tive. Thus for the Hopi Native Americans of the Southwest the time for their great Sun Dance cannot be specified in clock-time but only "when the time is ripe, has the right feel" for the whole tribe—much to the frustration of the tour-bus operators who want to situate it on their schedules at some precise clock-time. Native Americans who have passed over into "the white man's culture" have said one of the hardest things was giving up their qualitative sense of time and taking on this new, impersonal, purely quantitative one. There is gain in precision, but also loss in qualitative depth and texture in living by our machine-age clock time.

Internal biological and psychological time. Despite the uniformity of public sun and clock time for social purposes, each one of us has his or her own private time: the rate and rhythm of our own internal time, both biological and psychological. Our biological time is measured by the rate of our individual metabolic and other biological processes, the best measure of which seems to the rate at which our wounds heal. This seems to be different for each person and to vary according to age. This and the different metabolic rates in different people bring it about that some people live faster or slower than others in the inner intensity of their lives within the same clock-time. The rate is fastest in childhood, slows down for older people (all?).

All biological life on our planet is now believed on good evidence to have deeply implanted in each living organism its own "biological time-clock," adjusted to the basic diurnal rhythm of day and night, forming a 24-hour cycle, regulated directly by the proportionate span of sunlight and darkness—a proportion which changes with the seasons—regulating migration, procreation, etc. We humans, like all material beings, are beings-in-time.

Psychological time, as experienced from within, also apparently differs with the individual. In disturbed mental states the time-sense can be markedly distorted; there is also "dream time," in which a great deal can happen in a very short clock-time; in special altered states of consciousness, also, the consciousness of time can speed up or slow down, or even transcend time entirely into a kind of intense timeless presence (mystical states as reported, etc.).

Conclusion of the above four-step analysis.   The ingredients that make up the meaning of time for us in its full social dimension can be summed up as follows:

1. The real foundation of time is some process of real change or succession in the objective world. Since this process has not yet been formally "timed," it might be called *potential time* = real succession capable of being timed.

2. *Actual or formal time* is the unifying of this real succession by some consciousness, which holds together the changing phases, gathering them into a single mental presence so that it can compare them as before and after each other in reality. Time here becomes a synthesis of real and mental being: successive real being gathered together into a mental presence by a consciousness which recognizes them as before and after.

3. *Time as measured.* This is done by comparing the motion to be timed to some other motion taken as standard of reference, so that units of the former can be measured or numbered in terms of units of the latter. Any convenient standard, private or public, can be chosen by the conscious "timer."

4. *Conventional or public time.* This is the standard commonly agreed upon as shared public time by a given social group. This is, in fact, sun-time, or its derived clock-time, for most of the world, although it need not be and would not be in some other planet or solar system.

Summary: Time in its full social meaning = real succession unified by some consciousness so that its phases can be recognized as before and after in reality, measured by comparison with some other convenient, publicly agreed-upon motion taken as a standard of reference.

Aristotle's definition of time. All of the above is really only an expansion of one of the most famous, terse—and brilliant—definitions of time in history, that given by Aristotle: "Time is the numbering of motion according to before and after." Motion is the basis in reality; numbering is done by a unifying consciousness, in terms of another motion taken as a standard of reference (*Physics,* Bk. IV).

II. Further Questions on Time

1. Human time as a continuous flow. The kind of time we humans live in because of our insertion in the material world, and so tend to identify with the meaning of time without qualification, is time as a continuous flow, an unbroken continuum of many phases succeeding each other without a break. The type of such motion is local motion, partly because all the changes we are familiar with in the material world involve some continuous local motion, partly because our public standards of measurement of time are all based on local motion (e.g., sun-time), which, at least as it appears to us in our world, is a continuous flow.

But we should not conclude that all time is, or must be, of the same continuous type. Outside of our material world, in a world of immaterial spirits (like angels), there would indeed be real change and succession. But it would consist in a series of instantaneous leaps of spiritual action (knowing and willing), which succeed one another but have no time flow within them, each coming to rest but without any internal motion between the instantaneous, indivisible acts. This would be a process of discontinuous change and time, quite unlike ours. It does not seem that such time could be measured by any outside standard, though it could be numbered internally (e.g., a five-act angel, a ten-act angel, etc.—the more powerful the angel's mind, the fewer the acts needed and the richer the content in each one, according to St. Thomas's and other medievals' speculation). The medievals called these discontinuous phases in the life of a spirit, not an hour, or a year, etc., like our time, but an *aevum* (an epoch, or era), i.e., one instantaneous spiritual act, followed by a motionless rest, then another such act, and so on. Beyond this lies the timeless NOW of God's eternal mode of being beyond all change and succession, present to all moments of change in their successive "nows," but not pinned down within any, transcending all time-sequences of all types of change, material and spiritual alike. Thus we cannot properly "time" the duration in existence of either God or angels, though the acts of an angel's spiritual life could be compared as before and after.

2. *Flow of time not under our control.*   Why is it that the flow of time as experienced by us humans seems to flow at the same even, regular rate, outside of our control, so that we would like to speed it up or slow it down, according to our changing desires, but cannot? We must be resigned to waiting for things to happen in their own proper time, not under our control. This is because most of the real changes that are the basis of time for us are physical processes beyond our conscious control (growing up through fixed stages, biological and psychological, beyond our voluntary control, etc.) and also because all our public standards of reference for measuring time are themselves objective physical motions we cannot control, like the orbiting of the earth, the cycles of the moon, the tides, the seasons). As embodied spirits, destined to fulfill our potentialities by a journey through this material world, we must put up with the fact that our conscious lives are imbedded in the physical processes of our bodies, which in turn are imbedded in the vast interlocking network of physical processes that make our material cosmos—our temporary home as "earthlings."

3. *Psychological time.*   St. Augustine was not satisfied with Aristotle's definition of time, considering it much too physical and external as describing only public, physically-based time and leaving out the rich interior psychological experience of time, time as experienced from within. He gives us instead remarkably subtle and insightful analyses of what constitutes the present or the now for consciousness in its own inner flow. This is not some infinitesimally small point of time, but a kind of psychic span of attention, constituted by our own inner act of attention, which varies in breadth according to the intensity and power of this act. It consists of three elements: (1) the immediate past, still held vividly in

memory; (2) the immediate present passing before us; and (3) the immediate future made present by a kind of projective anticipation. This "space" or span of attention constitutes the psychological "now" for us, a "now" which has a temporal "thickness" varying with each act and each person. This is the present we actually live in consciously, constituted by *remembrance, attention, anticipation.*

4. The Reality of the "now." One of the aspects of our language about time is that we speak of the present phase of the flow of time as "now." "What's going on now?" "Do it now!" etc. This is legitimate and has a basis in reality. But just what is the basis in reality of this "now"? We tend to project it out uncritically into the real order as though time and the change underlying in were in fact composed of a whole series of distinct moments we call now's, really out there in their distinction independent of our thinking about them. Even some philosophers, who should know better, speak of time as though it were a succession of distinct objective now's.

This is an illusion, but a widespread and persistent one, which a closer metaphysical analysis should quickly dissolve. For there is not, and cannot be, any such thing as an objective "now," out there in reality independent of any intervention of mine, either in the flow of change underlying time or in the flow of time itself in my consciousness. Why is this impossible? First of all, the now cannot have any temporal thickness within it, for then it too would have a succession of parts within it— some past, some present, some still to come; and the whole span could not be called present or now all at once. If a *now* does exist, it would have to be an absolutely dimensionless, timeless point in itself, infinitely thin, so to speak, like a point on a line. But if time and change are made up of a succession of timeless *now's,* all these points would in fact coincide with each other both in time and in space, to form a single timeless *now,* with no succession or flow at all, either in space or time. As Aristotle showed long ago, in answer to Zeno's paradoxes, no addition of dimensionless points can make an extended line, nor can any number of timeless points of time add up to a successive flow of change or time. Time, like change and motion, is a seamless continuum, that cannot be broken down into an actually existing multitude of distinct dimensionless points. Any real continuum is actually undivided, though potentially divisible into as many distinct points as one wishes, though never all the possible ones at once, since they are infinite.

So it follows that any real successive change, and the time flow that measures it, cannot be composed of a series of distinct dimensionless points in space or timeless moments in time, but is a continuous seamless flow in space and time that is actually undivided, with no really distinct points of either space or time, but a continuum into which I can intervene any time I want and by some gesture or act create a distinct moment by declaring a "now," thus freezing it, so to speak, and lifting it out of the flow, for reasons of my own. Thus if I do not actively intervene, there is just the constantly flowing present in reality, which I can observe passing before me without breaking it up at all. I don't need a *now* to be aware of or even to measure the passing of time. But any time I want, as often as I want, I can intervene by my own action to create a distinct *now,* freezing the flow at that point, so to speak. So there are no distinct objective *now's* either in our world of change or in the flow of time within a human consciousness independent of human intervention; but we can create them, as often as we want, but only one at a time, by our creative interaction with the real world of changing being. So to the question, "Are there any *now's* out there in reality?", the answer must be, "Not until you make one." "When is now?" "Whenever you want it to be."

Philosophical objection: The passage of time from past to present to future is only an illusion of consciousness. In one interpretation of Einstein's theory of space and time as constituting a single four-dimensional space-time matrix, according to some scientists and philosophers following them, all world events are already given complete in this space-time whole, with their "world-lines" all sketched out complete from beginning to end, with no real succession or motion, hence no real passage of time. The only thing that moves is our human consciousness, which moves up and down these lines successively, dividing up the whole into past, present, and future according to its own subjective movement. The real world itself is timeless, unchanging. Real successive change, as well as the time resulting from it, is simply a subjective creation of consciousness, and an illusion if we think it is real. Einstein sometimes seems to speak this way, and the Minkowsky space-time mathematics confirms it.

Response.   This is a perfect example of a flawed philosophical method, of taking a static mathematical abstraction and mistaking it for an adequate model of existing dynamic reality. In this model no real action exists, hence real being, which is intrinsically dynamic and self-expressing in action, disappears too. Nothing really *does* anything; nothing ever really happens; all is statically given and motionless from the beginning, like a geometrical theorem. Hence all free will decisions disappear too and with them all moral responsibility, since nothing ever moves from potentiality to actuality and all decisions are already made, timelessly. But then even the movement of consciousness itself becomes illusory, and there cannot be even the illusion of any distinction of past, present, or future. Thus the very theory itself self-destructs and vanishes as not coherently thinkable. The theory eliminates the very data it is intended to explain!

Lesson: Mathematical entities are such extreme abstractions that they are totally static, emptied of all ability to act on their own, hence of all real being, and can only be mental beings, mental constructs, and despite their usefulness as tools for thinking about the quantitative aspect of real beings, can never be projected out of the mind to become real beings on their own. Hence they can never provide adequate models for the dynamic world of real being, Their stark clarity and precision have always proved misleading whenever metaphysicians have tried to use them as models in metaphysics, as the history of philosophy eloquently shows. Mathematics and metaphysics do not mix well!

Appendix I: Time in Einstein's Relativity Theory

This represents a dramatic shift away from the old pre-Einsteinian view that time was the same for everyone, no matter what his or her location in space. Every event in the universe had one definite time when it took place: "Now-here" was also "Now-there" and everywhere. This was partly because it was implicitly taken for granted that light delivered its messages instantaneously across space.

Aristotle, following the Ptolemaic astronomy, like most of the ancient world (sun goes round the earth), believed that the cosmos was enclosed by nine great revolving crystal spheres with the earth at the center and each lower sphere moved by the next higher one (like gears) up to the highest or "ninth heaven." The regular, continuous circular motion of this sphere—the circle was the most perfect motion for the ancients, because without beginning or end—was the ultimate measuring standard of time for the whole universe, reflected on a lower level by our sun motion.

Newton believed that his gravity-governed universe had to be set within the background of an *Absolute Time,* conceived as flowing like a great river, at its own fixed unchanging rate, in which all physical bodies were immersed and which was the absolute measure for all physical motion and time in the material universe—the "River of Time" concept, as it was called.

Einstein's Relativity Theory abolished all absoluteness of time as well as unity of time measurement for the whole universe. All measurement of time now became relative in two ways:

1) *Relative to the position of the observer in space,* i.e., his distance from the event observed and distance from other observers in space. *Reason:* Based on the newly discovered finite speed of light = 186,000 miles a second. It was formerly taken for granted that the transmission of light was instantaneous, since no one suspected that any physical entity could move as fast as it apparently did. Now, since the fastest means of communication, and hence of possible observation of things at a distance, is light, and since light is now known to be finite in speed, it follows that the time of an event as reported by an observer situated at a given distance from the event will be different from the time of the same event reported by another observer situated at a significantly different distance from the same event: the light will take longer to reach one observer than the other, so that the event will appear to happen later for one observer than for the other, precisely proportionate to their distances. This makes no significant difference on our little planet, where the difference anywhere would be in mini-seconds. But it would make a great difference in the huge distances of outer space, even in the time it takes for light from the sun to reach us compared to light from the moon.

Conclusion. Time has now become intrinsically relative to location in space, forming a new four-dimensional space-time matrix for locating and timing all physical motions and events. Now when one asks, "What time did this event occur?", the answer will have to be, "What time as observed from where?" We can no longer say, "Now here, there, and everywhere," but rather, "Now-here, there-then." Time and space are now inseparable in our cosmos. It also turns out that in the Einsteinian universe the speed of light is the absolute maximum limit of all speeds.

2) *Relative to the speed of motion* both of the body being observed and of the body of the observer. The relativity of time as depending on

location in space is easy enough to understand, once given the speed of light as finite. But this new source of relativity was an unpredictable surprise. It now turns out that for any body with mass, in motion with respect to another body, the faster one body moves with relation to the other (up to the ultimate threshold of the speed of light), the more its mass increases and the more all its own internal motions slow down with respect to those of the slower-moving body. This means that all its clocks or measuring devices slow down too with respect to those on the other slower-moving body. The astonishing conclusion follows: all possible physical measuring standards of time—clocks or whatever—on a body moving faster in relation to another body will themselves slow down with respect to the clocks on the slower-moving body, so that there is no longer any fixed standard of time measurement the same everywhere in our physical universe! So now, when one wants to know, "*When* did this event take place?", the answer must be, "As observed from where in space, and how fast was the observer moving with respect to the body observed?" Time has now become relative not only to the location in space but also to the speed of motion of the observer relative to that which he is observing and also with relation to all other observers in the universe. Hence in the Einstein universe, which is the one we are living in now, there are no more fixed times or standards of measuring time that hold the same all over the universe. There is no more center—all is relative with respect to time! Hence the question, "What time is it *now* in the universe?" is a meaningless one. This would have been a major surprise to the ancients and medievals, and is still hard to get used to for many ordinary people even today.

Paradoxes of Relativity. 1) If you could ride on a photon as it zipped around the universe at the speed of light, you would never age with respect to the rest of the world, since your clocks and bodily processes would have slowed down to their maximum compared to the rest of the world.

2) Twin Paradox: Given two twins, one takes off in a very fast space ship at half the speed of light, while the other remains at home. The first returns home after twenty years in flight—but he has aged only 10 years compared to his twin! Many claimed this impossible; but it seems to have been verified by very precise measurements from a space ship or plane breaking the sound barrier in speed. It seems to hold up both in theory and in test.

Appendix II. Space: Its Status in Being

Aristotle's Universe.   It has no need and no place for any concept of *space*, empty space in which bodies are placed, but only for *place*. His physical universe is a fixed, finite one, enclosed within the nine great spheres. Outside of this there is nothing into which anything can go. And inside of it there is no empty space at all: everything is chock full of something material, either physical bodies or air, with everything touching something else real. *Place* is the surrounding surface of all the bodies touching the body in question; and everything had its definite place. There was no need of any further concept of space between bodies. Hence it had no place in his scientific description of the universe—surprising as this may seem to us.

   Newtonian Absolute Space.   As the picture of our universe expanded with the empty space of the new Syrian astronomy, the introduction of the telescope, and the new Copernican astronomy of Galileo and 16th-century science, the vast distances between the heavenly bodies (sun, moon, planets, stars) and the earth forced the re-introduction of the notion of space (first held by the Presocratic Democritus with his atoms falling in an infinite void). Newton organized this mathematically and spelled out the properties required by this space as interpreted through *Euclidean geometry*, i.e., infinite empty space as a kind of container *for all bodies, with a reality of its own, endowed with the* properties of Euclidean geometry. It is this concept, which all of us today have inherited and according to which most ordinary people still live their lives and speak the standard language of space—bodies are "in space," "move through space," "out into space," etc.—that raises serious metaphysical problems as to its status in being. Can it possibly be some mode of real being, as Newton himself thought? Our answer will be "No," that it can only be a mental being, a mathematical construction of the mind that cannot exist as a real being, but does have a foundation in the real world, in the relational movement of bodies toward and away from each other, in a word, *Leibniz*'s conception of space as a relational system of bodies in motion.

   Properties of Newtonian Space.   They are the following, according to him: (1) It is an infinite field, extending infinitely in all directions, in which all physical bodies are "contained" and through which they move. (2) Yet it is absolutely empty of all bodies, not even a field of real energy, but pure, empty extension, devoid of any action of its own. (3) Its only properties are geometrical ones: i.e., it is homogeneous everywhere, governed by the two great laws of Euclidean geometry: the shortest distance between two points is a straight line; and parallel lines never meet. (4) Metaphysically, it is conceived by Newton as a *reality,* underlying and supporting our whole material cosmos. It is so real for him, in fact, that because it is infinite—a property belonging only to God—he calls it "the sensorium of God"—a kind of immaterial "sense organ" or medium for the divine presence to all bodies.

Critique. Such a concept cannot be thought through metaphysically as referring to anything real in itself, existing objectively outside of our minds and imaginations.

Reasons: 1) It is declared real but is absolutely empty of all real bodies and yet is not a spiritual entity, nor does it have any action of its own at all. But action is a primary property and criterion of all real being; without action there is no way of knowing that any real being is present

2) It is an actually infinite quantity, which is impossible. Every real quantity must be definite, hence finite. Also actual infinity can only be a qualitative property proper to God alone. It certainly cannot be an immaterial sense organ of God, distinct from him. If it is God himself as omnipresent, then it is a purely spiritual active presence and cannot be anything extended, which is a quantitative notion.

3) It is declared to have the properties of Euclidean space only, as though this were the only possible mode of geometrical space. But we now know there are other possible kinds of space, equally coherent as Euclidean and actually more useful for the great distances in outer space, e.g., Riemannian space, where the space is curved, and the shortest distance between two points is always a curve. For all these reasons it is impossible for space as Newton conceived it to be a real entity in itself.

What is Newtonian space, then? It is as such a mental being, or "being of reason" (*ens rationis*), an abstract construction of the mathematical mind, extrapolated outside the mind by the creative imagination as a convenient image for talking about the world we live in. We get so used to it that we end up treating it as though it were a reality in itself. It is convenient because we constantly speak of particular things being "in" something else (in this room, in this city, country, solar system, etc.); so it is easy to think of all bodies as being inside something, the ultimate container of all things, empty space, the ultimate "empty box" in which all things are located.

But it is not a pure projection of the imagination; it does have a certain foundation in the real world, in two data of our experience: (1) physical bodies do have real extension within themselves; (2) these bodies, in relation to each other, are really distant from each other, and take time to move toward and away from each other. What is real, then, is the set of relations of bodies to each other as regards distance and motion. And all that needs to be said about "space" can be said in terms of these relations of bodies towards each other. There is no need at all to speak of these bodies as located "in" something, or moving "through" something, or out "into" something which we call space. This is an extra importation of the imagination for convenience. Leibniz showed this brilliantly long ago when he proposed the relational concept of space as closer to reality than Newton's. But it never caught on with ordinary people; the container concept of space won out, and we all are caught up in it now, partly because of the great prestige of Newtonian physics, which seemed to depend on it, though in fact it doesn't. It is all right to use "space-as-container" language; but don't be taken in by it philosophically!

Note that the same critique holds against any concept of space that is declared to be real yet empty, and with no action of its own, especially if its dimensions are said to be infinite.

Space in Quantum Physics. In some interpretations of it space is no longer considered to be empty, but as filled with a high-energy-vacuum-field of electromagnetic waves from which particles pop in and out again in quantum randomness. Such a field is indeed very mysterious physically—what is going on within it when we cannot yet measure it directly in any way? But because it is not empty, and has its own reality with its distinctive action, it does not raise any radical metaphysical problems about its status in being, unlike Newtonian space. It does, however, raise other interesting and difficult ones as to what kind of reality it is, one "substance" or many?

Cf. Nick Herbert, *Quantum Reality* (New York: Doubleday, 1995), on quantum physics in general. On space, Max Jammer, *Concepts of Space* (New York: Dover, 1995); and "space" in Encyclopedias.

On Time: Richard Gale, *The Philosophy of Time* (New York: Doubleday, 1967); J. Callahan, *Four Views of Time in the Ancient World: Plato,*

Aristotle, Plotinus, Augustine (Cambridge, Mass.: Harvard Univ. Press, 1948); Georges Poulet, *Studies in Human Time* (Johns Hopkins Univ. Press, 1956); Charles Sherover, ed., *The Human Experience of Time: The Development of Its Philosophic Meaning* (New York Univ., 1975); Stephen Toulmin and A. Goodfield, *The Discovery of Time* (Chicago: Univ. of Chicago Press, 1982)—"the most important moment in human history"; J. B. Priestley, *Man and Time* (New York: Doubleday, 1964); Eva Brann, *What Then Is Time?* (Lanham, Md.: Rowan Littlefield, 1998).

QUESTIONS FOR REVIEW AND DISCUSSION

1. What is the problem of time for metaphysics?
2. What is the meaning of time (preliminary)?
3. Why does time imply real change or succession as its ground? Why cannot Newton's Absolute Time, "the river of time," be something real?
4. Why can time exist formally only in consciousness?
5. How is time measured? What public standards do we use?
6. How do biological and psychological time differ from public social time?
7. What is the full final definition of public time? What is Aristotle's definition? Are all our elements in there?
9. Must all time be a continuous flow? Other types of time?
10. St. Augustine's analysis of psychological time?
11. Explain the status of the "now." Objectively real?
12. Can time be only a subjective movement of our human consciousness (Einstein)? What has gone wrong here?
13. Explain Einstein's Relativity Theory of time.
14. Explain space in Aristotle's world. Newton's Absolute Space: Why can't it be real? What then is the being of space?

CHAPTER TWELVE

The Extrinsic Causes of Being and Becoming

A. The Efficient Cause

The first part of this course, now completed, might be called *The In-trinsic Principles of Finite Being.* In it we started off with the fact, given in our experience, of many different beings, which participate in the common bond of actual existence and in the common nature proper to their own particular species, and also undergo changes, both accidental and essential. We then uncovered the three intrinsic metaphysical com-positions that go to make up the internal metaphysical substructure of all finite beings: (1) existence-essence, (2) form-matter, (3) substance-accident—all of which turned out to be but different modes of a basic all-pervasive act-potency relationship. The first part of this course, therefore, was concerned with establishing the inner structure of all such beings, given the fact of their actual existence in our experience.

New Problem. In this second part of the course we probe even more deeply into the intelligibility of these beings, by raising the more ulti-mate question about the very existence of the whole world of these be-ings given to us in our experience. Granted that, if they exist, they must possess these intrinsic metaphysical structures, we now go further and ask: *Why* is it that this whole world of finite being actually exists at all? How come there is a community of real existents actually present for us to experience? And what explains *why* these beings actually undergo accidental and essential changes? The contemporary metaphysician

Martin Heidegger, in his *Introduction to Metaphysics,* has pointed to this as the most fundamental of all questions, not *what* things are like, but "Why is there anything at all, and not simply nothing?" Only metaphysics can raise such a question, presupposed by all other disciplines, and hopefully provide a basic answer, although Heidegger himself never got that far.

Method of solution. This is a new application of the Principle of Sufficient Reason (= another name for the basic Principle of the Intelligibility of Being) which has sparked our whole metaphysical inquiry, but this time applied to understanding the very *existence* of this world of our experience. Here the broader Principle of Sufficient Reason turns into the more precisely focused Principle of Causality. It works thus:

I. Every being must have the sufficient reason (i.e., the adequate grounding of its intelligibility) for its own real existence), either (1) in itself, or (2) in another. Otherwise it would be totally unintelligible, which is radically meaningless, not acceptable as an explanation for our real world.

II. But if (1), then its existence is self-sufficient or self-explanatory, and no further questions need be asked. If (2), then it must have its sufficient reason in another, something else in the order of real being. This sufficient reason in another is called its *efficient cause,* i.e., that which is responsible by its action for the real existence of another (either in whole or in part). Since such a cause must be "outside" the being whose existence it explains, it is called an *extrinsic cause* of the latter.

Thus this second part of the Metaphysics Course is the search for the extrinsic causes of the very existence of the beings of our universe, if they can be shown to need them. If they can be shown not to be self-explanatory, cannot provide the sufficient reason for their own existence in the real world within themselves, then their sufficient reason must be found in some adequate efficient cause outside of them. At this point the more general *Principle of Sufficient Reason* turns into the narrower *Principle of Efficient Causality:* Every being that does not possess the sufficient reason for its own existence in itself must have an efficient cause.

In this second part of the course, devoted to tracking down the extrinsic causes of the beings of our experience, we shall try to show that (1) every real being of our experience—in fact every finite, composed, intrinsically changing being in any universe—needs an efficient cause to explain its existence in the real world, in a word, that no being of this

kind can be self-sufficient for its own existence, but needs help from another, an adequate efficient cause; (2) every efficient cause needs
within itself a final cause, i.e. a goal-to-be-aimed-at in its action; and
(3) there must be one, and only one, self-sufficient being in the universe that is the Ultimate Source of all real being—and this we call God,
or Ultimate Reality, etc., according to our different cultural traditions.
Thus the discovery of God, or some equivalent principle of Ultimate
Reality, with the deduction of the basic attributes this Source must have
to do its "job" adequately, is the crown of the Metaphysics Course; the
search for the ultimate intelligibility of the whole universe of real
beings. The present Chapter XII will treat of the need of all finite beings
for an efficient cause of their existence.

Note on the Principle of Causality.   The proper formulation of this
principle, certainly in St. Thomas, and in fact in all the great classical
metaphysical traditions, is this: Every being that lacks the sufficient
reason for its own existence in itself must have an adequate efficient
cause. But the empiricist tradition, beginning with David Hume and extending down through John Stuart Mill, Bertrand Russell, and many
contemporary philosophers—who keep repeating this tradition uncritically—consistently (perhaps deliberately?) leave out this qualification and quote the principle as: "Every being requires a cause." The
result is to render a priori impossible any argument for God as ultimate
Uncaused Cause. But no valid reason whatever is given, or can be given,
for holding such an unqualified principle—and in fact no serious metaphysician has ever held it! But this does not keep philosophers in the
empiricist tradition—and not a few others besides—from repeating
this tradition uncritically (frequently, I think, in simple ignorance) to
this day, and using it as a base to refute any possible argument for the
existence of God. In fact Bertrand Russell cites it as the main reason why
he gave up believing in God at the age of 17, following the example of
the young John Stuart Mill. A striking example of a negative tradition in
philosophy that keeps repeating itself uncritically against an imaginary
opponent that is simply a straw man of its own creation! Cf. W. N.
Clarke, "A Curious Blind-Spot in the Anglo-American Tradition of Anti-
Theistic Argument," *Monist* 54 (1970), 181–200.

Note, too, that St. Thomas himself never *explicitly* appeals to this
general principle of causality, or even the principle of sufficient reason,
as we have done above. He prefers to invoke particular forms of the
principle as applicable to particular needs, i.e.: "Every being that begins

to exist needs a cause"; "Every finite, composed being needs a cause"; "Every changing being needs a cause." Some contemporary Thomists, like Gilson, insist it is against the spirit of Thomas to appeal to any general principle of sufficient reason. The reason they give is the danger of confusing it with the rationalist Principle of Sufficient Reason first explicitly introduced into modern philosophy by Leibniz, the great rationalist. But the Principle as explained above is quite different from the Leibnizian rationalist one. The latter interprets the sufficient reason as some reason from which we can deduce by rational necessity the existence of the effect. It looks forward: given an adequate cause we can deduce the effect as flowing necessarily from it. It follows, of course, that no efficient cause can be free, and that God creates the world out of necessity, not freely, i.e., that to be rational God must create the best possible world. Our Thomistic interpretation is quite different. It does not try to deduce anything; it looks *backward,* i.e., given this effect, it needs such and such a cause to explain it. The cause must be adequate to produce it, be able to explain it once this is there. But in no way does this require that the cause has to *produce* it; in a word, our world needs an infinite Creator to *explain* it. But this is no way implies that such a Creator had to create it. It is not, like that of Leibniz, a *deductive* principle, deducing the effect from the cause, but as St. Thomas expresses it, like most other metaphysical explanations, it is a "reductive explanation," tracing a given effect back to its sufficient reason in an adequate cause. Given this key difference from any rationalist principle like Leibniz's, it seems to me that this general Principle of Sufficient Reason is a quite legitimate development of Thomism, with the advantage of summing up in one basic formula the principle of the intelligibility of being that is implied in all of Thomas's specialized formulas of the Principle of Causality. So we shall use it from here on.

THE SEARCH FOR THE SUFFICIENT REASON OF THE ACTUAL EXISTENCE OF OUR UNIVERSE

I. Principal Reasons Why Beings Need Efficient Causes

1. Every being that begins to exist needs an efficient cause. This is the most obvious case. For such a being first of all does not exist, then comes into existence. If it were the sufficient reason for its own existence, it would have to give existence to itself. But this is impossible: nothing can give what it does not have; what does not have existence cannot give it, either to itself or to another. To do so it would have to pre-exist its own self, which is absurd. Hence every new being that comes into existence, in whole or in part, must be initiated into actual existence by another real being, which is its efficient cause.

Note.   When it is put in this general abstract form, there are always some people, even some philosophers, who do not see clearly the compelling force of the argument: "Why can't at least a few things just pop into existence every now and then without any cause? Who knows for sure?" To get an insight into its cogency and necessity, which is not a logical but a metaphysical necessity, try to deny it and see what happens. If this were the case in reality, then nothing at all would be required to produce anything at all: an elephant, or a hotel could appear suddenly on your front lawn out of nowhere, with no cause needed. If nothing at all were needed to produce real things, then it should be the easiest thing in the world for them to be popping up all the time. But they never do. It takes effort, work, to produce real things. But why, if nothing is required to bring something real into existence? When translated into concrete examples, the insight suddenly lights up that the opposite of this principle is radically unintelligible, hence impossible in the real world. But note that this is an insight into the *dynamic intelligibility* of being, governed by the Principle of Sufficient Reason, not into a logical impossibility, governed by the static Principle of Non-Contradiction. It would indeed be a logical contradiction to say, "Being *is* non-being"; but not "Being *comes from* non-being." That would be an unintelligibility in the dynamic order of being, which is precisely the order of efficient causality. There is no strictly and purely logical proof of the need for an efficient cause.

2. *Every being which undergoes real intrinsic change requires an efficient cause.*   We restrict this application to the case where a being acquires some new mode of real being which it did not have before (at least in some equivalent way, e.g., as stored up energy in muscles, etc.); for example, growing in body by taking in food, learning something new you never knew before, receiving a suntan, etc. Such a being cannot be self-explanatory of its new mode of being, for nothing can give what it does not have, at least in some equivalent form. Hence such a being needs at least some help from without from an efficient cause, to initiate its acquisition of new being.

Note. this principle must be applied strictly. Thus the efficient cause need not always be a completely other being: if a being has many parts and only one part acquires something new, then the efficient cause may be another distinct part in the same being, e.g., energy stored in one place to be poured into muscles in another. If nowhere in the whole being is the equivalent of the new perfection now possessed, then the cause must be some efficient cause outside the being.

Note 2. Aristotle, the ancients generally, and the medievals applied this argument to what appeared to them as one of the most obvious examples of real change, i.e., *local motion,* especially of the stars, the planets, and the other heavenly bodies, from which they argued to a Prime Mover as First Efficient Cause of all local and other motion in the universe. (St. Thomas is careful in his *Summa Theologiae* not to restrict his arguments just to local motion.) They believed that all local motion was an *intrinsic change* that required the constant application of an outside cause as long as the motion lasted. Since the acceptance of Newtonian physics in the 17th century, however, it now seems clear that uniform straight-line local motion, once launched, needs no further cause to keep it going; it is merely a change in external relations to other bodies, maintaining its motion by an intrinsic force of inertia. Only a change in motion—acceleration, deceleration, change from rest to motion—requires an outside efficient cause. Hence one can no longer validly, or safely, argue that all local motion requires an outside efficient cause. This invalidates some of the older arguments for God, if they argue purely from local motion of the stars, etc.

3. *Every composed being requires an efficient cause.* The datum here is any being which, at the deep level of its essential—not merely accidental—being is constituted by a real metaphysical composition of essence-existence or matter-form.

Argument. A being whose very intrinsic being is thus composed results from and depends on its components for its sufficient reason. But if we examine these component principles, each one turns out to be not self-sufficient by itself alone for its own actual presence in the composition. Each is an incomplete, intrinsically correlated metaphysical co-principle, which cannot exist unless its correlative partner already co-exists with it, supporting and complementing it. If asked for its sufficient reason, each one, if it could, would point to the other and say, "Ask it; I couldn't be here without it." Hence each one needs the other to be already co-existing in order to be present itself. Hence their actually existing composition needs some outside efficient cause as *unifying composer* to bring them simultaneously into existence together as co-existing. Hence every intrinsically composed being needs an active composer to join its constituent parts into unified co-existence.

Objection.   In the physical world we often see physical agents—atoms, etc.—which join together to form new compound beings with no outside efficient cause needed.

Response.   These agents first exist already on their own as complete beings, not metaphysical co-principles, and only after do they actively join together as cooperating efficient causes.

4. Every finite being requires an efficient cause.   A finite being is one that possesses a limited degree of qualitative perfection in its nature, such that at least one higher degree of perfection is possible, i.e., it participates in some perfection, such as existence itself, or intelligence, or power, or whatever, in some limited degree, but without exhausting it.

Argument.   Such a being cannot be the sufficient reason for its own actual existence in this limited mode. For something has to determine it to exist in this limited mode and not some other one possible. In a word, there must be a *principle of selection* among the range of possibilities of other different modes or degrees of the attribute in question. Why should it exist in this degree only and not some other one possible? It is impossible for the being itself to answer this question by itself. It cannot determine its own essential being to be such and not otherwise: to do so it would have to pre-exist its own self in some real but not yet determined state and then actively determine itself to be in this mode of being and not some other. But this is absurd, unintelligible. Nothing can determine its own essential being to be what it is *before* it actually exists in that mode or some other.

Hence the conclusion: No finite being, which only participates in perfection to some limited degree—above all the central perfection of actual existence—can be self-explanatory of its own existence in this particular mode. Therefore, every such being needs an efficient cause.

Another argument for the same.   If this limited being were the sufficient reason for its own existence and all the perfections in it , it would have to be the ultimate source of the perfections that it possesses in this limited degree, since obviously it could not receive them from elsewhere and still be self-sufficient. But then, if it is the very source of this perfection, it makes no sense why it does not possess this perfection in the total fullness of which it is capable. Why should it possess only in a limited and deficient way that of which it is the very source, whereas the same can be possessed in a higher way elsewhere? No answer can be found within the limited being itself. *Conclusion:* Hence every limited or participated being points back to some other being as its causal source, or efficient cause, and from it receives the limited degree of perfection it does possess. As St. Thomas sums it up: "Whatever possesses something by participation is referred back [for its explanation] to that which posesses it by essence as to its principle and cause" (*Compendium of Theology,* Ch. 68).

Corollary. It is easy to see how these two arguments—from internal composition and from finitude—can be put to work in the search for the ultimate intelligible ground of the universe, which we call "God." For if no composed and no finite being can be self-sufficient for its own existence but needs an efficient cause, and, as we have seen earlier, every real being save perhaps one must have at least the composition of essence-existence and therefore a limited participation in existence, it follows necessarily that there can be only one self-sufficient being in the universe. It, therefore, must be the Ultimate Source of all the others—the unlimited plenitude of all existence and of all other perfections that can exist and are compatible with God.

Cf. W. N. Clarke, "The Meaning of Participation in St. Thomas," *Proceedings of Amer. Cath. Phil. Assoc.* 52 (1952), 147–57; reprinted in my *Explorations in Metaphysics* (Univ. of Notre Dame Press, 1994), ch. 5.

5. *Every being which, in order to exercise its natural properties, must belong to a system, requires an efficient cause.* Such a being is one whose whole nature, in order to exercise its natural powers (active propeties), requires correlation with the other active members of a dynamic system of interacting beings. Thus every hydrogen atom in our universe is intrinsically correlated to combine regularly with every oxygen atom in the proportion of 2×1, and reciprocally every oxygen atom with every hydrogen atom in the reverse relation, and so for all the other elements in the basic atomic scale with their fixed chemical valences. The natural capacities for action and mutual combination of any one member of such a system are therefore defined by correlation with the others. But such a being, whose active nature is defined by relation to others, cannot be self-sufficient for its own existence as this dynamic nature. For then it would also have to be responsible for the existence for the

whole rest of the system, without which it itself cannot act, since it pre-supposes it. But it is impossible that the same being should at the same time be responsible for, i.e., the efficient cause of, the existence of the whole dynamic system of interacting beings with their intrinsic correlations and yet dependent on the same system in order to act itself independently to set up the system!

Conclusion.   Hence all members of such a dynamic interdependent system—and the system as a whole—need a unifying efficient cause outside of themselves to set up the whole system as a unified, interrelated, interdependent whole. It also follows that the adequate efficient cause must be outside of, not dependent on, the system itself. Otherwise, it would be both dependent on the system for its own ability to act, and yet be the cause that brings the system itself into existence—a vicious circle and impossible!

Note.   This argument can be used to show the need of an efficient cause of any dynamic system that is by nature interdependent (not just by some recent stage of evolution), and hence be applied to the dynamic physical system of our whole material cosmos, but including only the basic fundamental substructure of fixed, system-wide laws: gravitation, electromagnetism, the weak and strong forces in the atom, the fine tuning of the basic constants, the basic chemical valences for combination of elements, and the like, on all of which later evolution builds, but which do not themselves evolve. Later in chapter 14 we shall develop this into an argument for the existence of God from order in the world, requiring an intelligent efficient cause of the whole system.

Implications of the Above Arguments

We are now in a position to step back and take a new look at the entire universe of real beings in our experience—from the vantage point of efficient causality and dependence in being. Looked at from this point of view, it turns out that all the beings of our experience—indeed all possible universes of composed, finite, changing beings—suffer from a lack of self-sufficiency for their own existence, and so must depend on some other being(s) as their efficient cause(s). They need help, in other words, to get into the community of real existents. Our cosmos now appears as a vast system of interacting beings, each in turn receiving from and dependent on others not only for their basic existence but for their continued growth, and yet also giving to and supporting others in their turn. Thus to be a finite being is to be dependent on another, both for the origin of one's being and for its continued growth in being. This new integrating vision yields a significant new level of metaphysical understanding of what it means to be a member of the community of real existents that makes up our universe. To pretend we are self-sufficient is, for any of us, an illusion—a profound self-misunderstanding!

Corollary. It follows as an immediate implication of the above five reasons for needing an efficient cause that, if there does exist a self-sufficient being, it would have to be the opposite of all the above ways of being. It would have to be: (1) *uncaused;* (2) *eternal*—no beginning and no end; (3) *unchanging,* in the sense of not being able to rise to some new higher level of perfection that it did not possess before, though it could certainly express its plenitude by sharing with, acting on others; (4) *simple, uncomposed,* in the sense of possessing no inner metaphysical compositions, even of essence-existence; (5) *not a part of, or dependent on any system* of mutually interdependent beings; (6), *qualitatively infinite in perfection,* the infinite plenitude of all perfection. This is precisely the procedure followed for discovering the existence and main attributes of God philosophically, as we shall do in chapter 14. This central treatise on efficient causality is already pregnant with most of these main attributes.

II. The Nature of Efficient Causality

A. Nature of efficient cause. *Cause,* in general = that which contributes positively in any way to the being of another, which is called its *effect.* An *efficient cause* = that which contributes positively to the being of another by its action: it is the agent that makes something to be, brings it into being, in whole or in part. It thus involves more than the mere regular sequence of two beings or two events such that, given A, B regularly follows (this is the watered down version of Hume). It involves an *efficacious, productive power* in the cause such that the cause makes the effect to be, in whole or in part. It is the positive overflow of one being into another, "the ecstasy of one being in another," as Etienne Gilson has put it, rooted in the radical fecundity of the act of existence as inner act and energy of every real being, in virtue of which, given the opportunity, it naturally flows over and communicates being to others according to its capacities.

B. Origin of the term "cause."   In our Western history it originates in the Greek law courts, where it meant successively (1) *Aitios* = the person judged guilty of some crime by a judge or a jury (2) *Aition* = whatever is guilty or responsible for this harm done; (3) *Aitia* = whoever or whatever is responsible for something happening or coming to be, good or bad (generalized outside the law courts). This was taken over by Aristotle and made a technical philosophical term for *cause,* in general, any kind of cause.

Note that this meaning is very broad and flexible. It says nothing about regular recurrence of the same sequence, B following A, nor about the need of any direct empirical observation of the sequence, but only about a relationship of dependence, judged by a competent knower to be the case, based on good evidence—a derivation quite different from Hume's attempt to do so only on the basis of repeated observations. Since it leaves open what kind of cause the cause itself is, or how it causes, it is a broadly flexible and analogous term, similar to "action" and "being" itself, and takes on specific meaning only from the context. Hence it is an arbitrary restriction to limit it, as Hume tries to do, to empirically observed events following in regular sequence, or like Kant, to chains of finite, phenomenal, this-worldly causes only. If the context demands it, it can legitimately be applied to any being required by the principle of sufficient reason, including God, or to whatever sufficient reason is needed to solve a given problem. Thus its scope is just as wide as that of the inquiring mind at work, an intellectual tool to help the mind answer whatever relevant question comes up in its unrestricted drive for total understanding of all being—which, as we saw earlier in Chapter 1, is the very nature of the human spirit as intelligent. It is important to remember this history in the face of the various arbitrary restrictions of the meaning and legitimate application of the term brought in by later thinkers, primarily empiricists and Kantians, and widely but uncritically accepted by many contemporary thinkers who do not admit officially to being empiricists. Recall the metaphysician's theme song: "Don't fence me in!"

C. How do we first discover efficient causality?   This is somewhat controverted by psychologists. According to Piaget, the experimental psychologist, it takes the child up to about the age of six to become explicitly aware of the notion of causal efficacy as a general category. Up to that time it tends to explain the movement of clouds, trains, etc. animistically, that is, that it is because "they want to go over there and see what's going on." This is understandable, since the affirmation of causality requires a judgment, on good evidence, not a mere sense observation, and children are not yet able to make such good judgments. It seems that this evidential basis in our experience derives most likely from our own direct inner experience of actively controlling our own bodies, making our arms, legs, muscles work, deliberately exerting effort to make things happen outside of us (build something, push something around, etc.), where we experience that we are responsible by our own action for this happening, that it happens in proportion to the energy or force I deliberately apply, and that if I don't do this it won't happen.

We then extend by analogy this power we have discovered within us to other beings outside of us, which also seem to initiate happenings just like ourselves, e.g., animals, natural forces like winds, water, fire, etc. Thus we discover efficient causality by our experience from within, then extend it by well-grounded analogous intepretation to things outside of us, looking for an adequate cause when we judge one needed—an interpretation learned spontaneously very early and constantly confirmed by social usage and practical effectiveness in solving problems ever since. When we get down to the inanimate world, however, we must be more cautious in assigning the responsible causes, since it is no longer so easy to isolate clearly one single cause that is the decisive initiator of an event as we can do more easily in the case of animals or humans.

III. BASIC AXIOMS OF EFFICIENT CAUSALITY

These are the most important implications that follow from the very nature of efficient causality:

1. Actio est in passo: The action of the cause takes place in the effect as from the cause. This is in answer to the question: Just where is the effective action of the cause located: in the cause itself? or in the effect? or somewhere in between?

Response: It cannot be back in the cause, where the imagination tends uncritically to situate it, because to cause is precisely to give being to *another,* to make something happen, come to be, in the effect, not in the cause. For no matter what goes on in the cause itself, it cannot yet be called actually causing until the effect is actually produced in the being acted on. The causal action is thus identically the producing-of-the-effect, which takes place in the effect, not in the cause. It certainly does not take place somewhere in between, since until it actually produces its effect in the recipient it is not yet an effective causal action. Thus efficient causality is the immanence of the cause at work in the effect, as long as the effect is still being actually produced—a presence not by identity of essence but by a continuum of power as the cause pours over and communicates being in some way to the effect, "the ecstasy of the cause in the effect," as Gilson aptly puts it. This self-communicating overflow of being, manifesting itself through efficient causality, should actually be a thing of wonder and mystery, if we reflect deeply enough upon it, revealing "the intrinsic generosity of being," as Maritain puts it. But we take it for granted because it happens all around us every day, so that, as the poet Shelley expresses it, "The mist of familiarity obscures from us the wonder of our being." (Unfortunately, this making something new to come into being can be either creative or destructive, good or harmful, according to the context.)

Thus where is the act of causation located? In the effect as from the efficient cause. As produced in the effect and belonging to it, it is called the category of *passion,* or being acted upon; as coming from the agent cause responsible for it, it is called *action.* These two categories of being, action and passion, are identical in the order of real being, different in their relations: the causal act is in the effect, as from the cause. Mysterious as this sounds at first, any other explanation turns out to be incoherent, not faithful to the data before us. From this axiom follows immediately Axiom 2.

2. *Cause and effect are simultaneous,* that is, the cause as causing (the act of causing) and its effect must be simultaneous—although the cause as existing being not yet causing can of course be prior to its effect. *Reason:* to cause, as an efficient cause, is precisely to-produce-its-effect. But this must take place within the effected being itself, not somewhere else, back in the cause or in between the cause and the effect. For if there is any time gap between the causing and the being caused, then the cause at the moment of its causing is actually causing nothing, since the effect has not yet been produced. And the effect, if it is produced later than the act of causal production, is actually produced by nothing at that moment. But this is clearly impossible, absurd. If the act of causing is precisely the production-of-the-effect, then to say at the

same time that the cause is producing its effect and the effect is not yet produced, is a clear contradiction. For example, take the cutting of an orange by a knife: the cutting-of-the-orange-by-the-knife must be identical with the-orange-being-cut; otherwise the knife is not cutting anything at the moment of its cutting, nor is the orange being cut by anything at the later moment of its being cut—all of which is clearly contradictory.

It follows that in any genuine case of efficient causality the act of causing and the actual effect come together to form a *single ontological event,* with two different relations: the effect as produced is located in the cause being, but as originating from its efficient cause. The interpretation of cause and effect as *two events,* happening one after the other—as has been so widely taken for granted by so many modern philosophers since Hume and Kant—is a serious misunderstanding. The choice is clear: either (1) one accepts efficient causality as a genuine act of productive power, of communicating being from the cause to the effect—and then the causal action and its effect must form a single ontological event in time; or (2) one accepts a two-event interpretation of efficient causality—and then one cannot also hold that the causal act is a genuine effective producing of the effect, and the cause and effect relation sinks back into a mere sequence of one event occurring after the other in time, with no ontological bond of dependence between them at all—a conclusion that Hume and his empiricist followers are quite willing to accept. For them, the effect follows regularly the cause in time, but without any link of dependence between them, with the result that the cause can no longer be asserted as the sufficient reason or explanation of why the effect actually occurred. The traditional terms "cause" and "effect" remain, but emptied of the original core of their meaning and purpose as explanatory terms. Here we have a striking example of the reduction of metaphysics from explanatory inquiry into the intelligibility of being to a mere empirical reporting of an observable factual situation with no necessary connections between the contents.

Objection: But is it not quite legitimate, and generally accepted, to say that "the cause is prior to its effect?" *Response:* Yes, but only if a crucial distincion is made: every efficient cause is prior to its effect in the order of dependence, of the origin of its being, but not in the order of time. This is often forgotten, giving rise to such crude objections against

God being Creator as the following (actually in print): If God is time-less, outside of time, then he cannot be the cause of the world; for the cause must be prior to its effect in time!

Note, too, that it does not follow—as has often been objected—that every causal action must take place instantaneously. It often takes time for a cause working through a physical body to unfold its power phase by phase by motion across space, or for the parts of the effect to be pro-duced one after the other. For example, it indeed takes me time to push a chair across the room; but there is no time at all between my pushing the chair and the chair being pushed!

Another reason for the confusion between causality and time-sequence comes from the methodology of modern experimental science, which for its own legitimate purposes has reinterpreted cau-sality as *predictability according to law,* such that, given event A, one can predict event B, according to some kind of law, whether deterministic or merely statistical. Such an interpretation obviously requires a time interval beween events A and B. But this is not a description of the actual ontological action of the immediate producing cause. The event from which it predicts the other event is actually not the immediate cause but a more remote one in the temporal chain of causes leading up to the event predicted—not the "father" cause so to speak, but the "grandfather" or "great grandfather" cause.

For futher details see my historical and metaphysical analysis in "Causality and Time," in *Experience, Existence, and the Good* (Univ. of Illinois Press, 1961), 143–57. The honoree himself, Paul Weiss, a distin-guished metaphysician and not at all an empiricist, was astonished at my denial of any time gap between cause and effect, which he had always taken for granted until then.

3. *Causing as such does not imply that the cause changes or loses any-thing.* This also follows from the very nature of efficient causality: to cause is to make something new happen or come into being in another, the effect, whereas to change is to acquire something new in oneself. Hence the exercise of efficient causality as such says nothing whatever about any change within the agent. On the contrary, an efficient cause must already possess, in some equivalent way, what it will communicate to its effect. One cannot give what one does not have.

Hence if in fact a cause undergoes change on the occasion of its causal activity—as most of the causes we know in our material world do—this is not because they are causes, but because they are imperfect causes, which need to prepare for their action and come in contact with their effect by local motion. Thus if I want to punch someone in the jaw, I must first move my fist through the air up to his jaw in order to actually land my punch and produce its effect. I am not yet the actual cause of knocking him down until my fist contacts his jaw directly. A cause fully in act, totally present to its effect and not having to act through local motion, would remain perfectly motionless in its causal acts. To cause is to make another change or come to be, not to change oneself. Thus God's action in creating this world, as well as all his responses to us, takes place in us—where else would we want them to take place?—and imply no motion, change, or existence in time on God's part.

Another important conclusion follows from this: to cause as such does not imply to lose or give something away so as no longer to have it. It implies only to make another richer, not to become poorer oneself. Thus a teacher does not lose his knowledge when he communicates it to another; nor does the will become weaker by acting, but stronger. In our material world, however, whenever a material cause produces an effect requiring transfer of material energy, this is always in fact accompanied by an equivalent loss of energy in the cause. But this is not because it is a cause, but because it is a *material* cause, and in our material world there are always positive forces of inertia (a measurable force) that react on the causal agent proportional to their own strength to cancel out some of the motion or energy imparted by the agent by applying a counter force to move it in the opposite direction. This results in a "composition of forces" proportional to the respective energies of each, thus preserving the physical law of the conservation of energy and matter in the universe. This does not hold at all in the exercise of causality by spiritual agents, such as the human will or angelic and divine willing. Thus a totally spiritual cause like God, acting out of an infinite plenitude of actual perfection, undergoes no loss or change when he causes by a pure act of his all-powerful will, which simply wills efficaciously that something come to be in a creature outside of him.

4. Causal power as such is not directly observable by our external senses. *Reason:*   Since the act of causing is not another being really distinct from the effect produced, but identical with it, it is not something really distinct from both the cause and the effect, in between the two, so to speak, which could be seen, touched, or felt by one of our senses. We don't literally *see* something passing from the cause to the effect. The presence of efficient causality in a given case can only be understood and judged by the mind interpreting the whole context and recognizing that this being is responsible for the coming to be of this effect. It is a judgment of where to locate the sufficient reason for a datum of experience that reveals itself to be not self-explanatory. This cannot be done by mere external sense observation. This does not imply that what cannot be seen or touched is not in fact there, although it is beyond the reach of the scientific method, relying on quantitative measurement.

5. *No effect can be greater than its cause.*   That is, it cannot be qualitatively superior in perfection to the efficient cause, or to the sum total of efficient causes, which produce it. *Reason:* If it were, then the surplus of higher perfection in the effect over its cause could not come from the cause—for nothing can give what it does not have, at least in some equivalent way—hence would come from nothing, have no sufficient reason for its existence. But this would be unintelligible, metaphysically impossible. Hence in this case there must be some other hidden cause(s) at work, perhaps even some that are not subject to detection by the senses or quantitative measurement. Thus the mere fact that a higher level of being does, in fact, emerge in a time sequence after a lower level, and at least in part out of it, in no way implies that the later is fully explained by the earlier. This would be to fall into the famous fallacy: *post hoc, ergo propter hoc* (after this, therefore because of this). This is most important when seeking a philosophical explanation of evolution in our cosmos. Science does not strictly speaking have to be concerned about this, since its method of inquiry need only discover laws of regular predictability according to law, not locate the actually operating adequate efficient causes.

Problem of evolution.   How then explain the undeniable fact that often in the course of time the higher does emerge after, and in one sense from, the lower, as is clearly evident in the whole process of the evolution of life on our planet, with its slow, groping, but persistent movement upwards: from the inanimate to plant life, from plant to animal, and finally from animal to human, with its rational intelligence, one level following the other in time? For the fuller metaphysical analysis of the phenomenon of evolution, see the special Chapter XV devoted to it. For now, let us propose two general types of metaphysical solution, which can be applied as the data demand.

Explanation I.   While each of the newly emerging beings is higher than any *one* of the previously existing entities, still the whole system of the latter taken together contains a latent active potentiality, not yet given the chance to manifest itself, such that if enough causes combine, the system as a whole does possess the adequate power to produce the higher effect.

This can probably explain much in the process of evolution, especially in the lower levels. The notion of deeply layered active potentiality is a very fertile one, and we are not sure from our limited observations just how far it can reach. But it does not seem probable that it can explain by itself the few really large qualitative leaps in the history of evolution. The three main ones are: (1) the passage from the inanimate, from large molecules, to living cells, with their extremely complex ordering of many parts to a common end—science itself has not yet been able to propose an adequate scientific explanation for this crucial step upwards; (2) the passage from plant life to conscious sense knowledge in animals, with its intentionality and ability to interpret sense images as signs of the outside world, implying a new level of immateriality transcending merely physical and biological properties; and above all, (3) the transition from sense knowing in animals to rational self-conscious knowing in human beings, with its ability to transcend the whole order of spatially extended material properties by its powers of abstraction from space, time, and particular material conditions to form abstract universal concepts, appreciate values, moral obligations, etc. that are not specifiable in any sense images or spatio-temporal terms at all—all of which take place in the operations of the human intellect and will. The intervention of higher-level causes on the immaterial level is needed here to supply an adequate sufficient reason.

Explanation II. At crucial points in any process of upward evolution, where there is a major leap to something intrinsically higher on a qualitative level, a higher cause or causes—not discernible by empirical observation or quantitative scientific measurement of any kind—would be needed to intervene in the process to "beef up" or elevate the causal power of existing agents to a new, higher level of operations not possible before, or even to infuse a whole new supra-material power into the process, as in the case of the human spiritual soul, responsible for the higher spiritual operations of the human intellect and will. Thus the total causality needed to adequately explain the higher effects would indeed be present in reality, but not all of it detectable by sensory observation or scientific measurement. The most powerful and deeply illuminating application of this type of hypothesis is to see God as the constant hidden collaborator with the whole process of evolution. Thus creation would not be just a one-shot deal at the beginning of the universe, but a constant, open-ended operation unfolding constantly in the world, both supporting the active potentialities initially infused into nature and infusing new higher ones at crucial transition points along the way as needed, observable in their external effects but not in their hidden causal origins. Thus God should not be looked on as some alien, outside cause interfering with the process of nature, but an intrinsic, though hidden factor—at once transcendent and immanent—in the whole vast unfolding drama of what we call "Nature, the powers of Nature." All this is further explored in chapter XV.

6. *Causality in Science.*   Modern science since Galileo and Newton has given up the search for the ontological efficient causes at work in nature, in the rich metaphysical sense outlined above. And wisely so, since this is not possible for their method, based on empirical observation and quantitative measurement expressed mathematically. It has substituted what is more easily discoverable and subject to validation by rigorous scientific methods: a regular sequence of events, such that given event A, event B can be predicted from it according to some law, whether deterministic or statistical. Thus causality in science has become in practice predictability according to law. But since scientists are not always aware of the change in meaning of the term from the much richer philosophical one, much confusion has arisen—perpetuated unfortunately by philosophers who should know better. When a scientist finds a situation—as in the Heisenberg Indeterminacy Principle as applied to the subatomic world of quantum physics—where it is impossible to predict the action of a single subatomic particle, such as a photon of light—he will say, "Causality does not hold in the subatomic world." What he really means is that predictability does not hold there in individiual cases. But just because an event is unpredictable by us, it in no way follows that it has no efficient cause in the philosophical sense, i.e., no sufficient reason for its action. This might be some kind of spontaneous self-determination within the particle at the last moment, or some other hidden cause: an efficient cause, but not predictable by us. No violation here of the causal principle!

7. *Hume's Theory of Causality.*   This is the theory of causality most radically opposed to the classical metaphysical one expounded above and the keystone of empiricism ever since. Since, according to Hume, we can assert nothing of the real world save what we can observe with our senses, and since all we can observe is a temporal sequence between

an antecedent event and a consequent event, never any actual passage of causal power between the two, we have no right to assert anything more than a mere temporal sequence between the two, no intrinsic link of productive power or dependence of one on the other. Rather, by repeated observation of a regular sequence between A and B, we form the purely mental habit of joining the two together as though there were some necessary connection between them. A purely mental projection, with no grounding in reality as we actually observe it! Thus the whole explanatory power of the efficient cause as the reason why, by its productive power, the effect exists, has been evacuated, with only sheer factual sequence and predictability left. This may well be enough for scientific purposes, but not for the philosophical mind seeking understanding or even for making sense out of ordinary everyday experience, where we try to understand "What happened here? Who or what is responsible for what happened?" *Implication:* Hume's interpretation of causality renders impossible any argument for the existence of God as cause of any created effect.

For readings on efficient causality, see end of the next Chapter on Final Causality.

QUESTIONS FOR REVIEW AND DISCUSSION

1. The second part of the course from here on takes a new turn. What is the central problem that dominates the inquiry?

2. Explain the relation of the Principle of Efficient Causality to the Principle of Sufficient Reason?

3. Five principal reasons are given why beings in our world need an efficient cause to explain their existence or change. Summarize the argument in each: beings that a) begin to exist; b) undergo intrinsic change; c) are composed in their essential being; d) are finite or limited beings; e) belong by nature to a system of interdependent beings.

4. What new vision of our universe as a whole emerges from this new causal perspective of inquiry?

5. What then is the nature of all efficient causality? How do we come to discover efficient causality in our experience?

6. Explain the basic axioms as to the nature of efficient causality: 1) Where is the action of the cause located? 2) Cause and effect are simultaneous. How does the explanation of causality by Hume and Kant

differ from this one? 3) A cause does not change or lose anything by causing. 4) Causal action as such is not directly observable by the senses. 5) The effect cannot be greater than its cause. How does this fit in with evolution, where apparently the greater or higher emerges from the lower, especially in the case of human beings?

7. Causality in science: how different from causality in metaphysics? Does Heisenberg's Indeterminacy Principle violate the principle of causality?

8. Explain Hume's understanding of efficient causality.

CHAPTER THIRTEEN

The Extrinsic Causes of Being and Becoming

B. The Final Cause

Discovery of final causality.   Our quest for the full explanation of the actual existence of contingent beings cannot rest with the discovery of their efficient cause or causes. Since efficient causes frequently have a wide range of actions they can perform, the question now arises: Why does the efficient cause produce this effect rather than some other which it could also produce? The problem shows up most clearly in those agents that have a wide range of possible actions; the most obvious example is that of the free actions of a rational agent like a human being. The answer is also clear here. A human agent determines itself to do this or that by choosing some goal or end-in-view and then acting to achieve this goal. Its action is goal-directed or purposeful.

   This goal or end-in-view of an action plays the role of a new kind of cause, called the *final cause* (from the Latin *finis* = end or goal), which contributes positively to the being of the effect by determining or focusing the active power of the efficient cause from within to produce this effect rather than some other. It is a distinct kind of cause because it answers a different question: not *what* caused this effect? (efficient cause), but *why* did the efficient cause produce *this effect* rather than some other? It is called an *extrinsic cause* because it resides not in the effect itself but outside it within the efficient cause guiding its action to this particular effect.

Metaphysical problem. All agree that such final causality as guiding purpose is found in conscious, free human action, and is a necessary condition of possibility for determinate action by a free agent with more than one possible action open to it. But the wider metaphysical question now arises with respect to the whole spectrum of active being: Is this final causality or goal-directedness of action required only in a free agent, or is it a necessary ontological property of all action whatsoever, done by any being whatsoever = a property of all being as active? This is the properly metaphysical question.

Many philosophers deny this, claiming it is illegitimate and anthropomorphic to extend the goal-seeking character of human conscious activity to the activities of nature below the human, which act unconsciously out of blind necessity of nature, for example, *William of Ockham, Descartes, Spinoza, Hume* and empiricists generally—the latter on principle because it is impossible to observe empirically the final cause at work until the effect is produced, at which point the final causality has ceased. For the most part, modern scientists do not allow final causality into their work for the same reason, which is proper according to their mathematical, quantitative-measurement methodology. But it is infiltrating more and more into biology because of the more obvious goal-directed activity of living things. Most of the modern philosophers who deny final causality as a property of all efficient causes also do so because they understand final causality too strictly as requiring conscious focusing on an end, which is not the case in sub-human, or at least sub-animal nature. The classical metaphysical notion is broader, more analogous, extending to the whole range of active being. *Two parts: I. Every agent acts for an end. II. Final causality requires an intelligence as its ultimate explanation.*

I. Every Agent Acts for an End

That is, every efficient cause needs a final cause to determine its action to produce this effect rather than that.

Argument. The argument is drawn from the very nature of efficient action itself. It can begin from the side either of the cause or of the effect to reach the same conclusion.

1. From the side of the cause. If the efficient cause at the moment of its productive action is not interiorly determined or focused toward producing this effect rather than that, then there is no sufficient reason why it should produce this one rather than that. Hence it will produce nothing at all: indeterminate action is no action at all, hence can produce no determinate effect. But the effect as a real being must be determinately this or that, and this determination must be explained by, or find its sufficient reason in, the cause which brings it into being. This dynamic pre-ordination or predetermination of the cause toward this determinate effect, as precontained in the cause at the moment of its action and perduring throughout the action as its guiding form, is precisely what is meant by *final causality*, or focused efficient causality, efficient causality focused toward a determinate end or goal = the effect-to-be-produced as guiding the action of the efficient cause as it produces its effect. The final cause resides, therefore, in the efficient cause but as focused toward its future effect-to-be-produced.

2. *From the side of the effect.* Every effect of an efficient cause must be some determinate being or mode of being. But precisely because it is an effect depending on its cause, with its sufficient reason for existing located in its cause, its efficient cause must contain the sufficient reason not only for its existence but for its particular mode of existence, for its being this particular effect and not some other. Otherwise, it would have no sufficient reason for its being as it is. It follows that the agent at the moment of its action, and throughout the execution of the same, must contain within itself an interior determination or pre-ordination of its power toward producing this effect rather than some other. This inner determination of the causal agent toward the effect-to-be-produced is precisely *final causality* = the influence of the end or goal of the action, i.e., the effect-to-be-produced, on the causal action itself.

Conclusion. Every efficient cause, in order to be an efficient cause in action at all, must act for an end, i.e., its action must be finalized, directed, focused from within toward the effect to be produced as end or goal to be attained.

Final Causality as Analogous. The final causality thus shown to be necessarily inherent in every exercise of efficient causality does not imply in its meaning any conscious explicit intending of its end. The minimum required to satisfy the demands of the argument is simply an intrinsic dynamic orientation of the cause toward its end, the effect-to-be-produced. This is realized analogically, in a way partially the same, partially different, according to the different levels of being of the agents involved: (1) *consciously and freely* on the level of human persons, or higher personal beings; (2) *consciously but not freely* on the level of animals; or (3) *unconsciously,* as built-in natural tendency on the level of plants and below. This analogical character of the concept saves it from anthropomorphism (reading our human way of action uncritically into all of nature below us), nor is conscious intending of the end implied in any of the arguments given above.

Note. Ignoring this analogous character of final causality as it stretches all the way up and down the scale of active being is one of the principal reasons why so many philosophers have denied its applicability below the level of rational beings.

II. THE NATURE OF FINAL CAUSALITY

1. As a *cause* it is something that contributes positively to the being of another. But it does not do so as an active force, making something to be by its action, like an efficient cause. Its influence consists in specifying or determining the action of the efficient cause toward one effect to be aimed at, to be attained, rather than some other. It role is not to supply the power of the efficient power or exercise it, but simply to *focus* it, to supply the sufficient reason why *this* is actually done and not *that.* It is the effect itself to-be-produced in the future as present here and now, precontained in the efficient cause at least at the moment of its action, as a determinate orientation of its power to this effect-to-be-produced rather than that. A completely equipped efficient cause, therefore, is *focused power* = an efficient cause guided by a final cause.

The final is distinct from the efficient cause because it answers a different question. The efficient cause answers the question: Which being is responsible for this effect's coming to be? The final cause answers the question: *Why* did this efficient cause produce this effect rather than that? For in many cases the same efficient cause can produce several different possible effects. In a non-free nature the final cause is written into the very nature of the agent. In a not fully determinate or free nature, the efficient cause must select its final cause among several in order to actually produce this effect rather than some other one possible. For, since every real effect must be determinately this or that, not vague or indefinite, and since this effect, as effect, is explained precisely by this efficient cause—that's what it means to be an effect—then it follows that the determination of the efficient cause to this determinate effect must be pre-contained as dynamic orientation in the efficient cause itself, either before the action or at least at the moment of action. And as soon as the effect is actually produced in reality, the influence of the final cause ceases. As a guide for action, the guiding ceases when the action ceases.

2. As an end sought for, the final cause or end of an action has the character of *a good for the agent,* that which is *desired* in the widest analogous sense or *sought for* by the agent. The agent is not neutral towards it but tends dynamically toward it, whether unconsciously or consciously, freely; hence in the widest analogous sense the end is a value or good for the agent.

3. The final cause is therefore called "the first of all the causes," since no action can begin and effect be produced until the final cause of the action is determined. So it is said, "The final cause is *first in the order of intention, last in the order of execution.*" This is the metaphysical intuition behind Dante's great line in the Divine Comedy, "Love makes the world go round."

Two Kinds of final cause. In analyzing the final causality at work in any action, we can distinguish—and often have to, to answer the questions that interest us—*two kinds* or levels of final cause, especially in an agent that is acting by conscious free choice:

1. *The Goal or end-in-view of the action itself (finis operis)* = the immediate goal or end sought intrinsic to the action itself; for example, the immediate end of the action of a sculptor is to produce a statue, say, of Mother Teresa.

2. *The Goal or end-in-view of the agent* = *why* the sculptor is carving this particular statue now, e.g., in order to fulfill a commission and make money from it, give it as a gift to someone, or simply to produce it as a work of art for its own sake—in which case it coincides with the End of the Action above. Note that the first kind is always subordinated to the second, since the agent's own personal goal is the primary motivating force for his action. We often distinguish the two by asking someone at work, "*What* are you doing?" followed by, "*Why* are you doing it?" The two do not always coincide.

II. Final Causality Requires Intelligence as Ultimate Adequate Cause

This is the most controversial part of the metaphysical doctrine of final causality, for the obvious reason that if one accepts it, it leads immediately to the necessity of an intelligent Designer of our universe—

which is not a conclusion that a good number of philosophers today want to be forced to admit by reason itself, even though they might be by religious faith of some kind. Also, it does not have quite the same austere logical cogency that some other metaphysical arguments can command, but rather derives in the last analysis from a kind of reflective insight into the role of intelligence in nature that may take some time to come into clear focus. But if you can see it, it opens up a whole new profound insight into the very heart of what it means to be an active existing being in our world: every real nature, no matter how material, as long as it is active, has an idea at work within it which it has not thought up itself (except the Ultimate Designer). Put on your metaphysical diving suit as we plunge into the heart of the dynamism of being!

Argument. Step 1.   The final cause, as determining the action of the efficient cause to produce this effect rather than some other, must be somehow present in the agent, guiding its action, before the effect is actually produced in its own real being. But it cannot be present in the mode of *real being*, since the effect does not yet exist in its real being until it is actually produced by the agent, at the term of the action. The final cause, therefore, must exist in the agent as a present orientation or dynamic relation to a not-yet-existent-future. Such a presence, as the term of a relation to a not-yet-existent future, cannot itself be that of a *real being*. Hence it must be present in some mode of *mental being*, or idea, even though it is not necessarily recognized as such by the immediate agent in which it resides, i.e., in all non-conscious agents.

Step 2.   Now the only adequate sufficient reason for the presence of this not yet existent future in the form of a mental being within the agent must be that power which alone can make the future present, in the mode of mental being, and that is precisely *intelligence,* which can make present a future effect in its consciousness as a goal to-be-produced and think up appropriate means to achieve this end. The ordering of means to achieve a not-yet-existent end is in fact one of the defining characteristics of intelligence itself.

This requirement of a planning intelligence, however, can be filled in two ways: (1) if the agent itself is intelligent and can determine itself to its own goals of action; or (2) if the immediate agent itself is not intelligent, then somewhere along the line an intelligent planning cause has constructed the nature of this agent so that it has an innate natural tendency toward the production of this end, even though quite unconscious of why it is doing what it does, since this dynamic orientation is infused deep into its very nature before it can perform the actions leading to this end. These innate goal-oriented tendencies are like *incarnate ideas,* thought up by another and projected into natures which cannot think their own natural drives—ideas put to work in matter, so to speak, by their intelligent causes, in a way analogously similar to the way a human maker of a machine imbeds the idea of its purpose into the very internal order and "being" of the machine, so that it can carry on its work even if the maker of the machine ceases to exist. Thus every dynamic natural property of a non-conscious agent is an innate ontological "intentionality" toward a determinate type of effect, which it will carry out whenever the conditions of the surrounding environment permit.

Conclusion of Argument: The ultimate condition of possibility, or adequate sufficient reason, therefore, of all determinate action of an efficient cause must finally reside in some designing intelligence somewhere along the line, either in the immediate agent itself, if free, or else in some intelligent designer, either immediate or at least as the initiating origin of an ordered chain of causal events. Thus we end up with a remarkable confirmation from metaphysical reason of the opening words of St. John's Gospel: "In the beginning was the Word" (the *Logos,* the creative Thought)! Or, as Carl Jung puts it, "Final causes, twist them how we will, postulate a foreknowledge of some kind" (*The Interpretation of Nature,* New York, 1955, p. 107).

Note that we have here uncovered a new—and wonderfully creative—mode of participation at work in the universe: participation not just of real finite natures in the central perfection of actual existence—a participation in real being—which we have seen in the first part of the course (Chapter V), but also a further mode of participation in the order of mental being, where ideas first thought up by, and existing within an intelligence, are projected outside their originating minds to be participated in a less perfect way by beings which have the potential to receive and be molded by them without being able to think them consciously and freely on their own—in a word, idea-plans of action thought up by someone else and implanted within the agent, but which the agent itself cannot rethink but can only execute. What a marvelous creative invention of mind itself! The whole of nature can now be seen in much greater depth as *ideas at work in matter,* woven into it by a Master Planner.

How does this work in an evolutionary cosmos? Before the discovery of evolution as a feature of our universe came into Western science with

Darwin (1871), it was commonly believed that the Creator of the universe directly created the natures of everything in it roughly at the same time (or in a brief period) and so directly designed each nature for its characteristic activities—all in a fixed, unchanging order. Human beings had a history of development within the framework of cosmic nature, but nature itself was unchanging, without a history. Now, not only life on earth but also the entire material cosmos reveals itself as a single great developing history or story from the original Big Bang to the emergence of intelligent human beings as the latest cutting-edge chapter of this great adventure, shot through with unpredictable creativity deriving partly from the play of chance and built-in spontaneities partly from other as yet unknown or hidden higher causes at work.

In this context—which the present pope, John Paul II, has recently urged Catholic thinkers to accept in its general lines as the most solidly established and probable hypothesis (with the exception of the special origin of the human soul as immediately created by God) and to reflect on it to discern what it reveals to us about the wisdom of its Creator—it no longer seems reasonable to require that God immediately designed every nature in its present state of adaptation to its evolving environment. Rather we have the picture of an even more creative and powerful Designer who has shared more of his power and creativity with created nature itself all through its unfolding history in an ongoing creative process working immanently and unobtrusively within nature itself. In a word, creation is seen not as a one-shot, once-and-for-all event at the beginning, but as an ongoing process throughout cosmic history, God working with nature from his eternal Now outside of time.

One way of conceiving this is to think of God's designing and infusing final causality into created natures in this way: God could design directly the great fundamental laws of nature (gravity, electromagnetism, the strong force holding together the nucleus of atoms, and the weak force governing radioactive decay, with their extraordinarily finely tuned interrelationships), and also perhaps the fundamental dynamic relations or potentialities for combination of the basic table of atomic elements (pretty stable now around 105) as well as build into these the fundamental active potentialities for combining further into ever more complex types of compounds as the evolving environment allows them to be actualized in reality over time out of a wider spectrum of possible outcomes.

In other words, the Creator-Designer could build into creation from the beginning a great overall master plan of evolution with built-in active potentialities such that when one level of combinations emerges into actuality it makes possible new levels of combination of ever growing complexity in an overall ascending hierarchy of being. The details of just which potentialities would be ready for actualization at which time could be left partly to chance encounters in the vast developing matrix of space-time unfolding from its Big Bang beginning. They could also be due partly perhaps to hidden guidance or infusion of new information codes by divine providence itself when a really big jump to higher powers is ready to emerge (perhaps at crucial jumps such as the emergence of life from non-life, the jump to sense cognition, then certainly with the quantum leap to human immaterial self-consciousness and power of abstract thought and moral willing).

Thus only the general types of dynamic orientation of active potentialities in nature to future types of combinations in ascending series would have to be directly designed by God, but just how and when these latent active potentialities would be activated would unfold over time as the conditions of the evolving matrix of the space-time system would make possible at each stage—somewhat analogous to the way a child's potentialities become slowly actualized from lowest to highest as its development unfolds from embryo to adult. At every stage, though, the fundamental causal axiom must be at work: that the effect can never be greater than the cause, i.e., than the total available causes at work at the moment of emergence, whatever these may be, observable or hidden—in which case not discernible by the quantitative mathematical measurement techniques of the contemporary natural sciences.

IV. Chance: Its Meaning and Explanation

Data.   We frequently use such expressions as, "A game of chance," "This happened by chance," etc., to refer to various types of situations in our experience. This seems at first glance to deny the above thesis on the need of final causality to explain all action, as we have just established. What does this term *chance* mean, then, and how does it fit into a world of determinate causality? Upon analysis, the term "chance" turns out to refer to two basic types of experience:

Meaning 1: = the intersection of two or more lines of causality as unforeseen by a given observer. This is the situation in games of chance, in which the intersection or result may in fact be predetermined and foreseeable by some observer (at least by God), but not by the one to whom it appears as chance. (If it, in fact, turns out to have been foreseen by someone in the game by rigging it, we protest, "Foul! Fraud!") This meaning has no further philosophical problems involved.

Meaning 2 = the intersection of two or more lines of causality that are objectively independent, i.e., independently initiated (or at least the influence of one line on the other is so slight and remote as to be negligible). This is a more objective ontological situation, not depending on the subjective state of any particular observer. Whether or not it may, in fact, be foreseen by some observer who can know the future (e.g., God) does not change the objective fact that the occurrence is by chance and not predetermined or pre-planned, that the initiators of each line of causality are acting independently of each other.

This situation would prevail, for example, if the two lines of causality are initiated by the independent decisions of two free agents: for example, suppose a truck is coming down the street fast and a baby suddenly runs out into the street to pick up a ball, oblivious of the truck. It is too late to stop the truck in time, so the truck runs over the child. Even though the onlookers can predict exactly what is bound to happen, this does not change the fact that the accident happened by objective chance. The same would be true of spontaneous actions by beings lower than human, e.g., animals, and perhaps to a diminishing degree plants also, and even the ultimate particles of subatomic matter, which, according to the Heisenberg Indeterminacy Principle, are not predictable in their individual behavior but only on a statistical average. This could be an important factor in evolution, i.e., development by objective chance.

Chance in Relation to Causality.   Chance by no means entails a denial of efficient and final causality. It presupposes at least two lines of causality at work, each of which must have its own determinate inner orientation or focusing toward some definite effect, i.e., final causality, whether it attains its goal or not. What is by chance is only the intersection of the two or more lines, which is not itself an action done by any of the agents, but an unplanned meeting by several at once at a given point of space and time. Hence no chance can exist except within an underlying framework of efficient and final causality, neither of which is governed internally by chance. Thus chance cannot possibly be the explanation for everything in reality. The expression one sometimes hears, "Maybe it all happened by chance," is a nonsense statement. No calculus of probability, for example, is possible save given such and such elements with such and such determinate properties. Then the probability of their intersection can be calculated. But if there are no determinate properties at all, then anything or nothing can happen; the chances would be infinite, hence not calculable.

Thus at least the initial state of the universe must involve a basic set of elements with determinate properties of interaction, which must be planned by some intelligent cause. The later stages of intersection and combination of these elements may be due largely or in some degree to chance. Hence the actual development of an evolutionary world process can be the result of an interplay of inner causal determinations plus external chance, played out on the immensely vast stage of space-time that frames our universe. Thus divine Providence over our universe may well be—and probably is—a *flexible, creative synthesis of law and chance,* to achieve a grand overall design, pre-planned in its large lines, but not in every detail. The overall play of chance would include, of course, the chance interplay of free causes like ourselves.

ARISTOTLE'S FOUR CAUSES AS EXPLANATORY SYSTEM

Aristotle was justly proud of the fact that he was the first to identify explicitly and correlate together all the four causes—*formal, material, efficient,* and *final*—into a single integrated theory of explanation. Although not all explanation is through these four causes (one of the principal other modes is through relations), he maintained that the principal modes of explanation of any entity or thing that we discover in our experience are summed up by these four basic causes—once we have discovered first that the entity actually exists. They hold analogously for either a genuine real being or an artifact or a society. Two of these causes, *formal* and *material*—which we discovered in chapter VI—are called *intrinsic causes,* because they are found within the being to be explained; the other two—*efficient* and *final*—are called *extrinsic causes,* because they are found outside the being to be explained, in its efficient cause. Aristotle's theory of explanation through the four causes has now become part of all civilized thinking in some equivalent form.

BASIC DEFINITIONS

Cause = that which contributes positively to the being of another. This is the ontological aspect or role of cause. Once we know it, it also plays the epistemological role of principle of explanation (principle of intelligibility) for us. Cause must be distinguished from:

Condition = that which is required for a causal action to take place (a *sine qua non*), but does not contribute positively to the effect, e.g., a flashlight is a necessary condition for robbing a safe at night, but it does not itself contribute anything positive to the opening of the safe and taking money.

Occasion = that which is neither a cause nor a necessary condition for an effect to take place, but makes it easier or more convenient for an efficient cause to act, e.g., I make a business deal on the occasion of a golf game.

Formal cause = that in a being which makes it to be such, this kind of being. It answers the question, *What* is it?

Material cause = that in a being out of which it is made, e.g., this chair is made out of wood. It answers the question, What is this made out of? It is the determinable raw material which is determined by the form to be this kind of being.

Efficient cause = that which by its action makes something to be, or come into being, either in whole or in part. It answers the question, *Who* or *what* made this?

Final cause = that for the sake of which something is made or done. It is the goal, purpose, or end-tended-towards of the efficient cause itself, residing within it and guiding its action. It answers the question, *Why* was this made or done?

Exemplary cause. Later thinkers, interested especially in explaining creation by God as an act of intelligence, added on this refinement to the notion of final cause. The exemplary cause is the final cause in the mind of the efficient cause taken as a model or exemplar in imitation of which the effect is produced. This also applies to artists, architects, builders of anything; e.g., a blueprint expresses the exemplary cause in the mind of an architect, according to which he builds a house.

Role. Using the four causes as basic structure of inquiry is one of the most efficient methods of understanding a new being or explaining it to someone else, e.g., a new machine. It always presupposes, however, the more basic question about the actual existence of the thing in question.

Readings on Efficient and Final Causality: Louis De Raeymaeker, "The Metaphysical Problem of Causality," *Philosophy Today* 1 (1957), 219–30; also his book, *Philosophy of Being* (St. Louis: Herder, 1954); for both efficient and final causality; John Wild, "A Realistic Defense of Causal Efficacy," *Review of Metaphysics* 2 (1948–9), 1–14; Robert Faricy, "Finality," *New Scholasticism* 31 (1957), 189–207; R. Collins, "Finality and Being," *Proc. of Amer. Cath. Phil. Assoc.* 23 (1949); 36–46; Andrew Woodfield, *Teleology* (Cambridge Univ. Press, 1976); W. K. Thorpe, *Purpose in a World of Chance* (Oxford: Oxford Univ. Press, 1976); George Klubertanz, S.J., "St. Thomas' Treatment of the Axiom, *Omne agens agit propter finem,*" in *An Etienne Gilson Tribute,* ed. C. O'Neill (Milwaukee: Marquette Univ. Press, 1959), 101–17; C. Hollencamp, "Causa Causarum," *Laval Théol. et Phil.* 4 (1948), 77–109, 311–28 (in English); R. Hassing, ed., *Final Causality in Nature and Human Affairs* (Washington, D.C.: Catholic Univ. of America Press, 1997).

QUESTIONS FOR REVIEW AND DISCUSSION

1. What is the new question now arising out of the study of efficient causality itself? What is precise metaphysical problem involved in final causality?

2. Explain the Argument: Steps 1 and 2.

3. Why must final causality be understood analogously? Why is this so important, and how is it misunderstood by other thinkers?

4. Explain the nature of final causality and how it differs from efficient causality.

5. Why is the final cause called "the first of all causes"?

6. Explain the two main types of final causality.

7. Why does final causality ultimately require intelligence as adequate sufficient reason?

8. How does this work in an evolutionary cosmos like ours? How much must be planned by the Creator of the system?

9. Explain the two types of chance in the universe.

10. Can chance replace efficient causality?

11. How does Aristotle organize the four causes as basic explanatory system? Define each of the four causes.

CHAPTER FOURTEEN

The Final Unification
of All Being

The Search for the
Ultimate Source of All Being

The Final Problem of Metaphysics

The whole quest of metaphysics has been a search for the ultimate principles of intelligibility, the ultimate necessary conditions of possibility, of all the beings of our world of experience—and, by the extension of the same principles, of all finite and changing beings, whether known to us or not. We have pursued this quest first within the beings of our experience, discovering in the process the basic underlying *metaphysical structures* within them which make it possible for them to be as they are, i.e., multiple, finite, sharing common essences or natures, and undergoing change, both accidental and substantial. These structures were: *essence/existence, form/matter, substance/accident, act/potency.*

Next, in the treatise on *causality,* we traced out the basic lines of dependency linking all beings thus composed to other beings as to their extrinsic causes, discovering thus the two types of extrinsic cause: *efficient* and *final causes.* What now remains to be done is to trace out the lines of dependency thus discovered all the way to their ultimate source or ground, to some self-sufficient entity or dimension of being which does not point beyond itself to another. Here at last our quest for intelligibility will finally come to rest in the Transcendent Source of all being, to which the name "God" (in its philosophical meaning) can be given.

How the Term "God" Comes into Metaphysics.   When we have reached
the conclusion of our inquiry in this chapter we will find that what we
have discovered is at least partially the equivalent of what philosophers
and religious people call "God," the "Absolute," "the Transcendent,
"Ultimate Reality," etc. But it seems to me bad philosophical method to
say ahead of time that we are going to "prove the existence of God." For
from the point of view of systematic philosophical inquiry, the referent
of the term "God" has not yet risen from our experience or in the
course of prior inquiry. So it must be brought in arbitrarily from the
outside, from religion or the history of philosophy and then one has
the problem of defining ahead of time just what is meant by it, just what
it is one is trying to prove. But from where is one going to take this notion? From religion? But which religion? Christianity, Islam, Hinduism?
Or which philosopher? Why? And how does one know philosophically
ahead of time that the meaning of such a non-experiential term is truly
meaningful, not referring to something incoherent, as many analytic
philosophers have tellingly objected? One gets involved in hopelessly
complicated problems before even beginning such a project.

The proper philosophical method is not to mention God at all at
the start of the inquiry, but to ask rather: "What does the world of my
experience demand as its adequate sufficient reason, to render it adequately intelligible?" If the inquiry itself leads to the conclusion that
some Transcendent Source of all being is the only adequate solution,
then one can identify what has been discovered by the term "God," or
any other appropriate title, and define it precisely in terms of what the
path of discovery itself has forced us to postulate and nothing further.
The philosophical definition of God comes meaningfully only at
the end of the inquiry, not its beginning, and will usually be less full
than the various religious or theological meanings, since it contains
only what is demanded by the exigencies of reason itself building on
experience.

Our precise problem here: Is our universe of finite, changing beings
ultimately *self-explanatory,* self-sufficient for its own existence, or does it
necessarily point beyond itself to the existence of some Transcendent
Source of all being?

Does one need a philosophical argument in order to believe reasonably in God? No. There are several other paths open, which perhaps
most believers in God actually follow. (1) The path of faith in the word
of others, especially as passed on in a community of believers, because

one makes the judgment that one can reasonably trust them as being in possession of the truth. This can often be confirmed by (2) one's own personal religious or even mystical *experience* of some higher Transcendent power with which one is in touch. (1) and (2) are also usually confirmed by (3) one's own reflection on the meaningfulness of one's own life and the life of others, concluding from many convergent pieces of evidence that belief in God, both from the intellectual satisfaction that it gives and the good consequences that follow from it, is the most reasonable or the only reasonable explanation of the world available, and all in all the best for me. This procedure cannot be reduced to any formal, logically cogent philosophical type of argument, and it does require the individual judgment of the believer to decide how satisfying the meaningfulness is and how good the consequences are for him to make the decision. But this is still a deeply reasonable way of acting and responding to the deep human longing for ultimate meaning and happiness in our lives.

So strictly philosophical arguments for the existence of God are not *necessary* for one to believe reasonably in some Transcendent Reality that can be called "God"; but they can be a strong and even necessary support, especially for those who have a more highly developed critical intelligence and strong drive to understand what one believes, and who live in a pluralistic culture where belief in God is questioned by many others around one. And it is a good thing for any intelligent person to stretch his or her mind to understand as fully as possible the universe in which we live. This is also part of the fundamental drive of Christian intelligence, expressed so aptly long ago by St. Augustine and St. Anselm: "Faith seeking understanding."

Strength of philosophical arguments for God.   They are not rigorous strictly *logical proofs,* in the strict modern sense of "proof," which can in practice be verified only in matters of logic and mathematics, not of existential fact—outside of one's own existence. Any search for sufficient reason, especially the passage from finite to infinite being, requires a certain metaphysical insight into an exigency of reason beyond the merely logical, and a fundamental openness and commitment to the call of the intelligibility of being. The resulting *arguments*—we prefer this to "proofs"—present themselves as fundamental options between two or more ultimate explanations of the meaningfulness of the universe, such that the one for God can be shown to be the most reasonable or even the only reasonable one to choose—and one *must choose,* since this governs the way we live our lives in practice.

   Basic types of philosophical argument.   A. The Cosmic or Outer Path, taking the whole world around us, including ourselves, as starting point, and concluding to a single Ultimate Source of all being. This is the traditional path through efficient and final causality. *B. The Inner Path,* exploring the depths of our own inner conscious life to find God as the Ultimate Goal of one's inner drive toward the fullness of Truth and Goodness (Love). This Inner path reaches God as *my* ultimate Good and Goal, but not immediately as the Source of all being, the full notion of God. Hence it must be completed by the Cosmic Path to be philosophically adequate, though an individual may well be psychologically satisfied by the Inner Path alone.

I. The Cosmic Path of Efficient Causality

One need only follow out any of the lines of existential dependence opened up in the chapter on Efficient Causality, until they terminate in a self-sufficient being. The one given below begins with efficient causality to conclude that there must exist at least one self-sufficient being. To conclude to a single infinite Source of all being, however, one must make a second step, showing that any self-sufficient being must be infinite in perfection, and then that there can be only one such infinitely perfect being. This is what we call God.

Arg. I. From Any Conditioned Being to One Infinite Source of All Being

Prefatory Note: We could unfold this proof in the traditional way simply by following out the lines of causality left over from the chapter on Efficient Causality: "Every finite or composed being requires a cause," to conclude that the only sufficient reason for a chain of such causes is a single self-sufficient, infinite Source of all being. That is fine and easily understandable for those who have gone through this course in Thomistic metaphysics thus far. And they can do just that, if they wish. We would like here, however, to extend our reach and make this basic argument accessible to a wider group of readers who do not have the metaphysical training to understand an argument from efficient causality by itself. The difficulty lies in the notion of *efficient cause.* For many scientifically trained minds the notion of cause as used in science means only *predictability according to law,* not productive power. And for many modern philosophers the notion of cause is filled with ambiguity: is it Humean causality, or Kantian, or Aristotelian . . . ?

The notion of *conditioned existent,* on the other hand, is quite familiar to scientists, philosophers, and ordinary educated people. It is that of a being which needs certain conditions to be fulfilled in order that it can actually exist. Taken in its broadest sense, these necessary conditions include efficient causes as a principal ingredient, but go beyond to include anything else required, whether it be a strict cause or not. Hence to start from this wider basis one does not have to settle any arguments about what exactly is a proper cause and what is merely a necessary condition in the restrictive sense. This wider net includes all and hence gives a broader and more impressive sweep to the argument. It renders the argument more accessible especially to scientists, I have found, who are quite at home with the notion that physical phenomena need certain conditions to be fulfilled without which they cannot exist. (For those who wish to phrase the argument in the more traditional strictly causal language, simply substitute "caused" or "uncaused" for "conditioned" or "unconditioned" in the text.)

Structure of the argument.   The argument unfolds in three steps: (1) Given any conditioned being, there must exist at least one absolutely unconditioned, or self-sufficient being. (2) No being can be self-sufficient unless it is qualitatively infinite or unlimited in perfection. (3) There can be only one such being infinite in all perfections—which must therefore be the unique ultimate Source of all being. Such a being we can appropriately call "God."

Step 1: There must exist at least one unconditioned or self-sufficient being.   Let us begin with the beings around us. All of these manifest themselves to us as *conditioned existents.* That is to say, they are not self-sufficient for their own existence, but depend on other beings outside of them as necessary conditions for their own being, either to bring them into existence or to maintain them in existence, or both. Thus all human beings depend on their parents for initiating their existence, and on the air, temperature, nourishment, and many other factors around them to maintain themselves. The same is true for the whole realm of living beings, from humans, down through animals, plants, insects, bacteria, and whatever other intermediaries there may be. Alter the conditions necessary for life on this planet severely enough, and species begin to disappear, as we are coming to recognize with increasing concern today. The same is also true, we now realize, of all molecules, which depend on the atoms composing them and on many other conditions of space-time, fields or force, temperature, and so on, without which they could not hold together with their specific properties. The same now appears to be true of the whole domain of atoms themselves. All depend on external conditions: for example, atoms could not hold together as stable units until the initial temperature of the expanding universe cooled enough to allow it (several hundred years after the initial Big Bang). The same seems to be true even of the primordial particles making up the atoms. Thus what many believe to be the most elementary particles, the so-called "quarks," cannot exist alone, but must always be joined with two or three others. Everywhere around us, then, as far as our experience can reach, is a vast web of conditioned existents, none of which is self-sufficient for its own existence.

Now the question arises: Can all the entities of our universe be thus conditioned, not-self-sufficient, dependent on others for their existence? On reflection, the answer must be "No." Take any conditioned being A. It must depend on another entity B in order that its own conditions for existence be fulfilled. But now in our search for intelligibility we must ask the same question of entity B: Is it conditioned or not? If so, we must look further to entity C. And the same question will arise for C, D, and all other members of this chain of dependence. Can there be an *infinite regress* in this chain of dependence, so that it could extend endlessly, with all its members having the same existential status of conditioned existents, none of them self-sufficient for its own existence? Whether the chain extends backwards in time or simultaneously across the universe makes no difference; the problem remains the same. Again the answer must be "No." For if all the beings in the chain remain conditioned, dependent on another, then nowhere will the conditions for the existence of any member ever be adequately fulfilled. The search for the necessary fulfilling conditions will go on endlessly, be endlessly put off or deferred, and in principle be impossible of completion. Hence the entire chain remains suspended without a sufficient reason, or adequate grounding, for any of them to exist. But, as a matter of fact, the original beings we started with do actually exist, which means that all their necessary conditions must be already fulfilled. But they cannot be both fulfilled and unfulfillable at the same time!

Hence, under pain of the entire chain of conditioned existents remaining unintelligible in their actual existence, there must be somewhere in existence at least one absolutely unconditioned being, completely self-sufficient for its own existence, either at the beginning of the chain of dependence or outside of it, supporting the whole. There can be no conditioned beings unless there is at least one unconditioned one, which is the initiator (not necessarily in time) of the causal flow of existence into all the others in the series.

Nor can it be objected that, even though all the parts of the world system may be conditioned, the system as a whole may be unconditioned, self-sufficient. For such a system that is made up of parts, even though a higher mode of being may emerge from the parts, still depends on its parts, presupposes them as that out of which it emerges. It cannot operate as a whole unless the necessary parts are already there. If it is the ultimate source that generates its own parts, then it must be ontologically prior to and independent of them and the unified system dependent on them, in order to bring them into existence as a unified whole. The system cannot be at once the self-sufficient source of its own non-self-sufficient parts and yet dependent on them = contradiction.

Nor can it be argued that the causal dependence, or chain of dependence, might be circular: A depends upon B, B upon C, and C in turn upon A. For C would then be prior to A ontologically (not necessarily temporally), in the order of existential dependence, and yet posterior to A as depending on it. But it is contradictory for the same being to be at once prior and posterior to another in the same order of dependence. Such a circular, interdependent system must be placed there all at once as a unity by an independent cause, and then might maintain itself by reciprocal support. But none of the parts can generate their own mutual togetherness as an existing whole.

The rejection of an infinite regress might be put in another more austerely logical form. Given that being A here and now exists, categorically, not conditionally (i.e., as an "is," not an "if" statement). Now suppose one tries to explain the actual existence of A thus: A exists only if B, B only if C, C only if D, and so on to infinity, in an endless series of "only if" statements. In this case, since each member depends on the conditions for its existence being fulfilled by another, and these conditions in turn remain endlessly unfulfilled, the entire series remains conditional ("iffy") in its existence. Unless one of the members along the line exists unconditionally, categorically, with no more conditions to be fulfilled, then the original existence of A itself becomes only conditional. There could never be a categorical affirmation of anything at all (nothing but "only ifs"). But the original A *does* exist, categorically and unconditionally, as a fact, not "iffily." Hence we have failed in our search for the intelligibility of the existence of the A we started with, or of any other real being—unless we posit somewhere along the line the unconditional existence of a source of a being that is unconditioned, self-sufficient, self-explanatory of its own being, uncaused. Scientists and mathematicians tend to take systems as *givens* and then investigate *how* they work; but metaphysicians must also ask the deeper question: How come there is such a system here at all?

Conclusion of Step 1: There must exist at least one self-sufficient being. Many arguments stop here—as, for example, four of St. Thomas's famous Five Ways (only the Fourth concludes to a highest in the order of being that is cause of all others). The result is indeed impressive: it has taken us to a higher order of being transcending our world of dependent beings. But there is more to be done. What sort of being will qualify as self-sufficient? And how many such can there be? *Many* independent series, each with its own self-sufficent source? Or only *one*, the unique source of all being? The great Aristotle himself thought finally that there must be (for astronomical reasons) 55 unmoved, uncaused Prime Movers. So we must put an appropriate question to the self-sufficient being we have discovered that will smoke out its significant attributes further. After much searching, the crucial one has turned out to be this: *Is it finite or infinite in perfection?* This will immediately enable us to solve whether it is one or many.

Note 1: As far as we know at present, we do not know whether the whole universe makes up a single interdependent system, or whether there are many such independent systems of conditioned beings, i.e., many independent universes that have no contact between them. Hence we must continue further in our search.

Note 2: This argument does not decide whether our universe had a beginning in time, or existed from all eternity. The latter seems theoretically possible, as long as there exists an eternal cause eternally maintaining it in existence. The issue was hotly debated in the 13th century, St. Thomas opting with Aristotle that it was not possible to prove *philosophically* that the world had to begin in time; St. Bonaventure held the opposite view. It seems wiser to stick with St. Thomas here and not take on this extra burden of proof.

Step 2: Any being self-sufficient for its own existence must be infinite in per-fection, that is, unlimited in its qualitative fullness of all perfections. Or, put more tersely: *No finite being can be self-sufficient.* Why? Let us suppose it were finite. This means it would be one determinate, limited mode of being (limited in qualitative intensity of perfection) among at least several other modes possible, such that at least one higher mode were possible (i.e., this one does not exhaust all possible fullness of perfec-tion). Otherwise, it would not be finite or limited. Now there must be some sufficient reason why the being in question exists in this limited, determinate mode of being and not in some other possible. Why *this* being, or this whole finite world-system, in fact, and not some other? A principle of selection is needed to select this mode of being from the wider range of possibility and give actual existence (energy-filled pres-ence) to it according to this limited mode (or "essence," as the metaphy-sician would call it). But no *finite* being can do this selection of its own essential mode of being and confer existence on itself in this mode. For then it would have the impossible task of preexisting its own determi-nate actual existence in this mode, picking out what it wills to be before it actually exists, and then conferring actual existence on itself in this mode. All of this is obviously absurd, unintelligible. It follows that no de-terminate finite being can be the self-sufficient reason for its actual exis-tence as this particular finite being. Therefore it requires an indepen-dent efficient cause or source of being to determine it to exist as this finite mode of being. But since no *finite* cause can ever be self-sufficient, we must eventually come to some infinite cause or ultimate source of all these finite beings.

The same conclusion can be reached by a slightly different ap-proach. Suppose that a finite being were self-sufficient. This would mean that it would have to be the total ultimate source of all the attri-butes within it, including the central, all-embracing perfection of exis-tence itself. Now it does not make sense that the ultimate source of a perfection should possess this perfection in some limited, imperfect way, less than the full plenitude possible of the perfection in question, when it is the very source of this perfection itself. Nor does it make sense that it should deliberately restrict its own possession of this perfection of which it is the ultimate source to some limited degree when it could enjoy the full plenitude of it. The notions of ultimate, self-sufficient source of a perfection and limited possession of the same clash irrecon-cilably and cancel each other out. No being self-sufficient for its own existence, therefore, can possess existence—or any other perfection—only in some limited, incomplete, imperfect way.

Conclusion of Step 2: Any self-sufficient being must be infinite in perfection. No finite being can be self-sufficient for its own existence but needs an infinite self-sufficient source to draw it out of the range of possibilities and make it to be in this particular mode and no other. No finite being can do this for itself. It points beyond itself, as St. Thomas puts it, to some infinite, unparticipated source.

Step 3: There can be only one such infinite being. This is a quick and easy step, admitted by just about all metaphysicians, I believe, once the existence of an absolutely infinite being is granted. For suppose there were two such. Then one could not be the other, must be really distinct from the other. But this is impossible unless at least one of the two lacks something that the other one has. Otherwise, they would coincide into total indistinguishable identity. But if either one lacked some positive perfection, it could not also be absolutely infinite in all perfections. *Duns Scotus,* the great Franciscan Doctor, has added a powerful adaptation of this argument. If there were two self-sufficient infinite beings, they could not both *know* each other. For to know another real being one must either have caused it, or been acted on, caused, by it. But in this case one would have to be dependent in some way on the other, and hence could not be self-sufficient for its own existence and all its perfections. Hence there can be only one infinite self-sufficient being.

Grand Conclusion to the Whole Argument: Either the universe is unintelligible, or there must exist one and only one Infinite Source of all other beings, both of their actual existence and of all the perfections (goodness) within them. It is at once Infinite Being and Infinite Goodness, in which all finite beings participate both for their existence and their goodness (these two are identical in reality for St. Thomas, though distinct in our incomplete concepts of them). Our journey of the intellect, in search of the full intelligibility of what it means to be, has now finally arrived at the single Infinite Source of all beings, of the whole community of real existents. Journey's end!

Brief Summary of Argument: (1) Many conditioned beings exist in the world around us, i.e., beings which are not self-sufficient for their own existence but depend on others as necessary conditions which must be fulfilled in order that these beings can exist. (2) But not all beings in the universe can be conditioned beings depending on others. For then no matter how far the chain of dependence continued, even to an infinite regress, nowhere would the necessary conditions for any being ever be fulfilled. But unless somewhere along the line the necessary conditions for the existence of some being are in fact adequately fulfilled, nothing at all could exist. Hence somewhere along the line there must be at least one self-sufficient being, which is the source of existence for all the conditioned beings dependent on it. (3) Such a being must be qualitatively infinite in perfection, since no finite being can be self-sufficient. (4) There can be only one such unqualifiedly infinite being. For if there were two, at least one would have to lack something the other has, or be simply identical with it. Hence there must exist one and only one self-sufficient, infinite Source of all being.

Arg. II: From Any Finite Being to a Single Infinite Source of All Being

Note.   This is a much simpler and more direct path than the above, starting directly from Step 2 above, and preferred by many. But it does require an initiation into a metaphysical way of thinking and familiarity with the notions of finite being, efficient causality, and the impossibility of an infinite regress in non-self-sufficient causes, as in Step 1.

Take any finite being, limited in perfection, or any group of them. Because they are *finite,* they cannot be self-sufficient for the selection of their own limited participation in being among other degrees possible, but all require a cause, as shown above in Step 2. The same holds true of this cause, if it, too, is finite. Now, since no series of all insufficient causes can be self-sufficient, as shown above in Step l, the only adequate cause, or ultimate sufficient reason for any finite being, must be an infinite being. And there can be only one such being qualitatively infinite in perfection, as shown in Step 3 above. Hence all finite beings and causes in the universe point back ultimately to one Infinite Source of all being. Thus the single mark of finitude or limited perfection reveals our whole finite universe as not self-explanatory, not self-grounding in being, but pointing beyond itself to an Infinite Source.

Arg. III. From Many Existents to One Source

Note. This is the simplest, briefest, most elegant, and, some think, most profound and metaphysically beautiful of all arguments from causality. But it does require familiarity with St. Thomas's doctrine of participation in existence as the basic underlying core of all real perfections.

Argument. Step 1. General Principle: Wherever there is found a participation situation in reality, such that many different beings are *intrinsically similar* in that they all share in reality some one positive attribute common to all, this common property of similarity cannot find its adequate sufficient reason in these many diverse participants precisely as many and diverse. For similarity is a form of unity and cannot be adequately grounded in diversity. It is not because they are many and diverse that they share the same real property. Hence the only adequate sufficient reason for this common sharing, this real similarity among them, must be some one unitary source from whence this common perfection ultimately derives and is communicated to all the participants.

Step 2. Application to the basic perfection of existence itself. All real beings possess, share in common, the basic ultimate perfection of actual existence itself, the "act of all acts, and perfection of all perfections," as St. Thomas puts it. It follows immediately that all real beings possessing an act of existence point back to one single ultimate source of existence itself. And since there is no wider, more inclusive perfection than existence itself, such an ultimate source must be by that very fact not only self-sufficient, but unique, and infinite in perfection, since there is no wider span of perfection of which existence would be only some limited mode. Thus this argument reaches in a single step what takes two or three in the others.

So the entire quest for the intelligibility of being finally comes to rest in an *absolute One.* The Many are always secondary, derivative from the One. To understand is to unify, to see all things as somehow rooted in unity. As the great Chinese Taoist mystic, Chuang-tzu, once said: "Great thinking sees all as One; small thinking breaks down into the many."

Arg. IV: From the World as Ordered Whole to a Single Intelligent Cause

The argument from order in the world (or "design")—also called the "Teleological Argument" (from the Greek *telos* = goal or purpose)—is one of the oldest, most widespread and popular in almost all cultures and all times, because the order in the world is so evident and impressive to any reflective human observer and seems to point so plausibly and intuitively to an intelligent Designer. It is for this reason that St. Thomas himself calls it "the most efficacious argument for all times and all peoples." It is basically a good one and a powerful one, it seems to

me, too; but it must be carefully formulated, for there are many naive
and invalid forms, especially if they do not take into account *evolution* as
a partial explanation for the present order of things. The one we shall
present here does not move directly from the adaptation of living organisms for their survival and growth, since much of this may be explained by the play of chance within the space-time matrix of the basic
stable laws of the physical universe. We will therefore take as our starting
point only the basic underlying structure of the material universe with
its small number of unvarying (or at least stable) physical laws, which do
not themselves evolve but provide the stable matrix within which living
organisms can evolve—for without stable physical laws living things
could not learn from repeated experience, if the rules themselves were
constantly changing.

Starting point.   This is the world given to us as a *dynamic ordered
system* of many active elements whose natures (centers of dynamic active
properties or potentialities of action) are ordered to interact with each
other in stable reciprocal relationships which we call physical laws. For
example, every hydrogen atom in our universe is ordered to interact
with every oxygen atom in the exact proportion of 2 to 1, and reciprocally every oxygen atom is ordered to interact with every hydrogen
atom in the proportion of 1 to 2. So, too, of the chemical valences of
all the basic elements in their fixed proportions of interaction with each
other; so, too, all particles with mass move toward each other according
to the fixed relations of the law of gravity, and so of all the other basic
physical laws—electromagnetism, the strong force holding together
the nucleus of the atom, etc. In such an interlocking dynamic system
the active nature of each component is defined by its relation to the
others, and so presupposes the others for the intelligibility of its own
powers of interacting with them. Contemporary science also reveals to
us more and more that this world system is not merely an aggregate of
many separate unrelated sets of laws, but rather a tightly interconnected
whole wherein the action of one being has repercussions throughout the whole: "Pick a flower and you move a star!" The relation to the
whole affects all the parts. Thus the parts can no longer be understood
except in relation to the whole.

Argument. Step 1:   Where any such dynamically interconnected
system is given, such as is our universe, what is needed is an adequate
explanation of the unity of the system as whole, how each of the parts is
correlated with the others to form reciprocal laws, and then connected

with the whole. But no part can do that by itself, since each one presupposes the others present already correlated with it before it can perform its own action. Only some unitary cause of the system as a whole, which is itself prior to and ontologically independent of the system for its own existence and action, can fill this requirement and be the sufficient reason for the actual existence of the system as a whole.

Step 2: Such a cause can only be one possessing *intelligence.* For it must take into account many different beings, separated from each other in space (often at vast distances across the universe) and draw them together into the overarching unity of unitary laws governing all similar particles across the universe and then into an interconnected whole of all together. But only an *idea* or set of ideas can thus correlate and unify many different beings into cooperative action while leaving their distinct beings intact. And such an organizing idea, effectively guiding an agent, can only exist in an intelligent cause.

Another reason why such a cause of the unified activity of the system as a whole must be intelligent is this: It must correlate the parts with each other *before* they actually exist and go into action, since they cannot engage in reciprocal action with each other unless they are already oriented from within, in the dynamic properties of their natures, toward such distinctive correlated action. But not-yet-existent agents cannot be correlated with each other except by an agent that can make the not-yet-existent *present,* and this can only be done by an agent possessing conscious intelligence, which can plan ahead through the medium of ideas. In a word, only an intelligence can order means to a future end.

Conclusion: There must be a single intelligent organizing cause for our cosmic system as a whole: in a word, a Transcendent Creative Mind.

Further Question. Is this Mind itself self-sufficient for its own existence, and is it one or many? To solve this further question, and thus reach the full notion of God as Ultimate Source of all being, we must have recourse to the last part of Arg. I above, showing that this Mind can be self-sufficient only if it is *infinite* in perfection and that there can be only *one* such infinite being.

Conclusion: This argument, completed by the first, ends up with one infinite intelligent Source of all being. This can aptly be called "God" in the philosophical meaning of the term. It differs from the first argument only in that it begins with a richer starting point and concludes to a Source that is explicitly recognized as *intelligent,* one of the primary positive attributes of God. It should be noted that for most people, once they discover a Creative Mind as the Source of the universe they live in, this is enough to generate a deeply religious attitude of gratitude, reverence, and obedience toward the intelligent Planner of our world and our lives, even without going through the further metaphysical steps to the infinity and unicity of this Source. The philosopher demands this for completeness, but non-philosophers tend to take it for granted.

II. The Inner Path: From the Inner Life of the Spirit

Argument I: From the Dynamism of Intellect and Will

Instead of directing our drive to know toward seeking out the ultimate sufficient reason for the world around us (the Cosmological Argument, as it is called), we can also rise directly to the discovery of the Infinite Fullness of being through the interior dynamism of the human person as knowing-willing subject oriented toward the Infinite by its very nature, as to the only adequate goal that can fulfill its innate natural longing.

Step 1: Data. Reflective analysis of my conscious inner life of knowing and willing reveals that it is rooted in an unrestricted inner dynamism of my intellect toward the limitless horizon of all being as intelligible and of my will toward all being as good. This is revealed by the fact that every time I lay hold of some finite being as either true or good, my drive is at first temporarily satisfied, as I explore and enjoy it. But as soon as I discover the limits of the being—in either intelligibility or goodness—I spontaneously rebound beyond it to search for more. As Hegel noted insightfully, to recognize anything as finite is already implicitly to have reached beyond it, at least in desire. To recognize a prison as a prison is already to have reached beyond it in desire and imagination. This process of temporary satisfaction and rebounding desire is repeated over and over endlessly throughout my whole life here, surrounded by finite beings, all limited in some way in intelligibility and goodness

Step 2: Reflection on the implications of this experience. Rather than endlessly repeating this process and never reaching satisfaction, I can step back, reflect on its significance, and then totalize the whole process and grasp intellectually its basic law: my intellect and will are such by nature that they can never be completely satisfied or fulfilled by any finite being or good. I must always implicitly refer each one to a wider, richer horizon beyond, to which I then spontaneously tend. It follows that only an unqualified infinity, or unlimited fullness of being and goodness could ever satisfy this innate drive, which defines my nature as spiritual intellect and will. Thus my very nature as a human person is to be an ineradicable implicit drive toward the Infinite, which I implicitly affirm and desire in all that I explicitly affirm and desire. As St. Thomas puts it with his usual terseness: "In knowing anything, I implicitly affirm God . . . In loving anything, I implicitly love God."

Could not an endless supply of finites be enough to satisfy this drive? No. Once we knew this was all there ever could be or would be, we might be forced to put up with it in lieu of anything better, but there would still remain a deep unfulfilled void within us, a radical emptiness that nothing could ever fill. There would appear to be some deep unintelligibility, some profound lack of meaning at the root of our being as human.

Step 3: Radical option.   I am now faced with a radical intellectual choice between two ultimate alternatives on the meaning of my life:

Either there exists a positive Infinite Fullness of being and goodness, which is somehow possible to be attained by me—at least as a free gift—and then my human nature becomes luminously and completely meaningful, intelligible, sense-making, and my life is suffused with hope of fulfillment.

Or in fact, there exists *no* such real Infinite at all. And then my nature conceals in its depth a radical defect of meaningfulness, of coherence, an unfillable void of unintelligibility, a kind of tragic emptiness: a natural desire that defines my nature as a dynamic unity, but is in principle unfulfillable, incurably frustrated, "a useless passion," as Jean-Paul Sartre, the existentialist atheist puts it, oriented by its very nature toward a non-existent void, toward nothing real, kept going only by an ineradicable illusion. Sartre accepts the same analysis we have done above, but since he believes God does not exist, it is a fundamental illusion. That is why he declares, "Man is a useless passion," and human existence is basically absurd.

Thus *either* God exists, *or* I am absurd: that is the basic option that confronts me, if I am willing to go to the depth of the human condition. (Many people today are afraid of facing up to this radical option, and so

are "content" to live on the surface of life—at least for many years.)
Note that no strictly logical compulsion can ever force me under pain of
logical contradiction to opt for the total meaningfulness of my life, since it
is difficult to show that there is any direct *logical contradiction* in affirming that I or the universe is absurd. It can be shown, however, that
there is a lived contradiction between affirming theoretically that the
universe or myself is unintelligible and continuing to live and use my
mind as though it were intelligible—which we cannot help but do. Thus
it is finally up to each one of us either to accept his or her infinite-
oriented nature as meaningful and revelatory of the real or as an
opaque, illusory surd. But what good reason can one have for choosing
darkness over light, illusion over meaning, for *not* choosing the light?
Only if the darkness is more intelligible? But this does not make sense!
Why not then accept my nature as a meaningful *gift,* pointing the way to
what *is,* rather than to what is *not?*

   Conclusion. This unique kind of "argument," based on my own
inner experience, can lead me to a profoundly reasonable affirmation
that a real Infinite must exist as my final end, the ultimate condition of
possibility of my making sense as a being endowed with spiritual intelligence and will. But note that it does not deliver the full notion of God
as ultimate Source of all being, including all those below me and outside of me who do not possesses intelligence. But this does seem indispensable for the full satisfaction of my quest for the total intelligibility
of all being. To achieve this I must return, it seems to me, to the outer
or Cosmic Path to God. The two paths complement each other beautifully. The God of the *self* must also be the God of the *cosmos.*

Argument II: From the Moral Imperative of Conscience.

This is one of the preferred arguments of Cardinal Newman.

   Step. 1. Data of consciousness. As a mature moral person I experience within me the voice of *conscience* as an absolute, unconditioned
moral imperative: "You *ought* to do this good. You *ought* to avoid this
evil. You *should* do this, and avoid that." It is not a conditional statement
or suggestion: "*If* you want to be happy, or avoid punishment, or receive
a reward, or if this appeals to you, do it." It is "categorical": "You *ought*
to do this; do it!" The key point of this imperative is not the particular
content, this or that, of the act ordered or forbidden. This may vary with

a certain limited relativity according to the particular intelligence, sensitivity, upbringing, culture of the individual in a given society. But what remains as absolute, unconditioned in all cases is the core: "You *ought* to do good and avoid evil," or: "*Do* good; *avoid* evil" = Do whatever appears to our sincere reflective judgment as the good here and now, and avoid what appears to you as evil, *because* it is the good, or evil, and you ought to do good and avoid evil. Though I can dull the voice of conscience by continual deliberate violation of its commands, I cannot totally extinguish the basic imperative—"Do good; avoid evil"—without ceasing to be a rational, morally responsible human being, without ceasing to be truly human. This voice of conscience is both *antecedent,* warning me ahead of time what I ought to do, and *consequent,* judging my action afterwards as praiseworthy or blameworthy.

Step 2: Explanation. The only adequate sufficient reason, or source, of this absolute or unconditioned moral imperative within me, commanding me to do this or avoid that and judging my response afterwards, can only be an absolute Law-Giver and Judge who is the ultimate Source of moral obligation, dependent on nothing further, with absolute authority over my rational nature, and hence must be the very constituting source of this nature.

Why so? Because none of the other alternatives are adequate to generate authentic, unconditional moral obligation: (1) *I* cannot be the source imposing the command on myself. As both St. Thomas and Newman explain, if the command is in my power as its originating source, what I freely impose on myself I can also freely revoke. But I cannot simply at will revoke this warning, this unconditional command that speaks through my conscience. (2) Nor can my parents or society be the ultimate originating source. They can tell me: "Do this *or* you will get punished, be disapproved by us, be ostracized by us, become unhappy." This may be, and must be, the beginning of moral conscience in the child, but this cannot supply the unconditional *ought* for the mature, responsible, critically reflective adult. The characteristic of the moral conscience in the mature, morally responsible person whom we consider to be a good person is that the force of the moral *ought* becomes stronger and stronger in him or her as the person grows older and more mature, more independent of those who first taught or surround him/her now. Such persons now obey their conscience, the call of the moral good, not because someone clse taught them or told them (or tells them) to do so, but because they themselves now see that this is the *good* and they *ought* to do it. In fact, it is the case that the really mature moral person, especially the moral leader in a society, often transcends the moral vision of his social group, criticizing or even rejecting it in the name of a higher absolute Good speaking through the voice of conscience.

If the ultimate source of moral obligation were really only some human authority like my parents or society, once one came to recognize that there was no intrinsic moral *ought,* but some other human beings like oneself had imposed this command on him for their own ends, however sincere, the power of conscience as imposing an *unconditional command* would be broken. Other human beings can advise me, but never impose an unconditional obligation on me.

Conclusion: *Either* moral obligation, speaking through the voice of each person's conscience, is an illusion, foisted on me by the sheer power or persuasion of human society; *or,* if I take it seriously, as I must to be authentically and maturely human, then its only ultimate source must be an absolute unconditioned Law-Giver, Source of my human nature = another name for God.

Note.   For Newman, this was not an abstract argument, but a profound existential experience of the immediate presence of God as wise, just, and loving Law-Giver speaking within him and guiding him toward his own ultimate good. Many sincere professed atheists and agnostics also feel and faithfully follow this call of the Absolute Good within them, experienced implicitly as something greater than themselves, to be followed no matter what the cost, if they are to be faithful to what they perceive as their authentic human dignity. They might be called "anonymous theists."

Cf. A. Boekrad, "Newman's Argument to the Existence of God," *Philosophical Studies* (Maynooth) 6 (1956), 50–71; and his fuller book on the same, *The Argument from Conscience according to Newman* (Louvain, 1961). For texts from Newman, see *The Essential Newman,* ed. Blehl (New York: New American Library, 1963). For another form, see H. Rashdall, "The Moral Argument," in J. Hick, ed., *The Existence of God* (New York: Macmillan, 1964), 43–52.

III. Main Attributes of God

The two main questions about God are: I. Does God exist? II. What is the nature of God, i.e., what are the main attributes that can be truly affirmed of God? We are now exploring this second question.

Attributes of God already discovered in the arguments for his existence: (1) *Ultimate Source* of all beings. (2) *Infinite plenitude* of all perfections. (3) *Unique.* (4) For the existential metaphysics of St. Thomas, this means that the nature of God is to be the pure unlimited Act of Existence itself, in all its simple fullness, i.e., unrestricted by any limiting essence = *Ipsum Esse Subsistens* (Subsistent To-Be itself), which by that very fact contains within itself the fullness of all possible real perfection. This means that God is the highest possible qualitative intensity of all perfection, not that he swallows up within himself all the numerical diversity of perfection of all other existing finite beings, so that he alone possesses all perfection in all its modes. God + creatures = more beings, not more being (a higher degree of being) = *plura entia, non plus entis.*

Attributes immediately deducible from the above: (1) *Eternal:* always existing without beginning or end. Since God is self-sufficient for his own being and the ultimate source of all other being, there is no cause that can bring him into existence or take his existence away, annihilate him. (2) *Simple:* God can have no real composition of really distinct component principles of any kind, because all such compositions require an efficient composing cause, as we have already seen. (3) *Immaterial or Spiritual:* Matter implies composition of parts outside of parts, limitation, dispersal over space and time, hence imperfect unity. God is the pure infinite concentration of spiritual energy, lucidly and totally self-present in self-consciousness, with no dispersal of parts over space and time, no darkness of unconsciousness, "pure Light," as St. John says. (4) *Immutable:* Real intrinsic change in a being entails acquiring something one did not have before or losing something one did have. But since God is by nature infinite plenitude of perfection he can neither acquire or lose perfection, nor rise to a higher level or fall to a lower. This does not mean, however, that God cannot act on his creatures, manifest and communicate his goodness in diverse ways across time to his creatures. As shown above in the Chapter on Efficient Causality, since the act of causality takes place in the effect, causing something to happen in the effect, not back in the agent, God's causal action on the world implies no change, either acquisition or loss, in his own inner fullness of perfection. The effects of his action succeed one another in time, but not his own causal action in its source, since he is above and outside the whole order of time and change, acting from his eternal NOW contemporaneous with all our times and events.

Some philosophers complain, especially in the Process Philosophy School, that because God cannot change he must be indifferent, unresponsive, to all that happens contingently in our world. A serious misunderstanding: Because God in his eternal NOW is cognitively and actively present to all that goes on in our changing world, his intentional consciousness with respect to us is eternally contingently different because of what he and we do, but not *changing*—a distinction constantly missed by Process thinkers such as Whitehead and Hartshorne. "Different" means "could have been otherwise"; "changing" means "now one way, later another"—two quite different concepts. God can rejoice eternally, but contingently, in the free responses we make to the gifts and inspirations he has already freely given us—which are all limited participations in his own infinite goodness and power, never rising higher than the original source. For God to rejoice in his own freely given, but eternally decided participations is not to change.

Note that all the deducible attributes in the last section above start off as negative attributes: no beginning or end, no composition, no matter, no change. But they point beyond their immediate content at a mysterious positive fullness of perfection, the unlimited fullness of existence itself, whose content we cannot with our finite minds grasp directly and adequately. Hence St. Thomas insists that "we cannot know *what* God is, only that he is. . . . We can know *that* God is intelligent, but not *how*." This does not mean we know nothing positive about God. The *what* and *how* here are technical terms indicating the special infinite essence or mode of existing proper to God, which are beyond our grasp. We can know the divine essence, but only from perfections shared by God with us and extended analogously to point back to his own special infinite mode of possessing them, not directly accessible to us.

IV. How We Can Affirm Positive Attributes of God.

Can we do so truly and literally, not just metaphorically? We shall follow here the classic *Triple Way* pioneered by Pseudo-Dionysius and refined systematically by St. Thomas and other medievals.

Step 1. Affirmation of similitude between every creature and God.   This is based on the bond of causal participation between creature and God. Every effect must in some way resemble its cause, because what the effect has comes from its cause, and a cause cannot give what it does not

have, at least in some equivalent higher way. Hence every positive perfection in creatures must correspond to, derive from, some equivalent
perfection in God (e.g., visual power in us from knowledge in God).
The bond of efficient causality is the indispensable bridge by which our
minds can pass over the abyss between finite creatures and their Infinite
Source. Deny this bridge, and all we can say about God is by way of sug-
gestive metaphors, or direct religious experience which must remain in-
articulate or merely metaphorical.

Step 2. Purification of the resulting concept: the negative moment. How
can we aptly express this similitude? We cannot directly apply every
good quality in creatures to God literally, because many of these contain
imperfections built into their very nature that are incompatible with infinite perfection. Hence we must take every attribute drawn from creatures and purify it by examining whether it contains any imperfection
or limitation in its very meaning (e.g., all attributes implying something
material, like vision, hearing, speed, etc.). If it does, then it cannot
survive the purifying process so as to be applied truthfully to the divine
perfection. Only those attributes can survive which contain no imperfection or finitude in their meaning, although they do contain such
limitations as participated in us or other creatures. These are called
"pure perfections" (as opposed to "mixed"), and can be affirmed as
literally true of God, not merely metaphors. Thus we cannot say, "God
has the best eyesight, or is the fastest runner," because these imply in
their very meaning the imperfections of a material body. What does correspond to this in God are the pure perfections of knowledge and omni-
presence, which contain no such limitations, "no ceiling," in their
meaning.

How do we find such pure perfections in the world of creatures,
principally in ourselves, as the highest beings we know by experience?
We must search for those positive qualities which we recognize as de-
serving of our unqualified approval, as unqualifiedly better to have than
not to have, so that if God did not possess them he would be inferior to
us. There are only a small number which can survive this purification
process: e.g. existence, activity, unity, goodness, power, intelligence,
will, love, and others derivative in some way from these or implied by
them (justice, mercy, compassion, etc.). Among these, love especially
needs careful purification from connotations of desire for what one
does not have, all bodily implications, etc. For some oriental cultures,
love is too tied up with these limitations in their concepts of it to allow

this purification; and so they—correctly for them—are unwilling to affirm this of God.

Note that if you can find nothing good, worthy of praise, in yourself, you can say nothing positive about God. As someone has said: "Half of thinking well about God is thinking well about yourself."

Step 3: Reaffirmation and application to God + the index of infinity. These purified perfections are now affirmed as necessarily present in God—otherwise he would be less perfect than we are—but with the added index of infinity, i.e., possession in an infinite degree, beyond our positive vision or grasp by human concepts, pointing to the ultimate Mystery, the Infinite Being that is the wellspring of all reality, which we realize we must affirm as true even though we cannot directly penetrate the Mystery, "the Light too bright for our eyes to see," under pain of denying that there is a God at all. As St. Thomas puts it in his usual terse way, We know that God is intelligent, loving, etc., and to an infinite degree, but not how he is such.

Use of Analogy.   Such attributes, which apply in different degrees both to creatures and God, can only be expressed in analogous concepts (not univocal ones) which are not confined to the same rigid meaning all the time but are flexible, can stretch over different levels of being without losing their basic unity of meaning. See Chapter 3: Analogy, for how this is done. Since the divine being is beyond all determinate forms and limited essences, such analogous concepts that can be applied to God do not signify forms or essences but are action terms, signifying some mode of activity, which can be performed diversely by different subjects, each in its own characteristic way (e.g., existing, knowing, loving). This is not true of forms and essences, which indicate fixed modes of existing. Since the analogous application of all these concepts is grounded in the ontological participation of all creatures in the divine goodness according to various limited degrees, these concepts are "predicated of God according to the analogy of participation."

Can we put any more direct, quasi-experimental content into our knowledge of the divine Mystery as infinite, beyond the reach of all our clear concepts, so that it is not merely negative, "the cloud of unknowing," as the mystics call it? I think we can, by inserting what we do know positively about these attributes into the radical unrestricted drive of our intellect and will toward the infinite fullness of truth and goodness, which says of all finite realizations, "not enough, not enough." This yields an obscure but positive kind of *knowing* "through the heart," so to speak, hidden in the very experience of longing, a knowledge through desire itself. If we can recognize the absence of something we must somehow dimly know in silhouette what we are looking for, as Plato pointed out long ago. Precisely because such purified perfections applied to God are the objective correlates of the unrestricted innate dynamism of the human spirit, we cannot put any limit on them without putting a limit on the very dynamism itself, thus denying something in ourselves that makes us characteristically human. Thus when we apply these attributes to God, we project them beyond what we can directly see, along the ascending vector of these open-ended perfections, all the way to infinity. Such concepts are positive pointers to a mystery beyond.

Furthermore, it is frequently overlooked that this knowledge through longing contains implicitly a very precise item of knowledge about God that is essential for our religious relationshp of worship, adoration: "God is the *Number One* in excellence in all these domains, wisdom, love, etc." This is indeed all we need to know for religious purposes, that God *is* supreme wisdom, love, power, etc., not precisely how he knows, loves, etc. in detail. Whatever his mode of possessing these, he remains, with total precision, uniquely No. 1, with no rivals. Recall the stunning insight of Angelus Silesius, the 17th century mystical poet: "The abyss in man cries out to the abyss in God; tell me, which is deeper?" In the complementary extremes of fullness and emptiness they must match; otherwise, we are not really longing for the only God there is.

For an excellent summary of Aquinas' doctrine on what philosophical reason can know about God, cf. John Wippel, "Thomas Aquinas on What Philosophers Can Know about God," *Amer. Cath. Phil. Quart.* 61 (1992), 279–97; rich in texts.

V. THE DISTINCTION OF ATTRIBUTES

We have enumerated a number of different attributes of God above. Are these actually distinct in content or are they merely synonyms expressing the one simple identical perfection of the pure fullness of existence in God himself? Some philosophers have maintained the latter must be the case, under pain of contradicting the divine attribute of the absolutely simple, uncomposed being of God already established, so that only one positive attribute can be affirmed of God; anything else is a pure synonym or a philosophical error. This would negate the whole process of extending creaturely perfections to God as outlined above.

This is a misunderstanding of how human concepts work. Our human concepts of God are abstract concepts, each of which expresses a true but incomplete focus on the inexhaustible fullness of God in himself. No one of our concepts can express fully and explicitly in a single human concept this fullness; hence we need to use many. These are not merely synonyms, for one does not express explicitly what is included in the others. They all refer to the same identical simple reality of God, seen incompletely by us from different points of view. Yet since our ideas are not themselves real beings, they do not posit any real multiplicity of distinct parts or qualities in God himself. But although any one concept does not explicitly include the content of the others, neither can it exclude it—this would posit a real distinction in God. Neither does one say all that can be said about God in our language and mode of thinking through multiple focuses or "shots" on the same one reality. Hence we need many, justifiably so.

Historical Note. Some philosophical traditions, like the Neoplatonic (Plotinus, etc.), insist on an almost totally "negative theology," as it is called, allowing only one positive attribute of God (One or Good). But this, to my mind, is not just out of reverence, as they claim, for the Mystery of God as utterly One and Simple. In a Platonic realism of ideas, ideas are themselves the "really real"; hence any distinct intelligibility or idea-content implies a distinct real being, hence really distinct spiritual multiplicity in God. This cannot be tolerated in the supreme One, beyond all multiplicity, even spiritual, and can be admitted only in a second lower level of divinity for Plotinus, the divine *Nous* or Intelligence. But our human concepts, for St. Thomas, are not real beings in themselves, only abstract mental beings, whose only being is their "to-be-thought-about" by a real mind. There can be no adequate solution to the problem of the divine attributes unless one abandons, as all Christian thinkers finally did by the 13th century, the Platonic realism of ideas.

The Buddhist tradition(s) also allows no positive attributes about Ultimate Reality, since they are but anthropomorphic metaphors for what is in principle beyond all human concepts and language. Granted the partial truth in such a position, it seems to me there are also two dubious philosophical positions on which it implicitly rests. (1) Since it refuses on principle to engage in any theoretical metaphysical questions about creation or participation, it has no foundation for an adequate theory of analogy and the analogical use of concepts to cope with the problem and simply drops it instead. (2) The implicit understanding of being here and in many oriental traditions is that it signifies some finite, determinate essence or thing. Hence any reality that is infinite, beyond limitation of any kind, must be described in negative terms only, such as "emptiness" (*sunyatta*) or "non-being," more ultimate than being.

But there is no need to lock oneself into either one of these flawed or undeveloped metaphysical positions, either the Platonic realism of ideas, or an essentialist notion of being. The existential metaphysics of Aquinas shifts the center of gravity of reality beyond form and essence to the act of existence itself, transcending all forms and limiting essences, and thus escapes the principal Buddhist philosophical critiques, when they are willing to engage in philosophical discussion at all— which the Zen Buddhists usually are not, though I suspect these implicit metaphysical assumptions lie behind their silence.

V. Some Special Divine Attributes

We cannot here do a full treatise on the philosophy of God, so we will select only a few for special attention.

1. God as Creator. Creation in the strict philosophical sense means the production of some real being out of nothing. The "out of nothing" here, frequently misunderstood, means simply "not out of any pre-existing material or subject." In a word, it means that God is the cause of the total being of his effect, called a "creature." The causal activity of creatures, on the other hand, always presupposes something pre-existing to work on, and so is the cause only of the becoming, the transformation of its effect from this mode of being to that, not of the total being of its effect. Thus God alone is ultimately the Creator of the whole universe of finite being. This metaphysical notion of creation says nothing about a beginning in time, only total dependence of a finite being on God for its existence.

Theological notion of creation in Christian, Jewish, and Islamic theology: it adds on the notion of a beginning in time, as taught in the Book of *Genesis*. Since St. Thomas, following Aristotle, does not believe we can prove from reason alone that the universe must have had a beginning in time, he does not include this in the more austere meta-physical notion. Other medieval thinkers, like St. Bonaventure, and some moderns, disagree.

    2. *The Motive of Creation.*   Every intelligent agent, especially in a free action, must have an end in view or purpose that motivates it to do this action = *a motive.* What can be the motive for God's free creation of the world, granted that God is already infinite in perfection? (1) It cannot be to acquire any finite good outside of him, even honor, glory, adoration, etc. from any creature, since he already possesses the infinite fullness of all perfection. (2) The only motive for a divine action there-fore must be love of his own infinite goodness. (3) But there are two ways of loving one's own goodness: one is to *enjoy* it; the other is to *share* it, communicate it to others. The latter is precisely the reason, the motive—and the only possible one—why God creates the whole uni-verse, anything finite, outside of himself: simply out of pure gratuitous love that wants to share his own riches with us, to make *us* happy. As the 14th century mystic, Meister Eckhart, summed up the whole meaning and purpose of the created universe in one sentence: "God enjoys him-self, and wants us to join him." Period! That's what it's all about—sharing! Anything else would be unworthy of the being God is.

    The above conclusion often surprises people who have become used to an image of God handed down to them as very concerned, even jealous, about receiving the honor and glory due him, as though he somehow needed this for his own sake. But this is a serious misunder-standing, both philosophically and religiously. God does not need any-thing from us to maintain his own happiness. His only wish is to share his own happiness with us as richly as possible. But on our part, for our own sake, we must honor and glorify him as the best way to turn our-selves toward him and render us open and attentive to receive his gifts. In the same vein St. Thomas does not hesitate to say that the only reason why God is "offended by our sins" is not that they hurt him or threaten his dignity in any way, but because they *hurt us,* and he does not want us to get hurt.

    3. *God as Personal.*   Some religious thinkers tend to exaggerate the gap between "the God of the philosophers" and "the God of Abraham, Isaac, and Jacob," a strictly personal God, claiming that the God of meta-physics is too cold, abstract, impersonal to be the God of religious wor-ship. This does not seem quite fair to me. The God of historical, revealed religion has indeed a richer set of attributes of more personal,

free, historical relations with us than the God arrived at by philosophical reason alone. But the arguments we have presented lead necessarily to the conclusion of a God who is *intelligent* (wise) and *loving*, with a totally gratuitous, benevolent love for us, who wishes to share his own goodness and happiness with us as much as possible. But this is the very definition of a *person,* as a center of intelligent, free, responsible, loving action. The God of the philosophers and the God of Abraham are clearly pointing to the identical Ultimate Source of all Being; but the latter has a richer set of attributes than the former because it has a richer set of data to work from, supplied by Revelation. Christian thinkers, however, speak of God as "personal" rather than as "a person," in order to leave open the possibility of more than one person within the one divine nature, as taught by Christian revelation but not discoverable by philosophy alone.

4. Omnipotence. This is frequently misunderstood. It does not mean God possesses all power and holds onto it for himself. It means that he is the ultimate source of all power, which he then shares freely with creatures so that they can act with their own participated power according to the level of their natures. It also means that God has the power to bring into being anything that is intelligible as a participation in his own being (truly possible). It is *not* a limitation on his power that he cannot bring into being conceptual contradictions, like a square circle, since they cannot even be thought as possible. *Nor* does it mean that God can perform directly himself any possible action any other being can do; thus he cannot drink beer, have sex, smell roses(?), because all these presuppose a material body, which would be to introduce limitation into God. But he can experience to an infinite degree the delight and joy we get from doing these human actions, which is why we do them.

5. Omniscience. God knows perfectly and exhaustively all that is and can be known. *How?* Not by passively receiving the action of other beings on him; then he would not be self-sufficient, not God. Thus God does not know the world because it is there; the world is there because he creatively knows and wills it, by giving being to it. How is that compatible with our freedom? God works with every creature in all that it does (*concursus*), constantly feeding into them all the being they need both for their existence and their actions. But he allows creatures to use and channel this power according to their own natures, which are ultimately his own gift; thus he allows free creatures like ourselves to

channel and direct the power offered to them toward this or that particular goal determined by our free choice. Thus he knows what all creatures are doing all the time, including free ones, by knowing how we
allow his superabundant power to flow through, how we allow him to
work with us. Thus he knows what we are doing by actively doing with us
all we are doing, though we channel it through our own natures and
free decisions. He knows by actively doing, causing, not by first passively
receiving, as we who are not creators of the world have to do. A great
mystery *how,* but it must be so.

   Special Problem: Does God know our free future actions, all that will
happen in the future, and if so, *how,* without destroying our freedom?
All true knowledge must be founded somehow on something real, actually existent, for St. Thomas, at least on the action of some real mind
thinking it up (mathematical entities, etc.); it cannot just float somewhere on its own, independent of all real existence. But the future *as
future* does not yet have any real existence in itself. So Thomas does not
hesitate to say that no mind, not even the divine, can know with certainty the future as future, since there is nothing there yet to know. God
and we, too, can know the future actions of a non-free cause, because
they are already determined as flowing necessarily from its own nature.
But this is not the case with free agents, like ourselves. As free, the action
is not yet certainly determined until it is actually decided on by a real
agent; but it is then no longer future but present. That is why we, who
are locked into the passage of time, cannot know free future actions
with any certainty.

   How then can God know them, as is constantly asserted by religious
texts of all religions, including Christianity, and most theologies? St.
Thomas is clear and uncompromising on the point. God is *timeless,* entirely outside the flow of our time and all times, since all time is based
on some process of successive change, which cannot affect God. Therefore, he exists in an eternal NOW by which he is present to every real
being or event as it actually happens, "in its presentiality," as Thomas
puts it, not beforehand *to him,* though the event is future *for us* who are
stuck in the successive flow of earthly time. Thus God does not properly
foresee anything; he simply *sees* it as it is actually taking place. He sees
nothing as past or future to him, though he knows what time things
happen for us. God is always and only "the Present One," never the absent one to anything, especially to us, with whom he has such a personal
relation.

It should be clear why all this must be so. God could not know something not yet existent at all, because nothing can actually be or become real unless God actually works with it to make it real and able to carry on its action, and God's real action can only be in the real present, not in a non-existent future. Besides, have you thought that, far from being necessary for God to exercise his providence, as many believe, there is no knowledge more useless than to know all the future now? There is not a single thing you can do about it now, since it already will be and cannot be changed, or it would be false. If God did know all the future now as future to him "before" he actually worked with us to make it come true, i.e., by a passive spectator knowledge, then it would be impossible to exercise any providence at all, since everything would already be unchangeably fixed without his active cooperation with us that can only be in a real now—all of which is metaphysically impossible and absurd. There is no way God could see himself working in the future when he is not actually doing it. His action is the ground of all truth about creatures.

Thus God, who needs no time to work out his providence over our lives, works with us and guides us toward our futures right now in our present, adjusting creatively and instantaneously as needed, as history and our free choices with their consequences unfold. He might be said—in an at first perhaps shocking, but to me illuminating metaphor—to be the Great Jazz Player, improvising creatively as history unfolds. God certainly can and does plan out on his own initiative, "ahead of time" for us, his great overall objectives and divine interventions in world history, but the individual details depending on our free response are not determined except by his actually cooperating with us in our present, to which in his time-transcending NOW he is always present. The complete script of our lives is not written anywhere ahead of time, before it happens, but only as it actually happens, by God and ourselves working it out together in our ongoing now's.

This rigorously existence-based Thomistic theory of divine foreknowledge clears away a large underbrush of false problems often brought up by troubled people, e.g.: "If God foresaw me (or Judas) going to Hell, then why did he create me?" Response: If God actually foresaw this happening, it would be too late not to create you; then his foreknowledge would be false. God can know what will happen to you only if he first takes the risk of creating you and working with you all the way through to the end, trying to steer you in the right direction, but with the final outcome determined only by your last free choices at the end, to which God himself is always present, but only in the immanent order in which they actually occur existentially. God too must be a Risk-Taker! The "Ultimate Cosmic Gambler"? Understood properly, "Yes—but also an infinitely skilled player at the game!"

Flawed Solution: "Middle Knowledge of the Futuribles." A rival solution to the existentialist one of Aquinas outlined above has been proposed by the Jesuit theologian *Luis Molina* (1589) and is now becoming popular again, spearheaded by the Calvinist philosopher-theologian, Alvin Plantinga, and now being taken up by other Christian thinkers, including Catholics, e.g., Thomas Flint, *Divine Providence: The Molinist Account* (Ithaca, N.Y.: Cornell Univ. Press, 1998). The "futuribles" are our conditionally future free actions: what *we would* have done *if* we had been put in such and such a concrete circumstance, even though this may never actually occur: e.g., What would you do if elected president, even if you never are? According to this theory, since it is objectively true that, given this circumstance, we would in fact have acted freely this way and not that, God must know from all eternity all the free choices that all free creatures would have made in all possible circumstances in all possible worlds. These choices would have been made freely with no predetermination by God; so freedom is fully preserved. But God, seeing all the possible scenarios of human action, can now choose freely which of these total world scenarios he wishes to make actual by creation. Hence both the certain fulfillment of his providence, the world order in all its details, just as he wishes it, is preserved, because he freely wills this whole world-order, but also the freedom of creatures, since God does not predetermine their choices, but "sees" what they would do freely if placed in this world order.

Response: Brilliant logically, but fatally flawed metaphysically! It presupposes that a non-existent will can actually make free decisions, choose this rather than that. But free decision is an existential act that can only be done by a real existing free will. Non-existents can make no choices at all. Even God cannot possibly know with certainty what their free decisions would be except as they actually make them. He must create them before he or any mind can know them, except by wise conjecture.

The fundamental mistake was to consider these choices objectively true independently of their actual existence and prior to God's knowing them by actually working with them. The only truth there is in their futurible state is that, given this situation, they would have chosen *either* A *or* B, *or* C . . . , but not *which.* This is a fundamentally flawed, implicitly Platonic epistemology, that truth floats somewhere on its own prior to any actual existent being, and so, if true, God must know it. For Thomas nothing is determinately true unless grounded in some real existent or in some real mind creatively thinking it up. *Not:* "This is true, therefore God knows it," but: "This is true because it is grounded in something real and/or God knows it." Neither of these latter is verified in the futuribles. Molinism is a metaphysical impossibility!

Cf. Brian J. Shanley, O.P., "Divine Causation and Human Freedom in Aquinas," *Amer. Cath. Phil. Quart.* 72 (1998) 99–122; Katherin Rogers, "Omniscience, Eternity, and Freedom," *Internat. Phil. Quart.* 36 (1996), 399–412.

QUESTIONS FOR REVIEW AND DISCUSSION

1. What new problem now faces us? Is "Can I prove the existence of God?" the proper philosophical question to ask here? What is precisely the problem to be solved?

2. Do we need a formal philosophical argument in order to believe reasonably in God?

3. Identify the two great types of philosophical argument.

The Cosmic Path:

4. Summarize Argument I, Steps 1, 2, and 3 in its two forms.

5. Arg. II? Arg. III?

7. Arg. IV? Does this one get by itself to one Infinite Intelligent Source of the whole universe, or need completion?

The Inner Path:

8. Arg. I?

9. Arg. II from moral obligation (Newman)?

Divine Attributes:

10. What are the attributes already discovered from the arguments?

11. What are the ones immediately deducible from arguments? Does "immutable" mean God is indifferent to what we do, what we pray for, how we respond to him? Explain.

12. Explain the Triple Way by which we rise from creatures to legitimately affirm positive attributes to God. Steps 1–3.

13. Explain the role of analogy here.

14. How can there be a distinction between the various attributes of God, although his being is simple, uncomposed?

15. Explain and respond to the "Negative Theology" doctrine of Neoplatonism, and Buddhism?

16. What is the meaning of God as "Creator"? Philosophical meaning compared to richer theological meaning? Motive for creation?

17. Is God personal?

18. Is God omnipotent?

19. Is God omniscient? Can God know our free future acts? Is "middle knowledge" a viable solution for reconciling divine providence with human freedom? Explain.

CHAPTER FIFTEEN

The Metaphysics of Evolution

NEW QUESTION

Thus far we have worked out the basic metaphysical structure of a universe like ours, made up of a community of existents that are multiple, finite, changing, interacting with each other, all finally dependent on a single infinite Source of all being. But these all-embracing metaphysical laws and structures still remain very general, and would in fact apply to any possible universe with similar features. Special problems arise when we wish to apply these general metaphysical structures to the particular historical kind of universe we have now discovered ours to be, since Charles Darwin's revolutionary *Origin of the Species* (1859). We now know our material universe to be an *evolving* one in every dimension, not only on our own little earth but in the entire cosmic system, beginning with the initial Big Bang some 15 billion years ago, proceeding through the formation of stars, galaxies, satellite planets like our own, and the emergence of life on ours some 3 billion years ago. The subsequent slow development from the original, primitive one-celled creatures up through all the levels of plant life, animal life, and finally to our own human species of rational animals, each emerging in some way from previous stages in a general process, is what can be called *emergent evolution.*

I am speaking here only of the very general affirmation of some kind of evolutionary development from the beginning, as the most if not the only really plausible explanation of all the evidence we now have. But this general affirmation concerns only the "fact" that such an overall development occurred, that the more complex did evolve from the less complex, the qualitatively higher from the lower. Pope John Paul II himself, in his recent *Letter on Evolution,* urges Catholics to accept this general fact of evolutionary development as a well-grounded scientific theory—rather than fight a continued rear-guard rejection of it, as in the Galileo case—and then do creative philosophical and theological reflection on it to see how this helps us to understand better God's creative plan for this universe and our place in it. But this in no way implies that we yet have an adequate *metaphysical* (or even scientific) explanation of just *how* this process took place, what are the adequate causes at work to render it philosophically intelligible, whether empirically discoverable by scientific investigation or not. Thus the Pope in that same letter makes the explicit exception of the spiritual soul in human beings as not explainable by the natural process of evolution but requiring the special intervention of direct creation by God himself.

I. Main Problems Posed by Evolution

Scientific: Scientists are well on the way to working out how the main steps of the development of the physical universe before the level of life occurred. The more serious problems occur in explaining evolution in the biological world on our planet, especially the transition from one species to another, and in particular the crucial big jumps from non-life to life, from plant to animal life with the appearance of sense cognition, and above all the transition from animal to human rational life. The original Darwinian theory of evolution explained by a large number of small incremental steps, all occurring by chance interaction with the environment, and ending up with a new species, has come under strong criticism as lacking sufficient evidence, especially for the large jumps. More generally accepted is the theory of *punctuated equilibrium,* i.e., long stability of species once established, then sudden spurts of rapid change or jumps to new species under the pressure of severe environmental changes and threat to survival. It is the latter that cause the problem, since there are usually few if any intermediate forms remaining to mediate the change, above all in the jumps from non-life to life and from animal to rational human life.

   Problems for the Metaphysician: What is the basic causal process by which our material universe develops from simpler elements into more and more complex entities that are not just collections or aggregates of the component units but new *intrinsic unities* manifesting this by *new properties* that are not just the sum of or deducible from the properties of the component parts? There are two main phases of this development: (1) The development from simpler to more complex entities in the purely physical order below the level of life. (2) The development in the biological order: both the transition from non-living to the first living cells, capable of growth and self-propagation, and the progressive emergence of higher and higher qualitative levels of living, including the major "jumps" from non-cognitive plant life to sensibly cognitive animal life, and then from the higher animal species to the human dimension of rational life, animated by a spiritual soul.

Central Metaphysical Problem: Granted from science the fact that in the course of evolution more complex and higher beings have in fact emerged from simpler and lower beings, how can this be, how is it *metaphysically intelligible,* without violating the causal axiom: "No effect can be greater than its cause," and hence the principle of sufficient reason? Is the intervention of some higher cause outside the previously given system needed? And if such is needed, from what source does it come?

II. Inadequate Solutions

1. Reductive materialism. What seem to us higher levels of being are merely new collections of lower elements, arranged in different order, but without any new intrinsic unities with qualitatively new properties. This is the "Nothing But" School: everything is nothing but, reducible to, the lowest elements, rearranged in different order. Thus Carl Sagan, who declared: "I, Carl Sagan, am nothing but a collection of atoms bearing the name 'Carl Sagan.'" Held by the ancient Atomists (Democritus, Lucretius, etc.) and by many modern Reductionists: some holding total reduction of all higher levels to the most primitive, some only reduction of the biological to the physical, some only reduction of the human to the biological or animal.

Critique. Reductionism gives no adequate explanation, or even recognition, of the basic fact presented by evolutionary history, namely, that out of simpler unities new more complex ones emerge, with properties that are neither merely the sum of already existing properties of the simpler unities, nor deducible directly from them, but are distinctly on a new level. For example, hydrogen and oxygen taken separately are both highly flammable elements; combined into the new molecule water, the latter has the opposite property of extinguishing fires. Radical Reductionism just cannot do justice to these data.

2. *Emergentism.*   This theory came out of the British-American *Emergence Philosophy* school of the early 20th century (Lloyd Morgan, Samuel Alexander), which accepts as a basic law of being that the higher emerges from the lower, with no further cause needed. They refuse any further explanation; this is simply a law of nature, of being itself, and that's the end of it. This school has emerged again in recent times under the label *Emergentism.*

Critique.   In its pure form it seems to be really just a reassertion under a new name of the fact that emergence of higher entities from lower actually does occur in nature. It does not provide any explanation of *how* it takes place, in terms of the adequate causes involved. To state this is a "law of nature" may be adequate to fulfill certain requirements of a scientific law, i.e., repeated occurrence under similar conditions although not the requirement of predictability according to law; but it is certainly not a *philosophical explanation* according to adequate causes (sufficient reason). The repetition of such a factual law under the technical term "Emergentism" should not be allowed to present itself as a *bona fide* metaphysical explanation, as seems to be happening often today. Because of its non-explanatory, "quasi-mystical" character it has been falling out of favor recently. It has been absorbed into #3.

Cf. A. Beckerman, H. Flohr, J. Kim, eds., *Emergence or Reduction?* (New York: De Gruyter, 1992).

3. *Naturalism.*   Closely allied to the above but with a little more scientific explication: Nature is a single all-inclusive whole, of which human beings are a part. It has all the resources within itself to produce all the evolutionary movement from lower to higher, including to human intelligence, without any further intervention from outside or higher causes—even though many affirm that the whole process is first launched by God as Creator but then runs under its own power = a form of *Deism.* This is widely, and increasingly, held today by many scientists, philosophers, even by many Christian thinkers and theologians, principally Protestant, but spreading even among Catholics. In a nutshell, naturalism is the doctrine that nature is self-sufficient, i.e., completely capable of producing all the results of evolutionary history, from the lowest to the highest, including humans, by its own built-in resources or natural causes, without the intervention of any higher cause

from outside the already given system, especially not an intelligent designer(s). *Theistic naturalism* would add that the whole process was started off by God, but then left to develop by its own intrinsic resources with no further divine or other intelligent intervention. The whole process is in principle accessible to scientific explanation. And since intelligent design is not accessible to scientific methods of measurement and testing, any appeal to intelligent design from outside the system is in principle ruled out. The basic position of naturalism is laid out by George Gaylord Simpson, one of the founders of the new Neo-Darwinian synthesis:

> Although many details remain to be worked out, it is already evident that all the objective phenomena of the history of life can be explained by purely naturalistic, or, in a proper sense of the sometimes abused word, materialistic factors. [These phenomena] are readily explicable on the basis of differential reproduction in populations [natural selection], and the mainly random interplay of the known processes of heredity [random mutation]. Therefore man is the result of a purposeless and natural process that did not have him in mind (*The Meaning of Evolution,* New Haven: Yale Univ. Press, 1949, 343)

Critique. If the notion of innate active potency is included, this may take care of most of the evolution in the physical, pre-biological dimension of our world. But it is not clear that it is sufficient for the big jumps to qualitatively higher properties in the world of living beings, i.e., from non-life to cellular life, from non-cognitive plant life to cognitive animal life, and especially not from animal to rational human life. For if what emerges is clearly on a qualitatively higher level of being, then the surplus of new being over what was contained in the previously existing causes would have to derive from nothing, thus violating the principle of sufficient reason. The key point, therefore, is whether or not what emerges on a new level is in fact qualitatively higher in ontological perfection than what preceded: Is life a qualitatively higher level of being than non-life, conscious sense knowledge in animals higher than plant life, and especially rational human intelligence higher than animal sense knowledge? If so, then naturalism seems unable to provide any adequate metaphysical explanation of how this is possible, except to fall back on the Emergentism outlined above, namely, the reaffirmation that this is in fact a law of nature. In practice, therefore, most naturalists fall back on some kind of reductionism, that the later stage is not really intrinsically higher than the former but only a more complex ordering of the same, where the previously given causes, given the proper conditions, can produce the new results. Any appeal to intelligent design is really an appeal to religion, hence an illegitimate intrusion into science.

There is also developing now a very interesting and signicant new movement, now a minority but steadily growing and becoming increasingly articulate, among scientists (as well as philosophers), proposing a radical scientific critique of naturalism, and calling themselves *design theorists*. They claim that naturalism, relying only on unguided natural causes, is actually not a scientific theory at all, backed up by adequate scientific evidence, but a hidden metaphysical one, an ideology, based on an a priori philosophical view of the universe, not allowed to be open to scientific challenge, but simply taken for granted as the only responsible way for scientists to go.

On the contrary, they claim, more rigorous scientific analysis is now showing that the basic Darwinian theory, based on the play of chance, does indeed play an important part in the evolutionary process, principally in micro-evolution (within species and the same general kinds of entities), but cannot explain certain key points of innovation to new higher types of operation, and that this can be shown *scientifically*. These crucial points are already in the lower levels of pre-cognitive biological life: the origin of life (including especially the genetic code and multicellular life), the origin of sexuality, the absence of transitional forms in the fossil record, the biological big bang that occurred in the Cambrian era, the development of complex organ systems, and the development of irreducibly complex molecular machines. They are relying on powerful new, mathematically based scientific programs for deciding whether an object is the product of chance (or random factors), or intelligent design. These are now in use in various fields, permit reliable predictions, etc. The Darwinian theory of merely unguided natural causes, applied to these crucial transition points in evolution, simply does not meet the criteria for chance production but matches well the criteria for intelligent design. They conclude that in fact the basic Darwinian theory is not just an incomplete but an intrinsically flawed and failed scientific program. The design theory is a far more effective as well as simpler scientific theory and should be allowed its place as a reputable scientific competitor, not ridiculed and outlawed as an out of place appeal to a religious explanation. (*Caution:* highly controverted!)

Note that design theory, as a scientific theory (with strong philosophical backing, too) is not committed to specifying further what kind of intelligent designer is at work, whether divine or lesser. Hence it is not necessarily committed to a theistic designer. That is the further responsibility of philosophy and theology, not of design theory itself.

For a fine collection of articles on this new design theory movement, cf. *Mere Creation: Science, Faith, and Intelligent Design*, ed. by William Dembski (Downers Grove, Ill.: InterVarsity Press, 1998); William Dembski, *Intelligent Design* (same, 1999). *Contra:* H. Van Till, "The Fully Gifted Creation," in *Three Views on Creation and Evolution,* ed. J. Moreland and J. Reynolds (Grand Rapids: Zondervan, 1999), 161–218.

III. Thomistically-Inspired Solution

I think it wiser to divide up the problem into three areas: A. Evolution in the physical, pre-biological phase of the universe as a whole, from the Big Bang to the formation of our planet earth; B. Evolution of sub-human living species on earth; and C. Evolution of human beings with their spiritual soul.

A. Evolution in the Non-Living Universe

Basic scientific data. Our physical universe is a single vast matter-energy system, which exists not as a fixed, static order, but as an evolving system—a single great story. It begins with a single intense concentration of the whole reservoir of matter-energy (law of conservation of matter and energy) at extremely high temperatures in the so-called Big Bang. Then this energy-mass expands rapidly, forming the extended space-time continuum as it goes. As the temperature gradually cools down, the original simple elements begin to combine together to form more and more complex new entities with new properties different from the properties of the original elements and irreducible to them. Thus it took some thousands of years before it became cool enough for the fundamental elements making up the nucleus of an atom to coalesce and stick together by the power of the "strong force"; then,

more thousands of years until the nucleus of atoms could hold onto orbiting electrons to form the first simplest atoms, hydrogen and helium.

The vast numbers of these slowly coalesced under the pull of gravity
to form clouds of gas, then stars, then galaxies. Imploding stars then
cooked the lighter atoms into forming step by step the whole atomic
table of heavier atoms, carbon, iron, etc.; then exploding stars blew this
whole spectrum of heavier atoms out into interstellar space, where they
coalesced finally into other stars and planets like our own. Then atoms
of various weights combined under favorable conditions into more
complex unities of molecules, and these into more complex ones. It
seems that the highest intrinsic unities with new properties in this whole
pre-biological process are *molecules.* Everything else is merely a more
and more complex collection of atoms and molecules drawn together
by gravity and electromagnetism to form large systems bound together
by relations, but without constituting new individual higher entities
with intrinsic unity and new properties. Molecules are as far as we get on
the ascending scale of being in this pre-biological world.

Metaphysical explanation: the causal factors at work.   It would seem
that all that is strictly needed here for purposes of sufficient reason is
the infusion of a range of active potentiality within the original simple
elements present in the original cosmic soup, ordered to combine with
others as the external conditions permitted, and then for these new
compounds to combine with others as chance encounters and other
conditions allowed. This would be a kind of latent *active potentiality,*
layered in depth, with each set of potencies not just limited to the individual in isolation from the others but conceived together as limited
participations in a single great unified plan for the development of the
universe as a whole.

Where then would be the adequate causality for the production of
new, more complex entities with new properties? Not in the individual
elements taken in isolation, but in the combined presence of many sets
of active potentialities with their power of combining with each other.
The sufficient reason would reside in the whole existing set of individuals with their active potentialities for combining together, which are
built in to their very natures, as though they were precisely constituted
in view of their combinations with others to produce something new.
This would require, of course, the integration of all these distinct potentialities into a single great intentional plan for the system of the universe
as a whole—hence a plan in an organizing intelligence. But isn't this

just what we would expect from a wise creative Intelligence? And it does not seem that these various states of purely physical organized matter, though more and less complex, involve any jump to a radically higher qualitative level; so there is no significant disproportion between the combined potentialities of the elements and their combined effect. Hence after the original constitution of the system by God, with its built-in active potentialities, no further special intervention of the Creator or some higher cause would be needed for this move from the simple to the more complex in the purely physical order. This is not certain, but seems a plausible metaphysical explanation of the minimum causal factors needed, though God might also be creatively cooperating in some secret way even here.

B. *Evolution of Subhuman Life on Our Planet*

Data and Problem.   The fact of micro-evolution within a given species— already a well-established observable fact—does not seem to present any special philosophical problems, since it could be merely accidental adaptations of the same essential nature. Also, we now know from the new biology that the development of new active properties in a living organism is not the result solely of chance mutations of the genetic code from random sources on the outside: on the long chains of genes on the genetic code (DNA) there are a small number that are not ordered just to reproduce copies of themselves from the surrounding environment, as it was once believed all were, but are ordered precisely to monitor the environment for significant changes that could threaten the survival of the organism. When such changes are discovered, these genes can then jump from one spot to another on the DNA chain, say from position 9 to 12 in one case, and this will force a rearrangement of the whole chain to adapt to the new circumstances—that is why these genes are called "jumping genes." Such adaptations are not simply due to chance mutations but to the purposeful operation of these genes, already built in to the active potentialities of their natures. If such minor modifications in the genetic code were numerous enough and continued long enough, the cumulative changes might become so great that the later entities could no longer breed fruitfully with the earlier ones, and this could be judged to be a new species, by this useful scientific criterion. This would not necessarily imply, however, any qualitatively new level of ontological perfection, just a new manifestation of the same basic kind of life-energy on this same level. This would not require the intervention of some new higher level of efficient cause, but only the active potentialities of adaptation to the changing environment rooted in the already present inner resources of all the entities on this same general level.

The real metaphysical problems arise when there occur transitions from species on one level to a significantly higher qualitative level. The three crucial ones are (1) the transition from non-living matter to the first living cells; (2) the transition from non-cognitive vegetative life to cognitive animal life, and specially (3) the transition from animal to intellectual human knowing and willing—in a word, the emergence of the higher from the lower, the qualitatively more from the less. At each of the first two levels there occurs the emergence of a qualitatively new kind of active power, with a new interiority of the organism, now managing its own growth and improvement, its own internal evolution, not just entering into new combinations with other beings that change its nature to something else. What about the first two transitions, from non-living to biological life, then from vegetative life to animal life endowed with conscious sense cognition? I propose two possible metaphysical scenarios, with one preferred.

1. *Adequate causality is already present* in the cosmic system as a whole. This would be in the form of latent active potentialities instilled into the original elements for the whole subsequent development, in a kind of layered timetable: first, to combine with other, lower elements to produce more complex compounds; then for these to combine as the evolving environment permits to form still more complex new entities with new properties; and so on and on in an ascending spiral, each set of higher entities opening new possibilities and unleashing the latent potentiality to form new higher combinations, following statistical laws of emergent probability—each new step opening up new possibilities and probabilities for the next. This process would carry the system all the way up across the various thresholds of non-life to life, non-cognitive vegetative life to cognitive animal life, but not further. And the whole process would be guided from the beginning by a single great overall plan for the gradual ascent of the whole material cosmos up towards human being, a single final goal participated in by individual active potencies, not isolated in separate tracks but ordered to work together as the environment permitted towards a unified final goal—in a word, *participated final causality.*

What about this general theory of a deep potentiality in the original elements, participated diversely in them, but ordered to a single great immanent plan to combine and develop all the way up to, but not including the spiritual soul of humans? This is appealing and hard to rule out as clearly impossible or unintelligible, lacking adequate sufficient reason. This would come very close to a limited naturalism position with a theistic foundation, as outlined above. It is not easy to rule out this position definitively.

But on careful reflection it does not seem plausible (intelligible) that the active potentiality to produce something of a significantly higher qualitative level of being can actually reside in an ontologically lower being. The qualitatively more cannot come out of the less, the higher out of the lower, or even out of a combination of lower level potentialities, without a gap in sufficient reason: a cause cannot give what it does not possess in some equivalent way; the surplus would have to arise out of nothing. And remember that active potentiality means what a nature can do now, with its own resources, given proper conditions.

What is the special difficulty of explaining transition points like the origin of life—the first living cell—without intelligent design? As design theorists have pointed out, it is that the simplest living cell is now known to be an immensely complex example of what is called *irreducible complexity,* i.e., a system composed of many different parts, all of which must be present and working together simultaneously to produce any result at all. The slow addition of one or more parts at a time could produce nothing at all and would be of no use for evolutionary survival. It is a matter of all together or nothing. The odds are unacceptably high against this happening by some random chance, taken as a plausible explanatory theory, when another far simpler and more elegant one is at hand, intelligent design. The criteria of the new scientific programs for deciding between results produced by chance or by design are seriously violated by attributing an irreducible complexity system such as this to chance. Much discussion is taking place now among scientists on this topic. Cf. Michael Behe, *Darwin's Black Box: The Biochemical Challenge to Evolution* (New York, Free Press, 1996).

What is the difficulty in explaining sense cognition in animals purely by biological factors plus random mutation? It is the emergence of a qualitatively new and higher type of operation, namely, conscious intentionality, i.e., the power to interpret biological patterns of motion in the brain as images, that is, as signs of something outside the organism itself, even at great distances. Such an operation cannot be specified in any strictly material (spatially extended), or biological terms. A higher type of cause than a purely biological one—one that partially transcends matter, is needed to explain this higher type of operation. So I propose the suggestion of Karl Rahner:

2. *Creation of the material world by God is an ongoing process*—not just a one-shot affair in the beginning that leaves the system to evolve by itself with all its needed active potentialities for the whole process already contained immanently within it. Rather, God is constantly working creatively with the ongoing unfolding of the world's own built-in active potentialities, stepping up his creative collaboration at certain key thresholds to inject new information-sets—not necessarily new physical energy—into the process to enable new qualitatively higher ontological centers with new properties to appear on the scene. Such creative intervention, or perhaps better, creative collaboration of God, acting on a totally spiritual level, would entirely escape all empirical observation, quantitative measurement, or scientific detection in any way. Only the material results would be accessible to science, yielding empirical laws of succession, but not all the causal factors at work. Nature would *appear* then as a self-sufficient whole on the observable, scientific level, while the metaphysical account in terms of ontological sufficient reason would be much deeper and richer—although please note that the new design theorists deny even the scientific adequacy of such a scientific account. Such a creative collaboration of God might be necessary even down within the process of the early physical evolution, to nudge the ongoing process at key turning points with a bit of extra information, although neither we nor science might be capable of detecting this on our own. The key point in this metaphysical explanation is the notion of creation as a continually ongoing activity of God creatively forming his own universe as it unfolds, infusing new active potentialities into it as needed at crucial transitional thresholds, thus *collaborating creatively* with the whole process as it ascends slowly upwards: through inanimate matter to life; to animal cognition; and finally to a special, more intimate creative collaboration by infusing directly the spiritual soul into the evolution-prepared human body. God is thus seen as initiating a new chapter in the story of a more intimate personal union of himself with his creation through his created images, embodied spirits like ourselves, persons like himself, imperfect though we are. It seems to me

that the above is the most richly satisfying, if not the only truly satisfying, metaphysical explanation of the wondrous and mysterious gift that is our evolutionary universe—a single great story, with ourselves as the cutting edge, and the final *raison d'être*, of the whole profoundly unified process, God's own creative self-expression in matter.

Role of Chance. Note that there is plenty of room for the play of genuine chance as a partial explanatory factor in this whole God-guided process: namely, in the unpredictable movement of individual particles in the subatomic quantum world, and especially in the encounter between material agents within the vast theater of an expanding and changing space-time matrix, as to when they can actuate their latent active potentialities for combination or interaction with other active agents moving within it. The God of our universe seems to exercise his providence by a creative interweaving—inscrutable to us now—of law, order, and chance, and occasional direct personal intervention, possibly between the cracks of quantum indeterminacy.

C. Special Case of the Creation of the Human Soul.

The emergence of the highest and final level—so far—of this evolutionary process, that of human beings with their self-conscious intellectual life, poses a special metaphysical problem going beyond just the collaboration of a higher cause. Once the spirituality of the human soul has been established because of its higher operations that transcend the properties of spatially extended matter (abstract ideas transcending time, space, and all particular material contexts, understanding of values, self-consciousness, etc.), then the metaphysical question arises of what can be the adequate cause of its origin.

Since such an immaterial nature has no material parts, but is a simple, inextended center of spiritual energy, it cannot be made out of different material parts provided by different material causes, e.g., the father cannot provide half a spiritual soul and the mother the other half; it must be produced all of a piece at once out of no preexisting material, that is, out of nothing. But this is creation in its strict sense and is in the power of God alone, the only cause that has power over being itself directly, as the unique ultimate Source of all being. The parents can provide a humanized body, emerging from the whole history of evolution, apt for the inhabitation of a spiritual soul, but at this point God has to enter into a new, direct, and much more intimate relation with his creation by lifting it up to a new spiritual level with the infusion of a human spiritual soul transcending the whole evolutionary process so far and all its innate natural potentialities.

So the appearance in our world of a new human being is something very special, as the *Genesis* story expresses imaginatively: the collaboration of heaven and earth, the earth rising up as far as it can, and heaven reaching down to light a new spirtual fire in it from above—the production of an embodied spirit that we call a human person, with a corresponding destiny extending through but beyond this whole material world. Nothing less than the creative initiative of a transcendent cause can render adequate sufficient reason for the emergence at the end of the cosmic story of this amazing microcosm, the human person, that integrates within itself all the levels of creation from the lowest material to union with the highest spiritual, the Author of the whole story himself.

Conclusion.   It seems to me that only a metaphysical account that involves the ongoing collaboration of a higher cause with the immanent natural causes of our material cosmos can provide an adequate sufficient reason—and so intelligibility—of the central challenge presented by the evolutionary story of the universe we live in, with its two main aspects: (1) there is a hierarchy of being, i.e., different qualitative levels of the perfection of being from the lower to the higher, not just different quantitative expressions of matter on the same ontological level—a flattened out universe, so to speak; and (2) causes on a qualitatively lower level just cannot supply the sufficient reason by themselves for the emergence of something qualitatively higher—causes cannot give what they don't have in some equivalent way—and hence the collaboration of some higher cause on the same (or higher) level as the surplus of higher being in the effects must be introduced into the metaphysical account, though not the scientific one, to make full sense out of our universe.

Note.   The growing resistance of so many thinkers today, not only scientists but philosophers—and even a number of religious thinkers, both Protestant and now Catholic—to allow any intervention (they say tendentiously "interference") of God or any higher cause in the evolutionary process, even for the emergence of human intelligence, seems to me to derive, at least in part, from two insufficiently examined and deeply flawed premises: (1) the diminishing philosophical recognition of the irreducibly immaterial nature of the human soul, as the source of the irreducibly immaterial activities of human intellect and will; and (2) the underlying principle, rarely if ever submitted to full critical examination or justification but merely taken for granted, that Nature is an all-encompassing, self-contained whole, of which humans are an inseparable part, that contains within itself, with its own immanent resources, all that is needed for the entire evolutionary development of the cosmos, humans included. Otherwise we infringe upon the competence of Science—not itself open to question. We hold out against both!

Readings: One of the latest and most illuminating books in this ongoing controversy is *Three Views on Creation and Evolution,* eds. J. P. Moreland and J. M. Reynolds (Grand Rapids: Zondervan, 1999),—all three views by Christian thinkers with four commentators on each. The two most significant views correspond to the two solutions I have proposed above: (1) Howard Van Till: "The Fully Gifted Creation" (theistic evolution, or nature infused at creation with the active potential for all future earthly life forms); (2) Robert Newman, "Progressive Creationism" (progressively unfolding creative activity of God infusing new information where needed at crucial points of discontinuity along the way). The latter, favored by the majority of the contributors, corresponds in its main lines to the second solution I too favor in this chapter.

Cf. also J. Donceel, S.J., "Causality and Evolution," *New Scholasticism* 39 (1965) 295–315 very good; Karl Schmitz-Moorman and James Salmon, S.J., T*he Theology of Creation in an Evolutionary World* (Cleveland: Pilgrim Press, 1997), although they may concede too much to naturalism on the origin of the human soul; Ernan McMullin, "Biology and the Theology Of Human Nature," in P. Sloan, ed., *Controlling Our Destinies: Perspectives on the Human Genome Project* (Notre Dame: Univ. of Notre Dame Press, 2000); Lynne Baker, "Must a Christian Be a Mind-Body Dualist?" *Faith and Philosophy* 12 (1995), 489–504: "No." The last two present a theistically-grounded naturalism. *Mere Creation: Science, Faith, and Intelligent Design,* ed. by William Dembski (Downers Grove, Ill.: InterVarsity Press, 1998): articles by the new "design theory" scientists in criticism of Darwinian naturalism; James Reichmann, S.J., *Philosophy of the Human Person* (Chicago: Loyola Univ. Press, 1985): last chapters good.

QUESTIONS FOR REVIEW AND DISCUSSION

1. What are the principal metaphysical problems raised by the scientific theory of emergent evolution?

2. Summarize and respond to the following inadequate solutions: Reductive Materialism? Emergentism? Naturalism?

3. Thomistic Solution: a) Evolution in Non-living World? b) Evolution in Subhuman Life World: Two solutions? c) Evolution of Human Beings?

CHAPTER SIXTEEN

Being as Good

Status of the Question. So far we have discovered three great transcendental properties of all being—a *transcendental property of being* is one that is co-extensive with being, is found wherever being is found (it "trans-cends" or leaps over all boundaries of class, or kind, or mode of being). These are: every being is *intelligible, active, one* (true). Now, after discovering that every being is goal-oriented, striving dynamically for its own actualization, and as proceeding from the one Ultimate Source of all perfection, we are in a position to bring into explicit focus the next great transcendental property of all being, its *goodness*. This aspect of being corresponds to the other great drive of the human spirit as *will*, its drive toward being as good, as valuable, as desirable, as lovable.

Note. This property of being could, strictly speaking, be discovered before establishing the existence of God; and this is frequently done. But I think it can be done more adequately and persuasively within this broader vantage point: God as Source of all real being.

Main Problems: I. What is the meaning and nature of the good? II. What are the main kinds of good? III. Is every being, as being, good, and if so, why?

I. MEANING AND NATURE OF THE GOOD

1. Meaning. We discover the goodness aspect of being from our experience of positively desiring, valuing, loving various real beings, i.e., from the *appetitive drive* of our nature (in its original broad meaning "appetite" comes from the Latin *adpeto* = to tend toward something). Thus the good appears as the objective correlate in being to our subjective inner dynamism of desiring, loving, valuing, admiring, both in the sensitive and the spiritual orders. Thus Aristotle defines it as "that which all things seek." This is true, but it does not tell us just what it is in being we seek, or why. This appetitive tendency toward, or response to, something can thus be called an act of *valuing*, or *valuation*. Hence the good appears as the valuable: that which is, or can be, the object of any act of valuing or valuation, which in a very wide and analogous sense can be called an act of loving. Hence the good is that which is in some way *lovable*.

2. *Relational aspect.*   Note here the intrinsically relational character of the good, which distinguishes it from being a mere synonym for being. It does not signify some characteristic of a being taken purely in itself without reference to anything else. In that case we would call it merely a mode of being or perfection. To call something "good," although it still denotes something in the being itself, adds on the connotation—at least implicit—of relation to some valuer, some appetitive dynamism: good *for* something—which could even be its own self.

Historical Note: This explicit recognition of the intrinsically relational character of the good marks a significant development in the history of the concept. Although already present in Aristotle, it was not clearly understood or explicitly brought out by the Platonic and Neoplatonic traditions and early medieval thought, which tended to treat the Good as the ultimate Absolute perfection in itself, without reference to anything but itself, the proper name of God even prior to Being itself. St. Thomas is one of those principally responsible for introducing the more relational and personalist aspect of the good as intrinsic to its meaning, without denying the nature of God as ultimate, self-sufficient Source of all being.

Relation of the Good to Being.   The good does not add anything on to being from the outside that is really distinct from it, as an "absolute" or non-relative property. It is the *being itself* that is valued, called "good," not something else added onto it that is not it. Hence the good signifies the object or being itself that is valued, but considered precisely as the object of valuation with relation to some valuer, as valued or valuable *to* something—which could in fact be its own self. Hence the good is being as desirable, valuable, lovable.

3. *Good as synthesis of objective and subjective poles.*   This is important lest we fall into a radical subjectivism and relativism of the good. If we

go no further than Aristotle's definition of the good as "that which all things seek," there remains a certain ambiguity, often noted and exploited in the history of thought. If the good is defined as "that which all things seek," then the question immediately arises: "Is something good (or called "good") simply because we seek it; or do we seek it because it is good?" In other words, is the good a purely subjective aspect that we confer on things precisely by our seeking them, without it being at all objectively grounded in the thing sought itself? Or does the good signify something intrinsically in beings that makes them worth valuing by the valuer—or at least something he believes is worth valuing?

Subjectivist value theories. Spinoza seems to have held this, that "Things are good precisely because we seek them." Many modern value theorists hold the same: there is no objective goodness, no objective values in reality itself; value and goodness are a purely *subjective attribute* conferred on things by the valuer's interest in them: "I do not desire, value, love things because they are good; they are good, valuable to me because I love, desire, value them; things or actions are bad, evil to me because they displease me, make me feel unhappy, and I want to avoid them." This is an extreme version of the position, which perhaps not many would hold in its radical purity, but there are many mitigated versions, especially in ethics, aesthetics, etc. Ralph Barton Perry's famous *General Theory of Value* (1926) is a classic statement of this general position.

Critique. If this means merely that nothing can be called good save in relation to some valuer, this is quite true. But if it also means, as is quite clear in most cases, that there is no objective ground for its being valued or loved within the being itself, making it truly worthy of being valued, then it becomes purely arbitrary, irrational, and is contrary to our actual experience and to the ordinary meaning of the terms "good" and "valuable" as understood and used in practice by most people. For then someone could value anything at all, declare it truly good, for no objective ground in reality or reason at all, simply by sheer fiat or decree. But this is clearly against our experience. We strive for most things because we really believe (mistakenly or not) they will objectively, truly, fulfill us, make us happy, be good for us, so that without them we will not be happy. It is not enough for us simply to decree that something is good for it to turn out truly valuable for us—otherwise we could be rich or well-fed with a few pieces of dust declared to be precious stones or nourishing food, whereas it is clear that we will not be nourished but harmed by the wrong choice of foods, climate, and many other things. We also routinely argue with, try to persuade others that such and such is *truly* good, worthy of being loved or admired, and that if I am wise, reasonable, and in tune with reality, I *should* value it. This would not make sense in a purely subjective theory of value. Notice that in this view the good is determined primarily by the *will* in terms of what it wants, not first by the intellect, judging what is truly good; then chosen by the will under the guidance of the intellect, the good depending on the true, and that in turn on being itself—as is the proper order for human valuing and willing.

Hence the proper understanding of the meaning of the good should include both the objective and subjective poles. We are now ready to define it finally:

Definition: A being is good if it possesses some positive quality (or "perfection" as it is called by St. Thomas) that renders it apt or worthy to be valued by some valuer (i.e., by some appetitive dynamism that can seek, desire, appreciate it). Aquinas defines the good as "that which is perfect in itself and perfective of another." (Must be adapted to include self-love.)

Note 1.   Something does not have to be *actually* valued by something to be properly called good. It is enough for it to be apt or *worthy* to be valued, to be valu*able,* desir*able,* lov*able.*

Note 2.   This definition allows us to make sense out of what we call an "apparent good," i.e., something that seems good to something, or is believed to be good, but in fact is not. If the good were purely a subjective projection, this would not make sense: whatever appeared to be good would be good, as long as the valuer valued it.

Note 3.   The good does not have to be *consciously* valued or sought for. Any positive tendency toward something as a goal is enough to fulfill analogously the notion of "appetite." Thus we can say meaningfully "Water is good for a plant." It is clear enough how this applies to all living things. Does it also apply properly to inanimate, non-living entities, like atoms, molecules, electrons, etc.?? It is not clear what it would mean for such to be seeking something to fulfill them, since it is not clear that it is any better for them to be in one state instead of another. Does the notion of tending, seeking, appetite here become so attenuated as to practically disappear?? The metaphysical question remains open, difficult to decide!

II. Kinds of Good

The good is analogous in meaning, like being itself, since it is applied in many different ways to different levels of being: goods can be material, sensible, intellectual, spiritual, moral, or aesthetic. Equally analogous is the act of valuing, desiring, and loving, according to the subject valuing and the objects valued.

1. Moral goodness = the goodness proper to a moral act, as conforming to the moral norm of what ought or ought not to be done here and now by a free responsible agent. This is the concern of *Ethics,* and is *not* our concern here.

2. Ontological goodness belongs to the order of the *is,* not the *ought,* and signifies that which is in fact valuable or perfective for some valuer in the objective existential order, whether it is morally good to seek it here and now or not. Thus a chocolate cake is an ontological good of a modest order in itself, but may be morally wrong for a diabetic here and now (as is sex outside of one's marriage). The ontological good is our concern here as metaphysicians.

3. Kinds of ontological goods:

A. *Useful or instrumental goods* = those that are valued not for themselves but only as a *means* for achieving some other good: e.g., a can-opener, a shovel, a pen (though this can also be valued for its beauty). (Persons should not be thus valued.)

B. *Intrinsic goods* = those valued for themselves, as good in themselves to be sought for, possessed, loved, admired, not just to obtain some other good, e.g., friendship, love, beauty, truth, joy, etc. These in turn can be valued (1) either as to be possessed by the valuer, as perfecting, to be enjoyed by it, i.e., as good-for-me—this is called self-centered love, or love of "concupiscence" (desire to possess for myself); or (2) willed for others, as goods-for-others; or (3) to be admired, appreciated for themselves (as images of God, participating in their own limited way in the infinite goodness of God), or loved for their own sake (persons, friends)—this is called the love of benevolence or self-transcending love ("altruistic" love if for persons).

Note that this self-transcending love is possible only when we rise above our own narrow biological and pleasure-driven drives oriented towards our own self-perfection, to live with our intelligence and will in the wide horizon of being itself as truth and goodness. We then become able to recognize and appreciate (value) the good wherever and for whoever it is, thus tending as far as we can toward a subjective viewpoint that totally coincides with the objective viewpoint of being itself—which really means toward the God's-eye view of both knowing and willing all being as true and good as it really is in its total order and harmony under God, its Source. We can love even our own selves not as the center of the universe but exactly as we are in our proper place in the harmony of the whole.

And since it is the very nature of our spiritual intellect and will to tend toward the unlimited fullness of being as true and good, i.e., in reality toward the God's-eye view of both knowing and loving all being, the marvelous paradox results that we humans can in fact actually attain our full self-actualization and self-perfection only by such a self-transcending, "self-forgetting" love. As Jesus put it, "He who loses himself [= his self-centered self] will find himself [= his truest, deepest, most authentic self]." Or, as the great Zen Master, Dōgen, expressed it, "To seek enlightenment is to seek the self; to seek the self is to lose the self; to lose the self is to find all things."

Historical note. *Aristotle*'s analyis of the good tends to be restricted to the more biological viewpoint of self-perfection: the good is the actuality that fulfills our potency or need; he does make the exception for friendship, but does not go back to adapt his system in the light of this. *St. Thomas* follows him in his general metaphysics of the good for all beings, and this perspective certainly remains true: all beings do tend by their very nature toward their own good—that is the way God made them. It is only when he analyzes what in fact is the self-fulfillment of the human, what can satisfy our unrestricted drive of intellect and will towards the fullness of being as true and good, that he breaks out of the apparent self-centeredness of the human good to its *God-centeredness,* as images of God tending toward the fullness of this image—which is the ultimate synthesis of subjectivity and objectivity. But it seems to me that he should show us more explicitly how this paradox is solved; without this he leaves his analysis somehow incomplete, unsatisfying to other Christian thinkers, e.g., the Franciscan school. This lacuna can be easily corrected, as above, and should be.

4. When love is of an absent good, it takes on the character of *desire.* When it is of a present good, it takes on the character of fruition or *delight* in the good as possessed. Thus God's love for himself, the

plenitude of all goodness, can only be of the second kind, not something he desires but does not possess yet. The only adequate object of the divine will that can draw or "attract" the divine love is his own infinite goodness. But that does not mean that God is locked entirely within his own goodness, unable to will anything else. For there are two ways of loving one's own goodness: one is to enjoy it; the other is to share it with others, to communicate it freely to others out of a love of sheer gratuitous generosity. This, and this alone, must be God's motive for creation of beings outside himself, not to obtain some finite good from them, even glory.

5. *Note the existential, extroverted character of love* compared to knowledge. Knowledge is basically *introverted,* in the sense of drawing its objects within itself, to an immaterial presence within itself as idea, as mental being, even though referring to reality outside itself. Love, on the other hand, is *extroverted,* draws the lover out toward the object of its love as it is in itself, wishing to be united with it as it is in its own real being. Thus when I know a plate of ice cream, I turn it into a spiritual cognitive presence within me; when I love or desire it, I want to eat it in its reality (I can't eat, be nourished, by the idea). There is thus an alternating rhythm between knowledge and willing: I first draw the good in by knowing it, transmuting it into an idea (or sense image) within me; then, informed by the idea, my will follows the incoming path back out again to rejoin the known good in its original reality.

As a result, St. Thomas points out, knowledge draws everything it knows to its own level: it draws things below it up to its own spiritual mode of possessing by knowledge; it draws things above it down to its own imperfect mode of spiritual knowing by abstract concepts drawn from the finite world. Love, on the other hand, is drawn to the level of whatever it loves: it is drawn down by what it loves beneath it (sensible, material, non-personal things), but is drawn upward to what it loves that is above it (e.g., God). Thus St. Thomas concludes that to know things below us is to raise them up to our level, hence is more perfect than loving them, whereas to love things higher than ourselves (God) is to raise ourselves up to their level, hence is more perfect than knowing God—though both, of course, are still necessary and good in their own way. So too Plotinus, followed by the Christian Greek Fathers of the Church, teaches that you *become* what you love: if you love principally sensible things, sense pleasures, you *become* a sensual person; if you love spiritual things, you *become* a spiritual person; if you love divine things, you *become* a "divinized" person. Better do a check on the priority of your own loves!

III. The Ground of Objective Goodness or Value

If goodness, value, is not something purely arbitrary and subjective, but has some objective grounding or foundation in things themselves, in their very being, then the question arises, What are the objective grounds for discerning and judging this value in things?

There are two main ways of attributing good to beings, indicated very precisely by two distinct linguistic forms:

1. The Relative Order: the good for such and such a being.

Here the good in question is limited to the horizon of a particular being or type of being. Such goods are expressed linguistically as attributive adjectives, attached directly to their noun subjects, thus: "This is a *good man;* a *good friendship;* a *good painting, good Scotch,*" etc. Or it can be expressed in *"good-for"* terms: "Jogging is *good for* John; water and sun are *good for* plants; Scotch is *good for* Peter, not for George," etc.

Objective Ground of the Good in the Relative Order. This arises naturally out of the basic metaphysics of nature as dynamic center of action, with natural potentialities, final causality, etc. In a word, all natures are naturally oriented toward their own self-fulfillment or actuation. An objective good or value for a given being, therefore, is whatever fulfills in some significant way its own natural potentialities—always with a view, of course, toward the integrated harmony of these potentialities as contributing toward the unified perfection or fulfillment of the whole being as such. Thus a *good man* or *good woman* is one who has achieved a high degree of fulfillment or actualization of his or her natural potentialities as a human being, man or woman. So, too, good music, a good friendship, a good pen, etc. Thus the natural potentialities in a human being are not the result of arbitrary subjective whim or decision, but are built in to its very nature, ranging through a whole ascending spectrum from biological needs and corresponding desires to social ones such as friendship, belonging to and having a family, spiritual ones such as longing for truth, beauty, a religious relationship with our infinite Source, in a word, a meaningful life. These yield a whole spectrum of objective values for all beings possessing human nature, and so can ground objective value judgments based on them.

2. *The Absolute Order of Goods.* This kind of attribution of the good occurs when a being or kind of being is declared to be without qualification a good or value in itself, as seen within the whole horizon of being, i.e., on the absolute scale of all being as intrinsically good. This is linguistically expressed by using the good as predicate following the *is* of judgment: "Love *is good.* Beauty *is good,* Friendship *is good.* Humanity *is good.* Plant life *is good,*" etc.

Objective Ground for Goodness in the Absolute Order. Here the horizon of comparison is not limited to a single being or kind of being, but to the entire horizon of being. Calling any being good in this sense indicates that such a being participates in the basic perfection of actual existence in the community of real existents, corresponding to its degree of fullness of being in relation to the Infinite Goodness of God as Ultimate Source of all being. This degree of perfection is then objectively recognized, valued, admired for its own sake by our intellects and wills, which are themselves ordered by nature to positive response to all being as both true and good.

3. *Relation of the Relative to the Absolute Order of Good.* The judgment, "Friendship is good," is quite different from the judgment, "This is a good friendship," based on different grounds: one absolute, the other relative. What is the relation between the two? The Relative Order of goodness must ultimately be based on the Absolute Order. *Reason:* The fulfillment of a particular being is itself a good only because it is a degree of participation in the absolute value of being in itself.

Hence the order of intelligibility runs thus: (1) Friendship *is good.* (2) This is a *good friendship.*

IV. Good as Transcendental Property of Being: Every Being Is Good

A. Meaning. Every real being, precisely as being, because it has some degree of real existence of its own, stands out from the darkness of non-being, is good, and to be valued as such. This is one of the most profound and ultimate metaphysical questions, affecting one's whole attitude toward the universe according to one's answer. St. Thomas, consistently with his radically existentialist metaphysics, insists that only real, actually existent beings can properly be called good, and precisely because of their participation in the act of existence, the root of all perfection. This means that purely mental beings—ideas, possibles, mathematical and logical entities, hypotheses, etc.—are not good in themselves and worthy of being valued, loved, in their present state as unreal, except insofar as the projection of them as real draws us and we want to make them real. If possibles as such were good, desirable, valuable, just as possible, then we could all be perfectly happy now with all our possible wealth, friends, union with God, which are now possible. This does not make sense. We want *real* friends, *real* money, *real* happiness I can't enjoy *possible* friends, spend *possible* money.

   B. *Opinions.*   *1. Manichaeans* (third century Persia), an offshoot of the *Zoroastrian religion* (Persia, sixth century B.C.).

   They believed the world is a battle-ground between two Gods: *Mazda,* God of light and goodness, and *Ahriman,* God of darkness and evil. Beings made by the God of light are good; those made by the God of darkness are intrinsically evil. Matter is the main source of evil, hence the body, sex, and marriage, which propagate new bodies, are evil and to be avoided by the elect. Human destiny is to collaborate with Mazda, the God of light, for ultimate victory over darkness and evil. *St. Augustine* first held this and struggled long to get free of it. In this view not all real beings are good, only those from the good God.

   2. Neoplatonism. Plotinus (d. 230) and his followers. Matter is the principal source of evil, as being the absence of form at the lowest level of the universe, where the radiation of goodness and unity from the supreme One-Good through form finally dies out in sheer formless multiplicity. The soul loses its spiritual vision by clinging too closely to the body and matter, gets imprisoned by it. This idea was carried on by various Gnostic sects and medieval Christian heresies and keeps popping up all down the ages, even today in some form or other. Thus the recent *Course in Miracles* religion, flourishing in New Age circles, for whom the whole material world, though not evil, is still only a delusory dream of escape from God, which God himself knows nothing about.

   3. Judaism and Christianity.   All being is good because created by a good God in his image: based on Genesis 1:31: "God looked on everything he had made, and behold, it was very good," it can be supported by philosophical reasoning to show why this must be so. *St. Augustine* worked out the first philosophical explanation of evil as negation, as the privation of some good that ought to be there, not a real being in itself, but a parasite on real being. All real being, on the other hand, insofar as it is, is good as created by God. This is the great optimistic affirmation of Christian thought ever since, that no real being, as such, can be intrinsically evil in itself. Evil is only the lack of a missing good that should be there.

4. *Many Modern Philosophers,* including empiricists, atheistic existentialists (like Sartre) and others. Being as such is merely a brute fact, neutral, neither good nor evil, "value-free." Goodness and value are not in being itself naturally but imposed on reality from without by "man, creator of values"; or, for some German idealist schools, derived from a higher independent realm of values distinct from being, which we have to respect and try to incarnate in the real world (something like Platonic ideas, with which they have considerable affinity). Many, for moral and emotional reasons, consider the notion that evil is not something real as intolerable, unrealistic optimism in the face of all the obvious evil we see around us.

Note. Philosophers should remember, that, to be consistent, if they hold evil is something real in itself, they cannot also hold that every being is good.

C. *Argument: Why Every Being as Being Is Good.*

Arg. 1. The doctrine that evil is a positive reality in itself turns out to be unintelligible. Since every real being is some degree of participation in the basic perfection of actual existence itself, and all real being ultimately comes from God as its creative Source, it is impossible that anything real, precisely as real being, should also be intrinsically evil, not good, in itself—though of course it can produce evil effects in something else. It is also impossible that God could produce something as a participation in his own perfection that is intrinsically evil in itself precisely as real being. Hence every being as such in its positivity as real must be good, worthy of being valued for what it is. (See the next Chapter on Evil for a fuller development of this point.)

Arg. 2. Empirical argument: All living things exhibit a fundamental drive or tendency toward survival, toward continuing in existence (at least for their allotted life-span) and attaining the growth that fulfills their potential, and they devote all their energy to working at this. Hence their continued existence and growth is a good, a basic value for each one of them, to be striven for with all its energy. Below the dimension of living beings this becomes more obscure. But it can be said, as St. Thomas, Spinoza (with his *conatus essendi*), and others insist, that each real being has a natural drive toward its own survival, continuation in existence, so that its being appears as a good for itself.

It is also manifest from our experience of the world that most if not all things are good in some way for something else, e.g., to be used, eaten, enjoyed, admired, appreciated for their beauty, etc. *Objection:* How about something like mosquitoes, which seem to be an unmitigated evil for humans and many animals? They are certainly not good for us, nor for many other animals; but they serve as a main source of food for many birds, bats, frogs, etc., in the integral harmony of nature. We should not judge the objective goodness of anything just from its relationship to some limited kind of being, like ourselves.

Arg. 3. Every being is a good for every spiritual intellect and will. This seems to me the most universal, all embracing, and perhaps ultimately most satisfying of all the arguments. From the very fact that something *is* at all, it participates in the fundamental ground of all perfection, the act of existence, which is also a participation in the perfection of the divine nature itself, an image of God, however slight. Hence every spiritual intellect, since its fundamental natural orientation is the unrestricted drive to know all of being, all there is to know about all there is, is fulfilled in some way by knowing any real being. And since every spiritual will, following the guidance of its intellect, is ordered by nature to love, or at least respond by appreciation, admiration, to the whole unlimited range of real being, it then follows that every real being is a good, a value, to be appreciated, admired, as such, for its own sake—and as a gift from the Creator in some way—by every spiritual intellect and will. It is good for every intellect and will to know and esteem (love) every real being, each in its place in the total order of being.

This does not mean every being is good for me to possess or be physically united with. It is a purely contemplative relation that is one of the highest and noblest activities of the human spirit, indeed of any spirit, angelic and even divine. Even God takes delight in his own creation, as *Genesis* says: "God saw all that he had made and behold, it was very good." And as the artist, Margaret Holmes, has put it: "Living without wonder ends up with wondering what living is all about."

How, in this perspective, can we positively value the being of, say, a mosquito? Certainly it is not a good for our human bodies, but harmful. But if we can just step back from this perspective and look at the mosquito purely as it is in itself as a being, then, as any biologist can tell you, it is a tiny marvel of engineering, of elegant efficiency, to be wondered at and admired as such in its own niche in being. A fine challenge to the authentic metaphysician! Aristotle himself makes this point.

How do we judge beings as higher or lower?   This problem causes great difficulty for many modern people. By what right do we, a particular finite kind of being, judge that we, as humans, are higher in value than animals, plants, etc.? Is not that just an arbitrary, subjective point of view, a human-eye perspective on value? Might not animals have a different view? Thus many animal-lovers, as philosophers, and philosophers of "deep ecology," for whom all living species are of equal value. They are opposed to all "species-favoritism," as they call it.

Response.   This might be true from a limited biological viewpoint. But it is of the very nature of beings endowed with spiritual intellect and will, ordered to the whole of being as true and good in itself, to be able to transcend their own or any limited, self-centered point of view to judge and value things as they are objectively in the whole order of being, tending therefore toward a God's-eye view of all beings as they truly are. Thus we humans can judge quite objectively that we ourselves are limited, not perfect, in the order of wisdom, love, power, etc. If animals had spiritual intelligence and will too, they could do the same. But they lack these; they cannot even raise the question of the place of anything in the total order of being itself. *We* can judge *them,* objectively; *they* cannot judge *us,* and God can judge not only ourselves but also our attitude toward animals, plants, etc.

How do we in fact judge the relative level in being and value of other beings? What is our criterion for judging perfection? I think our main criterion is judging the level of a being by its characteristic actions—what can it *do?*, and making this judgment from a qualitative, not just a quantitative point of view. Thus plants can do more than inanimate beings. Animals can do more than plants—they can know other things, according to the abilities of sense perception. Humans can do more—know intellectually, rising above the restriction of here and now concrete material things, can creatively construct tools, think of and love beauty, God, etc. Angels can do more, not bound by the limitations of body. God is infinite in all perfections. Humans must guard against blind spots and biases coming from inherited culture; but as intelligent beings we can, if we are careful to look at the evidence, judge objectively the value not only of our own selves but of all the surrounding world. Is not this one of the principal vocations of a human being as such: to judge wisely and value accordingly the respective values of all that we come to know?

Cf. D. J. Hawkins, "Value and Value Judgments," in *Being and Becoming* (New York: Sheed and Ward: 1954); Scott MacDonald, ed., *Being and Goodness: The Concept of the Good in Metaphysics and Philosophical Theology* (Ithaca, N.Y.: Cornell Univ. Press, 1990) fine collection; Denis Bradley, *Aquinas on the Twofold Human Good: Reason and Happiness in Aquinas' Moral Science* (Washington, D.C.: Catholic Univ. of America Press, 1996).

Application to Life: It follows that it is an intrinsic part of the self-fulfillment, the vocation, of all human beings to *celebrate* all creation—and its Author—for their being, their goodness, their beauty, and be grateful for them as a gift. *Celebration* and *gratitude* are central components of any authentic religion—and human life! It is the special vocation of the artist, the poet, as one of them has said, "to be the voice of all creation," to sing the being, the meaning, the beauty of all things. The Dalai Lama has summed it up beautifully: "The universe has no voice. But it needs a voice. We are the voice of the universe."

QUESTIONS FOR REVIEW AND DISCUSSION

1. When we examine the relations between goodness and being, what are the main metaphysical problems that arise?

2. What is the basic meaning of the good? Explain the relational aspect of the good; how is it a synthesis of the objective and the subjective aspects? How finally should we define it?

3. Kinds of good: difference between moral and ontological?

4. Kinds of ontological good: What is the difference between useful goods and intrinsic goods? Extroverted nature of the good?

5. What is the ontological ground of objective goodness and value? In the "relative order"? In the "absolute order"?

6. The good as transcendental property of all being: what does this mean? Summarize the various key positions of: Manicheans; Neoplatonism; Christianity and Judaism; modern philosophers.

7. Why is every being good? Summarize Arguments 1–3.

8. What is the objective ground for judging some beings to be higher than others?

CHAPTER SEVENTEEN

Evil and Being

Data. The *presence of evil* in the world around us is clearly an undeniable and important part of our human experience. We all suffer
from evil in some way, physical, emotional, moral; we complain about it
and try to avoid it as best we can. Hence what we call "evil" must have
some objective status in the real world. Otherwise, we are all living in a
state of profound illusion, and could wipe it all way like a bad dream just
by clearing up our thoughts. Try it, when you fall down and break your
leg, or you discover someone is plotting to destroy you! If our statements about evil in the world are true—as many of them certainly are—
then the presence of evil in reality cannot be a mere subjective illusion.

Meaning of "evil." We discover its meaning from our experience
and how we express this in language. We call "evil" whatever we experience as the opposite of good in some way, i.e., whatever our appetitive
or valuing dynamisms turn away from or disapprove, disvalue, as not
good, perfective, valuable, lovable in some significant way, but harmful,
destructive, repugnant, unpleasant, etc. This negative dimension in the
meaning of all "evil" terms should not be a matter of philosophical argument. It is simply what we *mean* by the use of the term. The meaning
of any term in public common language comes from its use. We can
argue about the nature or being of evil, or which things are evil; we
should not argue about what it means: all philosophical arguments presuppose this.

Metaphysical problem. The "existence" of evil raises serious problems for all metaphysicians. If one holds, as we do, following Augustine,
Thomas Aquinas, and most Christian thinkers, that all real being, as
being, is good, then what is the *status in being* of evil? Pure illusion, or

non-being? If one holds that not all beings are good, but some are intrinsically evil as being, then what can this be in beings, if all participate in the basic perfection of the act of existence, and as such are participations, images, no matter how slight, in the perfection and goodness of God?

Hence main problems: I. What is the nature and status in being of evil? Is it a positive mode of being or merely a negation? How can a being be both good and evil at the same time? II. Is the existence of a good God compatible with the presence of evil in the world? If he is both good and omnipotent, could he not prevent all evil? If he does allow it and cooperates with it, is he not responsible for it, and therefore morally evil himself?

I. Nature and Status in Being of Evil

Opinions

1. Evil is a positive being or aspect of a being.   This answer to an old and vexing problem goes back well before Christian times. It came from the Middle East and was held by ancient *Mazdeism* and *Zoroastrianism* (Persia, sixth century B.C.) and *Manichaeianism* (heretical Christian offshoot of the above, Persia, third century A.D.). Both good and evil are positive beings, deriving from two ultimate Sources or Gods: Mazda, God of light and goodness, and Ahriman, God of darkness and evil, who are in conflict over the mastery of the world. Human beings stand in the middle, a mixture of good and evil (principally through our body, since matter is the primary evil) and are called to cooperate with the good God to bring about the final victory of light and goodness over darkness and evil in the world. St. Augustine records his long struggles to overcome this belief.

2. Matter is the primary source of evil.   Only beings mixed with matter, and matter itself, are evil in themselves, insofar as they have matter in them. This came into Greece from the ancient Persian religions mentioned above and had considerable influence on *Plato,* who hints at it with his doctrine that the body is a prison for the soul. It was taught more explicitly, but still with considerable ambiguity and obscurity by Neoplatonism. For *Plotinus,* matter is a kind of "real" non-being, formless, chaotic, unintelligible in itself, resistant to form, order and beauty—the last outpouring of the emanation from the supreme One-Good as it fades out into the darkness of matter beyond all form. The spiritual soul, which descends into it by a kind of primal "sin" of turning away from the pure contemplation of the divine ideas, becomes blinded, bewitched, by attachment to sense pleasures, so that the soul forgets its true spiritual nature and destiny, "loses its true self." The remedy is to flee from the world of matter, the body, toward the world of pure spirit, beginning by detachment from the body and sense pleasures in this world.

Many Gnostic and heretical Christian sects carried on this tradition underground from early Christianity through the medieval period (*Albigensians*, etc.), and tried to infiltrate orthodox Christianity, which fought fiercely against them in the name of the goodness of all creation. Forms of Gnosticism keep springing up again in every age, e.g., just recently in our own day the new *Course in Miracles* religion, widely popular in New Age circles and admittedly Gnostic in its roots, which holds that the whole material world is not evil, but an illusory dream of escape from God, that God himself knows nothing about. Sin itself is part of the dream. True wisdom is to wake up from the dream! Cf. the book I co-authored with its main theologian, Kenneth Wapnick, *A Dialogue between A Course in Miracles and Christianity* (Roscoe, N.Y.: Foundation for A Course in Miracles, 1995) on why this religion is incompatible with traditional Christianity.

3. *Evil is merely the metaphysical status of all finite beings as imperfect,* lacking some perfection possessed by God. This may appear to us as evil from our limited point of view, but is really only the necessary metaphysical status of any created, finite world. Defended by *Leibniz,* with his famous "metaphysical optimism," according to which he tried to demonstrate that this is the best of all possible worlds, since God as infinitely wise, able to make the infinite calculus of all possibilities, could not create anything less than the best possible.

4. Akin to this is the view of *Spinoza* and most other strict pantheists: *evil is a subjective illusion,* due merely to our incomplete finite view of the universe from a limited human perspective. If seen from the higher total viewpoint of God himself, everything in the universe is merely a finite mode of the one infinite Substance; hence all is really good, fitting into a total pattern of ontological goodness. True wisdom is to wake up to this higher point of view, where evil melts away like a mist dissipated by the rising sun. Also held in some form by various

oriental monisms, such as *Hindu Advaita* (Non-dualistic) *Vedanta*. Evil is only apparent, an illusion of our limited minds under the "veil of ignorance." Once we rise to enlightenment, the realization of the Brahman as "One without a second," it dissolves like a mist. Thus the contemporary Hindu yogi who, asked "If all is Brahman, how do you explain all the misery and sufferings in that poor village in the valley below you?", replied with a beatific smile, "What sufferings?" Behind the veil of ignorance, Maya, he saw God pervading all. While still blinded by Maya, there is a problem, with no solution; once enlightened, the problem disappears and cannot even be formulated!

5. *Many contemporary philosophers,* including Christians, who do not agree with the tradition of Augustine and Thomas. It is naively unrealistic and optimistic to hold that all cases of evil are merely negations, privations. At least acts of violence and especially deliberate hatred and inflicting evil on others are positive acts, hence must be called real. Thus John Crosby and the von Hildebrand-Liechenstein School of Values, and others.

Conclusion. The problem is important and not easy to solve.

SOLUTION: EVIL IS A PRIVATION OF A DUE GOOD

This solution was first worked out by *St. Augustine,* after freeing himself from the Manichaeans, refined by *St. Thomas,* and held by most traditional Christian thinkers since. It unfolds in two steps:

Step 1. Evil cannot be a positive being or mode of being. Any time we recognize a case of evil and try to identify just in what this evil consists, why we call something evil, we discover that it is impossible to locate it until we come to some negative or not-being element. As long as we stick to the purely positive properties of any being we cannot identify evil there yet. Thus a disease, say TB, is evil only because it deprives someone else of the positive property of health; it makes someone not-healthy. The TB germs in themselves are perfectly healthy, doing fine for themselves; they are not evil in their own being, but are called so only because they are the cause of the absence of health in human lungs. Blindness is evil because it deprives us of the positive good of vision that we would normally have; it is a not-seeing where there should be seeing. Death is deprivation of life, hatred is wishing evil to someone else, the opposite of love, etc. The core of evil is never located until we find some absence, some deprivation, some not-being that should be there. Until we hit this negative core, there is no reason to call anything "evil." Note that we attribute evil by a kind of extrinsic denomination to positive beings that bring about evil results; but the evil itself properly resides only where the negation, the deprivation resides. Thus evil must exist formally as such only in this non-being, this deprivation. The causes of evil are not evil in themselves, in their own positive being.

We could also argue the same point a priori, from our previous conclusion that all being as such must be good, since it is some degree of participation in the basic root of all perfection, the act of existence itself, and hence ultimately caused by God as a participation in his own infinite goodness; and God could not create something intrinsically evil in its very being.

Conclusion: Evil is not a positive being in itself but is rooted in some form of negation, non-being.

Step 2. Evil cannot consist simply in a negation, an absence, by itself. This is impossible, for then every finite being that lacks some perfection in some order, since it is not God, would have to be declared evil. But this is not what we mean by calling something evil. We do not call a tree evil because it cannot see; but we do in the case of a dog or a human being. Hence evil must be that special kind of negation that we call a privation, i.e., the absence of some good or aspect of being that should be there, according to the nature of this thing or this act. Thus evil is the deprivation of some good that should be there. It is precisely the gap between what is and what ought to be (for whatever good reason) in a given case. It is a "hole" in being, so to speak, essentially relational in nature, and can only be recognized by making a comparison between what is in fact here and what should be there, so that the gap appears between the *is* and the *ought to be*. Until that shows up, there is no reason to judge anything evil.

It follows that evil must always reside in some positive being. It is a lack in something of something else. Pure evil would thus be a contradiction: if there is no positive being present which lacks something, there is no evil either. Pure lack by itself is a lack for no one, hence no lack at all. Evil is essentially a parasite on positive being. Hence even the Devil, if there is one, is ontologically good in his being as intelligent spirit, but morally evil in the distortion of his moral attitudes and actions.

Conclusion of whole argument: Evil is the privation in some being of a good that should be there, or, more briefly: Evil is the privation of a due good.

Value of this solution.   Although it may seem paradoxical at first to affirm that evil is not a real being, but only a privation residing in a good being, this solution of the problem seems to me the most reasonable of all those proposed, in fact the only really intelligible one. It is the only one that does full justice to the essentially negative and relational character of evil and yet keeps the balance between these two truths: (1) evil is not a real being in itself, no real beings as such are evil; and yet (2) it is definitely true that many real situations contain evil within them, so for good reason can be called evil in their whole relational context. Let us look at one key objection.

Objection.   The above analysis may work fairly well for many evils, but not for all. Two principal cases resist reduction to evil as a privation only, not a positive being or action: these are pain (physical pain) especially when it is incurable and can no longer serve any useful purpose; and acts of hatred and willful harm or destruction of others.

1) *Pain.* This clearly seems to have a positive being to it, a positive feeling I clearly perceive and forces itself upon me, and is through and through unpleasant; I perceive it not merely as the absence of pleasure but as a positive unwelcome presence that intrudes itself upon my attention.

Response.   The feeling of pain is indeed a positive presence. But as such its nature and purpose is to be a positive messenger service to notify us that something is wrong somewhere in our organism and something should be done about it urgently, depending on its intensity. Without it, with only pleasant sensations, we would be in very serious trouble, since without it we would have no incentive to do anything about a malfunctioning in our bodies until it was too late—we lost an arm, died, etc. This messenger service must manifest itself as unpleasant if it is to fulfill its job of warning and spur us to action. Hence it is doubtful that it should be called an evil at all. Would we really want it not to be there? A very small number of people who lack pain sensitivity are well known to the medical profession, and their lives are quite dangerous and difficult to manage, since they lack a warning system to tell them something is going wrong (they are constantly getting burned without knowing it, etc.). It is true that from the limited viewpoint of pleasure we don't like it, but from the higher point of view of reason we should welcome it as something that should be there for our overall good. It is a positive mixed with a negative, for a higher positive result. Useless pain does seem at first to be a pure evil, serving no useful purpose. But this is an inevitable side-effect of an essentially good function.

Would we want to suppress an indispensable messenger service—which must work automatically if it is to be effective—just because the messages are unpleasant and sometimes nothing can be done about them? Pain is indeed a difficulty against our analysis, but it seems to be more accurately analyzed as a positive-negative mix than an evil, since it is something that should be here, is better to be there than not, in a healthy material organism.

2) *Hatred*. This means to deliberately will evil to somebody, the opposite of love. Although the evil willed may well be a privation, still the act of willing this evil seems clearly to be a positive act, filled often with energy and intensity. That the act of hating itself is only a privation, a lack, especially when it goes on to act positively to bring about harm to the other, seems hard to believe.

Response.   This is indeed not an easy objection to answer. There seems to be a kernel of truth in it. Two remarks: First, the core of the willing is to will a negation of being, a privation. Hence the intention that is the soul of the act is negative. What about the act itself, especially as it acts to carry out the willed harm to someone? The answer, I think, lies in this: The flaw in the objection consists in understanding all privation as merely static, the absence of some ontological perfection that should be there, like blindness = the absence of sight. What we are dealing with here is privation in the dynamic order of action itself. The privation is not *of action* itself, in the deployment of some physical or psychic energy and physical movement, so that there is no action. The physical or psychic action is unleashed and to that extent is something positive taken in abstraction from the rest of the action. But the action as a whole is vitiated by the privation within the act itself of a goal and intention appropriate to the nature of a deliberate, free human act. It is not that there is no action, but it is a fundamentally disordered action, torn loose from the good, positive goal and intention that should belong to it, tending toward disorder and chaos, toward destruction of the proper good order of human living in the world. And since in the order of free conscious action it is the goal and intention that determine the nature of the act as morally good or bad, and to try to separate the physical action alone from its indwelling goal and intention is an artificial abstraction from its full reality, the act as a whole then becomes evil precisely and only because it is vitiated by the privation of the kind of goal and intention that should be there in a well-ordered, free human act. The key to answering the objection, therefore, lies not in denying that there is an element of positive action, of deploying of psychic and physical energy in an act of hatred, but in seeing that the action is rotten at its core because of the privation of a properly human goal and intention within a positive act. In a word, a morally evil act is a good thing run amok in its disordered expression. It is a privation not *of* action, but *in* a positive action.

II. Kinds of Evil

Physical evil = A privation of some good due to a being or its action in the ontological order of its actual existence compared to what its nature is naturally ordered to be, e.g., blindness in an animal or a human being; injuries produced by an accident.

Moral evil = A privation of some good due in an action produced by some free responsible moral agent, compared to the moral norm of good and bad moral actions. This privation in the moral order is due principally to a disordered or evil goal and intention, e.g., physical injuries (physical evil) inflicted on another out of hatred, contempt, etc.). Note that a morally evil action can produce a physical evil as a result.

III. What Is the Cause of Evil?

There is a special problem here. A cause, as we have seen earlier, is something that makes another being to *be*, in whole or in part. But if evil is not a real being but a privation of some due good, how can it be the real effect of a cause? Strictly speaking, it cannot, although we speak this way loosely for brevity. Evil as a privation cannot be the direct and immediate effect of a cause. It must therefore be a negative by-product or "side-effect" accompanying a causal process that directly produces some positive effect, but in so doing excludes from being some higher good that should be there. It is not what is produced that is evil in itself; the act becomes evil because it excludes from being some higher good that belongs there instead of this lower one. This evil result can derive from one of two sources:

1) Evil can result from a defect in the power of the agent or some defect in the material the agent has to work on, so that the effect produced lacks the full perfection it should naturally have, e.g., a deformed

baby, because the mother is starving or drug addicted, or a defective chair because the carpenter used a half-rotten piece of wood.

2) Evil can result from the fact that the cause, in producing one positive effect or good, thereby excludes from being some other higher good that should be present. Thus if I continue to recline at the edge of a pool enjoying my glass of beer, while someone is drowning and yelling for help, which I could easily give, I am pursuing one modest good, drinking the beer, but by so doing I exclude the higher good of saving a human life—and an evil results. If this is done knowingly and freely, it becomes a moral evil, as well as a physical evil resulting. In a word, in whatever we do, we do some positive good; we cannot properly do evil; but in doing this good rather than that, we can exclude a higher good that should be there, and from this evil results, the privation of some due good in this situation. Thus moral evil always consists in saying "No" to some good that should be allowed or helped to be, instead of saying "Yes" as we should have.

IV. GOD AND EVIL

Problem.   This is one of the most difficult problems that a philosophy of God must face, and it is one of the most persuasive reasons cited by many either for why they became atheists or why they remain so. The classic formulation of the problem was proposed long ago by *David Hume* and has been repeated ever since: "God by nature must be both omnipotent and all-good (all-loving). Now if God is omnipotent, he *could* prevent all evil. And if he is all-good, he *would* do so, since it is the characteristic of a good person to prevent evil wherever possible. But in fact he does not prevent all evil, even though he could, but allows a vast amount of it, both physical and moral, as is evident in the world around us. Therefore, it follows that God is either not omnipotent or not all-good. In either case such a being could not be God. Hence there is no God" (at least in any traditional sense, although this would not exclude a finite God, who does his best but has limited power to prevent evil—a doctrine which William James, the Pragmatist, seems to have held, along with a few others, including some contemporary Jewish thinkers.).

General response.   There is a fundamental flaw in the form of this argument as an argument. The alternatives are incomplete. It is not the case that a morally good and wise person is bound to prevent any evil wherever it is possible to do so. There is another condition not mentioned, i.e., unless a greater good can be achieved by allowing this lesser evil, which could not otherwise be achieved. For example, it is well known that a wise parent can allow his children to suffer small hurts and failures in order to train them to learn responsible judgment on their own. Overprotectiveness, not allowing them to take any chances lest they get hurt, can produce far worse results in character development. Also, God could not endow us with the very lofty gift of intelligent freedom and allow us to use it unless he were willing to take the chance that we would misuse it and at least sometimes choose evil over good. It follows that an all-good person could reasonably allow some evil in order that a higher good could result therefrom that would not otherwise be possible.

Since this possibility must be left open, the burden of proof now falls on the objector to show clearly that there is no higher good possible that God can draw out of permitting this evil, even granting the possibility of a next life in which all these sufferings could be finally healed and an eternal reward won far out of proportion to the evils suffered in his life. But it is clear that with our extremely limited range of knowledge, especially of the future, we humans cannot possibly have all the evidence needed to settle such a question with any certainty or even probability and make a cogent case against God. God's positive reasons for allowing precisely the evil that he does allow remain for the most part a mystery hidden from us in this life, though Christian revelation does contain the promise that at the Last Judgment the full meaning and intelligibility of all human and world history will be finally unveiled for us. But the fact that the existence of evil remains a mystery for us in this life in no way entails that any valid objection can be drawn from this against the existence of a wise and good and omnipotent God, since any adequate evidence to do so is beyond our reach. It is very important for the theist to understand the faulty logical status and radical weakness of all such arguments and not let himself be involved in futile and unnecessary attempts to take the burden of proof on himself to defend God by proposing positive explanations of evil from our limited human viewpoint. The burden of proof is not on the theist, but on the non-theist.

Still, I think the philosopher can and should go as far as he can in proposing some general reasons why it is reasonable for God to allow both physical and moral evil in our world. I propose the following:

Physical evil. In this we include all privations of ontological good brought about by nature without the direct intervention of human free will, i.e., not resulting from moral evil: diseases, injuries, accidents, etc. God does not just allow these as part of the working out of natural laws, but is indirectly responsible for them as the initial cause of these laws of nature. Let us grant that God has decided freely to create a material universe that is ordered to develop according to an evolutionary pattern over time, and with embodied spirits like ourselves included, with other living things, among its inhabitants, called by God to live out this chapter of our lives and strive for our fullest possible human development precisely in such a world, under its conditions and great fixed natural laws. Such a world is not the only good one possible, but it is certainly one possible good one, with many unique values of its own, and God certainly has a right to try out this remarkable experiment.

Given such a world of evolving living organisms like our own, the great underlying natural laws that govern its dynamic operation must remain stable; otherwise, there is no way such living organisms could learn from experience if there is no chance of their getting hurt from anything they do in violation of such laws. For God to protect them and us from all physical evil would require constant miraculous intervention to suspend these laws, in which case they would not be reliable enough to learn about them from repeated experience, nor would we have any incentive to do so. But given such necessarily stable laws, it is inevitable that developing living organisms with their limited knowledge and their own spontaneity of action will run afoul of such laws inadvertently, at least occasionally, and so suffer physical injury. God wants us to learn how to live safely in such a world on our own initiative and change it where necessary and possible by our own creativity. This is the kind of being he created us to be, to learn how to live in such a world, to become masters and stewards of it under God. And given the promise of an eternal life after, beyond the reach of pain and suffering, of all physical evil—which the atheist cannot rule out—the unequal opportunities of this life can easily be compensated for in the next.

But, the objector might insist, would it not be even better to make a world wherein no physical evil were possible? But would this really be better in the long run? We would never be challenged to learn from experience, since we would never get hurt no matter what we did, and, worst of all, with no challenge most of our natural virtues would disappear since not needed: there would be no fortitude, courage, disciplined temperance, and many other virtues, since we could not get hurt by lacking them. We would remain like simple, spoiled children with no challenge to character development, in a word, quite unlike the human beings we know and admire today. Do not we all recognize from our shared human experience that no human reaches his or her full maturity of wisdom and moral excellence without the purification of some significant suffering? Are we so sure this new world of yours would really be a better one than what we have now, and not be in fact significantly worse?

But why not at least a world with significantly less physical evil, say crippling or lethal diseases? Would not that be easy and better for God to do? But maybe he has already done that by protecting us from a host of horrendous possible diseases that would make our world look like a picnic! And watch out! Once you start demanding that God remove such and such an evil ("If God can prevent an evil, he must") then there is no consistent way of limiting such demands until all physical evils are removed. We have no idea what such a world would really be like, nor what far more undesirable and now unforeseeable consequences might follow. Certainly nothing like the human beings we now know could exist—a strange objection that would eliminate the existence of the objector himself! Trying to reconstruct a better world than God planned with his infinite wisdom, by our own limited human wisdom, is an extremely dubious and perilous enterprise, with no guarantee at all of success rather than a giant cosmic flop!

Conclusion.   Why does not God prevent evils coming from chance disasters? May it not be precisely because it is our vocation as embodied spirits to work out our destiny in a world where chance is at work? To intervene constantly to block it would be to radically change, to annul, the basic nature of the world as a theater for human development: our world is a polarity of chance and order in vital tension. God is committed to help us meet the challenges of chance; we should not ask him to abolish the very experiment itself! God planned it to be both a deeply challenging and a profoundly rewarding one.

Moral evil.   In the case of moral evil, which is rooted in the disordered willing of a free created person, God is not the cause of moral evil, not responsible for it. God has committed himself, in creating us as dynamic agents, to cooperate with us in being and acting as we perform all our positive actions. But he does not cooperate with us in saying the "No" to the higher good that should be here, in which consists precisely the root of moral evil. This is not a positive action but a negation, and we alone are responsible for it. God cooperates with us in all our "Yes's," not in all our "No's." So God is not to be blamed for the moral evil in the universe, widespread as it is, nor for the many physical evils inflicted on human beings, other living things, and the environment itself resulting from these morally evil choices and actions. But he does allow such evil moral actions to occur, since theoretically he could prevent them by physically blocking the created agent from carrying out its evil intentions. This allowance by God of moral evil now becomes a problem for believers to understand and an objection raised by non-believers in God. Why does God allow so much moral evil, with its harmful consequences, to exist in the world? Since he could block it if he wished, why does he not do so if he is a good and loving God? For example, why did he allow Hitler and the Holocaust?

The full answer as regards particular cases is hidden from us in this life. But a general answer can be given. One of the highest perfections God has decided to give to humans and other created intelligent beings is the gift of freedom, intelligent free self-governance of one's life, the necessary root of our ability to love freely other persons and God. But to take seriously this gift he has given us and allow us to exercise it freely, God must take the chance of allowing us to make evil choices as well as good ones, without determining us from without ahead of time to make only morally good ones. Hence the achievement of this great good of freedom, and the freely given love that can proceed only from it, requires accepting the risk that comes with it of allowing the possibility of our misusing this power by deliberate evil choices. Apparently God esteems this gift of freedom and the freely given love that it makes possible as so precious a value that he is willing to take the chance. It is indeed a game of high stakes. But if God in his infinite wisdom and love has judged it to be well worth playing, where the odds are stacked on our side—we cannot lose by chance or ignorance but only by our own fault and self-induced blindness—and where the rewards of following God's plan are transcendently magnificent, who are we to object to playing?

But, the objector insists, could not God, and therefore should he not, at least prevent some of the most harmful evil moral choices, at least from execution, since the evil flowing from them seems to us to far outweigh any conceivable good that could be brought out of them? Two points in response: (1) It may well be that God has intervened directly to protect us from certain horrendous crimes that could have ended the whole human experiment prematurely, or other such evils—we have no way of knowing that he has not, and is not so doing all through our history; our ignorance cannot be a basis for blaming God for what he is already doing. (2) Once you put an obligation on God to prevent certain moral evils, there is no consistent way of limiting this obligation and not demanding that he intervene to block all moral evils with harmful effects. But this would require that he be constantly intervening all over the world and forcibly blocking people from doing what they want to do, no matter how stubbornly they are determined to follow through their evil intentions. It would follow that we would have no incentive for taking the responsibility, personally and as a human race committed to living together, to learn how to cope with these problems creatively on our own responsibility for the common public good. Instead, we would sit back passively and expect God to intervene and pull the fat out of the fire for us constantly, with no responsible effort on our part. It seems that God for good reasons does not want that to happen, but wants us to grow up in moral and social-political wisdom to learn how to do the job ourselves, for the most part, with all the inner help we need in good inspirations, grace, etc., to guide us in our human vocation. As one wise Jewish Rabbi has put it, "It seems that God, for his own good reasons, has taken a vow of non-violence in dealing with humanity." Perhaps only that way can we learn what it really means to be human, the heights and depths we can ascend and descend to, and hence what it takes to truly redeem us.

Furthermore, how can we exclude that God, in his infinite wisdom and tender love for us, knows just how, in the next life, to heal all the traumas and wounds suffered by us in this life, to comfort us to the very roots of our being far better than we know how to, and even heal and transform creatively the very memories of such sufferings?

Conclusion.   It is not up to the theist to provide the exact reason why God permits a particular moral evil, but only to show that no cogent objection can be made forbidding him to act thus, and that there are positive reasons for the wisdom of his plan.

Cf. John Hick, ed., *Evil and the God of Love* (New York: Macmillan, 1964); Bruce Reichenbach, *Evil and a Good God* (New York: Fordham Univ. Press, 1982); D. Cress, "A Defense of Augustine's Privation Account of Evil,)*Augustinian Studies* 20 (1989), 109–28; O. G. Ramberan, "God, Evil, and the Idea of a Perfect World," *Mod. Schoolman* 53 (1975–76), 379–92.

QUESTIONS FOR REVIEW AND DISCUSSION

1. What are the data about evil in our world that challenge the philosopher? What is the meaning (preliminary) of "evil"?

2. What are the main metaphysical problems resulting that we must face?

Problem I: Nature and Status in Being of Evil

3. Principal opinions: (a) Evil is something positive in being. (b) Matter is the source of evil. (c) Evil is merely the finitude or limitation in created beings. (d) Evil is merely a subjective illusion. (e) Contemporary philosophers. Explain each.

4. Solution: Steps 1 and 2.

5. Objections: How can pain and acts of hatred be merely privations?

6. What are the two main divisions of evil?

7. What is the Cause of Evil? Problem? Solution?

Problem II: God and Evil

8. What precisely is the problem of their compatibility?

9. What is the general response?

10. How does this apply to physical evil?

11. To moral evil?

CHAPTER EIGHTEEN

The Transcendental Properties of Being

The Many Faces of Being

Question. In classical metaphysics, from the high Middle Ages down through the whole Scholastic tradition, it has been customary to ask the question, "What are the transcendental properties of being, that can be predicated of every single real being, from the tiniest material particle all the way up to God"? The result was called "Treatise on the Transcendentals." We are now in a position to answer this question adequately. Throughout the course of our inquiry into the full intelligibility of being, we have uncovered these attributes one after the other, together with the reason why each must apply to every real being: every being is *one, active, true* (intelligible), and finally *good,* after establishing the existence of God as ultimate Source of all being. We can now pull them all together, and see how, though each reveals a distinct perspective on the meaning of being, they are complementary to each other, and taken together reveal the full richness of being, like so many facets of the same diamond, turned different ways. We shall also show why there are good reasons for adding, with the later St. Thomas, another transcendental property, *beauty,* to the traditional list. This is still a disputed point among Thomists.

I. What Is a Transcendental Property of Being?

Meaning. *A transcendental property of being* = a positive attribute that can be predicated of every real being, so that it is convertible with being itself; i.e., "Every being is good" can be converted to "Every good is being in some way," etc. Such a property is called "transcendental" (from the Latin *trans-cendere* = to leap over) because it leaps over all barriers between different kinds and levels or modes of being, in contradistinction to other, more limited concepts that apply only to certain beings or kinds of beings: intelligent, material, etc.

Relation to being. Such concepts signify properties that are *identical* in the real order with the being of which they are predicated, that is, the being itself, not something added on to it from the outside that is not itself being. But each one makes explicit some aspect of being that is not made explicit by the term "being." The concepts themselves are distinct from each other in what they explicitly affirm about being, but they refer to the identical reality as it exists in itself, grounding these different perspectives on it from the point of view of our limited minds that cannot say all at once all that can and needs to be said about any real being.

This is an important point to remember, since some non-Thomistic traditions understand truth, goodness, and beauty to be independent realms somehow above or apart from the order of real existence, which have to be infused into reality from without—e.g., the *Platonic Demiurge,* or the human mind for *Kant,* which imposes its a priori forms of truth, goodness, and beauty on the content of sense perception. For many empiricists, too, like *Hume,* the real of itself is sheer brute fact, value-free—the radical split between being and value, the *is* and the *ought*—so that we have to import truth, value, goodness, beauty into the real by our own subjective attitude. For Aquinas, however, it is *the real itself* that is one, true, good, and beautiful, but seen according to different perspectives and relations. Hume, and especially Kant, initiate the split between being and the other transcendentals, since unity, truth, goodness, and beauty are all projected onto reality from without by our minds. The objectivity of all four of these now becomes suspect or ambiguous once they have lost their grounding in being itself.

II. THE NUMBER OF TRANSCENDENTAL PROPERTIES

The doctrine of Transcendental properties developed piecemeal in Western thought. *Plato and Neoplatonism* introduced *unity* and *goodness* as attributes of every reality, descending by participation from the supreme One-Good. But they did not include *being* itself in the list, because "being" for them signified a limited intelligible form as part of the whole system of intelligible essences defined by relation to each other. But the ultimate One and Good was above this whole realm of determinate intelligible essences or forms, hence "beyond being," as they put it (though not beyond reality in the broadest sense), and even beyond intelligibility itself in the ordinary sense of clear rational concepts; the One and Good is known only by a mystical ecstasy of the soul beyond reason. Beauty is sometimes identified with the supreme Good, sometimes considered as on a lower level, because of the multiplicity implied in the notion of proportion, deemed essential to beauty.

For Aristotle, *unity* and *truth* were certainly transcendental properties of all being, but he is not that clear about goodness and beauty. In the 12–13th centuries the basic trio appeared: being is *one, true,* and *good;* and this remained the classic formulation from then on. But these tended to be understood mostly as absolute terms, at least goodness— goodness in itself—not in relational terms. *Beauty* was not admitted among the transcendentals, either because the pure simplicity of God was beyond all proportion and harmony, which were judged inseparable from beauty; or because beauty was identified as simply a mode of the good, with no distinct status of its own.

St. Thomas took over this position but with an original twist of his own. He was the principal one to introduce the notion of relation as intrinsic to the distinction in meaning between the transcendentals, at least for truth, goodness, and beauty. Being is true (= intelligible) with relation to all spiritual intelligences—the connatural affinity of mind and being; being is good with relation to all spiritual wills—the connatural affinity of will and being; being is beautiful with relation to both intellect and will at once—the connatural affinity of the whole spiritual soul, as a unity, with being: beauty is being insofar as its contemplation gives delight. At first St. Thomas, following the tradition, did not include beauty among the transcendentals but identified it with the good. But later, under the influence of the *Pseudo-Dionysius,* with his emphasis on the beauty of God that diffuses itself by participation among all creatures, he added it on as a distinct property. The question is still disputed among Thomists today. I have added *active* (self-expressive through action) to the list, making explicit what Thomas himself teaches quite explicitly, as we have seen, but never included in his official list, perhaps because not traditional.

III. Being as One

Cf. Chapter 4 for the full explanation of being and unity.

Meaning. *One* in its ontological (not numerical) meaning signifies: the intrinsic cohesion of a being by which it exists as a single undivided whole (whether with or without parts). *Technical definition: One =* that which is undivided in itself and divided from every other. It is so absolutely basic a property that it is very difficult to define in terms other than itself; hence the negative definition by contrast with what it is not: it is *not* divided in itself. How do we come to recognize its meaning? St. Thomas says it is by a process of comparison with other beings, thus: "A is a being. B is a being. But A is not B. Hence A is undivided in itself but divided from every other being." It stands on its own distinctly from every other being, even though it may be related to others. This is true even of God.

Why every being must be one. If a real being lacked this inner cohesion of all its parts to form an undivided whole, there would be no way to distinguish *this* being from a collection of *these* being*s,* and it would be impossible to block an endless regress of fragmentation into a dust of pure multiplicity, with no intelligible "this" or "it" remaining at all.

Analogy of Unity. Since unity is co-extensive with being, it is just as analogous in its meaning as being itself. Since the core of every being is its act of existence, which is not a static form but an act of self-presenting and an inner energy that expresses itself in activity, unity itself as identical with being must also be a *dynamic act.* In a word, it is the very dynamic inner act of *cohering,* the energy by which it actively coheres within itself, holds itself together as a unified whole, according to the mode of each essence's participation in the power of existence. This illuminates from within what it really means to be, since we usually tend to think of unity as a static state, not as an act of unifying. The unity of a real being is thus an achievement, not a static given!

Intrinsic unity. Unity as a property of real being = intrinsic unity as opposed to merely extrinsic unity, i.e., it signifies that a being has a single act of existence manifested by a single center of unified action, whereas an extrinsic unity is merely a collection of several real beings, joined together by relations of order, but with no unified center of action of the whole. To be is to cohere and act as a unit.

IV. Being as Active

Active is not on any of the traditional lists of transcendentals, but St. Thomas constantly speaks of it as though it were. So I have made it explicit here on my own as part of my "creative retrieval" of St. Thomas. It plays a central role in his whole metaphysics and deserves to be recognized explicitly as such. Chapter II gives a fuller development of the point.

Justification. As explained in Chapter II, St. Thomas says that every being, insofar as it actually exists, has a natural tendency to communicate itself, to pour over into self-manifesting, self-revealing action, expressing its own nature by its characteristic activities. "Each and every thing," he says, "shows forth that it exists for the sake of its operation; indeed operation is the ultimate perfection of each thing" (*Sum. c. Gent.*, III, 113). And there is the wonderfully explicit text: "Each and every thing abounds in the power of acting just insofar as it exists in act" (*De Potentia*, q. 1, art. 2). But this is exactly equivalent, practically word for word, to the proposition, "Every being is active." Therefore, St. Thomas's own metaphysics of being as dynamic act is not given adequate expression unless we add on *active* to the list of transcendentals.

It follows that all real beings connect up with each other by action to form a single universe or interacting system of beings acting on and being acted on by each other—a community of real existents woven together by the bonds of action. If this were not a property of all real beings, then the ones not possessing it would be locked up in their own isolation, making no difference to any other being—in fact, could not be known by any other being, since beings are known through their actions—and hence might just as well not be. *To be*, for St. Thomas, implies to be actively present to other real beings.

Cf. W. N. Clarke, "Action as the Self-Manifestation of Being: A Central Theme in the Thought of St. Thomas," in *Explorations in Metaphysics* (Notre Dame: Univ. of Notre Dame Press, 1994), ch. 3.

V. Being as True = Intelligible

Meaning. By this is meant the *ontological truth* that is in things themselves as known or knowable in relation to all spiritual intelligences, in a word, the intrinsic intelligibility of all being, as ordered by its very nature to be understood by mind, just as it is the intrinsic nature of every mind to be oriented toward the knowledge of all being. See Chapter I for a fuller development of this point. This radical built-in complementarity and mutual affinity of mind and being lies at the very foundation of all St. Thomas's philosophy and theology, in fact, the whole cognitive life of human beings.

Truth in general = the conformity between mind and being. But this conformity can be rooted either *in mind* or *in being*. If located in the mind as being conformed in its own knowledge to the real being that it knows, this is *epistemological* truth, truth as found in the mind as related to the being known. That is the concern of *epistemology,* not ours here. But this conformity can be located in the being itself as related to its knowers, actual or potential. This is *ontological* truth: the truth of things themselves as related to intelligence. Ordinarily when we speak of "truth" we are referring to epistemological truth, i.e., whether we know being accurately or not. Ontological truth is more properly expressed as the intelligibility of being, i.e., being as intelligible. This refers to the inner aptitude of all being to be understood by all intellects.

Diverse relations of being to the divine and human minds. The relation of created beings to the divine mind is the inverse of their relation to human minds. Every created being is conformed to the divine creative idea according to which God actively created it and sustains it in being continually. Its whole being is true to God's creative knowledge of it. As St. Thomas puts it, it is the divine mind that "measures" the being of creatures. Thus all beings are actually known by God's mind.

With relation to human minds, however, created beings are not conformed to, "measured" by our human minds, since we did not create them but have to receive knowledge of them from created beings themselves as they act on us, actively manifesting their being to us. Rather, our minds are conformed to them, "measured" by them. Thus the divine mind is the measure of all other beings; our minds are measured by real beings; in between are created beings themselves: measured, in relation to the divine mind; measuring, in relation to human minds. Our created minds are measures only of *artifacts,* things we have made, insofar as they are the result of our active making. Thus a well-made house conforms (more or less perfectly) to the plan conceived by its architect, expressed in his blueprints. But note that the ontological truth of real beings with respect to our minds does not mean that they are all actually known by all human minds, as by God's mind, but only knowable = intrinsically ordered, *apt de jure,* to be known by any human mind (or created intelligence). Hence the attribute *true,* as applied to all real beings in relation to us, means intrinsically intelligible.

Note that this fundamental relation of our minds to real beings as measured by them, open to receive from them and be conformed to their being, is the ground of all realism, or objective truth, of human knowing. Note how *Kant's* theory of human knowing runs directly contrary to this: for him it is not the real being of things that conforms our minds to them, makes our knowledge true; rather it is the human mind that is the master, imposes our own a priori forms of understanding on the not-yet-intelligible sense manifestations of things in order to render them intelligible—with the result that we cannot know real things as they are in themselves, but only as we can't help thinking them in ourselves. The receptive status of our minds with respect to real beings is the essential underpinning of the whole realistic philosophy of Aquinas, or of any authentic realism, i.e., that *our minds are true to the being of real things*—not perfectly or exhaustively, but adequately for our human needs in this life.

Having reached the philosophical discovery of God as Ultimate Source of all being, we are now in a position to understand St. Thomas's beautiful explanation of just why all beings are in themselves intelligible through and through, but yet are not fully and exhaustively intelligible to us. They are intelligible through and through in themselves, because they have been thought-created by an Infinite *Mind.* They are not fully intelligible to our human minds, cannot be exhaustively understood by us, because they are thought-created by an *Infinite* Mind. And as such, as images of an Infinite Original, they cannot be fully understood as images without knowing fully also the original which they are imperfectly imaging; but it is impossible for our limited human minds to know exhaustively the infinite fullness of being that is their Source. Hence all created beings conceal deep within them a certain inexhaustible depth of intelligibility that exceeds the grasp of our concepts. Hence they always remain for us in this life somehow touched with mystery, as *known-unknown.* As Einstein put it insightfully, "Whatever is real is mysterious; whatever is not mysterious has nothing to do with reality."

For a rich development of these ideas see Josef Pieper, "The Negative Element in St. Thomas," in *The Silence of St. Thomas* (New York: Pantheon, 1957), ch. II.

VI. Being as Good

Meaning,   *Ontological good* = that which is intrinsically valuable, i.e., apt to be desired, loved, enjoyed, appreciated in some way by some appetite (some dynamism that tends toward something). *Good* as a transcendental property of being = being as intrinsically related by its very nature as real being to some appetite that is by nature reciprocally related to all being. This is every spiritual will, since this is by nature oriented toward the whole unlimited horizon of being as good—just as every spiritual intellect is by nature oriented toward all being as knowable, intelligible. Cf. chapter 17 for a fuller treatment.

This human will can be related toward all being as good either because (1) this good is desirable, to be possessed by the desiring being as somehow perfective of it; or (2) it is apt to be loved, appreciated, esteemed, for its own sake, as a real being participating to some degree in the basic perfection of actual existence, which itself is ultimately a participation in God's own infinite perfection as pure unlimited fullness of existence and hence is an authentic, though limited, image of God, and for that very reason worthy of our appreciation and esteem as good in itself. Since every created intellect is made for the knowledge of all being as the fulfillment of its nature, it follows that to know any and all real beings, even without actual possession of them, is good for it. So too it is a fulfillment of the will to appreciate and affirm the intrinsic goodness of all beings—including God—hence *good* for it to do so. In so doing the human being comes closer and closer to realizing its radical potential for being an image of God who both knows and loves all real beings precisely according to their intrinsic value and place in the total order and harmony of the universe.

Note that, just as the intrinsic intelligibility of all being for every human intelligence is the basic ground of the objectivity of truth for us, so, too, the intrinsic value of all real beings for the human will is the basic foundation for the objectivity of goodness and value for us, so that the latter is not just a subjective imposition on reality from our side only. The loving power of our will is a response to the lovableness of beings themselves; God's love is the *cause* of their lovableness.

But note again that just as all real beings are actually known by the divine intellect, but only potentially by ours, i.e., all are apt to be understood by us, but only some are actually known by human minds, so too all beings are actually loved by the divine will, but only potentially so by our wills. All are *apt* to be loved, valued by us; not all are *actually* so.

VII. BEING AS BEAUTIFUL

Controversy. *Beauty* was not included in the traditional list of the transcendentals handed down to St. Thomas. The reason was that since it was commonly agreed from the Greeks that *proportion* was one of the essential ingredients of beauty, it was taken for granted that this could apply only to material things and hence not to God or purely spiritual beings. Thus St. Thomas never lists it when commenting on the official list. But in his later writings, under the powerful influence of the Pseudo-Dionysius, *On the Divine Names,* who speaks so eloquently of the beauty of God, Thomas begins to speak often of beauty as a transcendental property of all being.

The point is still controversial today. Most, I think, are now willing to include it among the transcendentals, but a fair number still hold out and claim it is merely a species of the good. I think there are very good reasons for following St. Thomas in his later works and including it, even applied to God.

Meaning. We are concerned here only with *ontological beauty,* the beauty belonging to real beings as such, not with *aesthetic* beauty, the beauty of works of art made by man.

Ontological beauty (according to St. Thomas) = that which, contemplated, gives delight (*id quod visum placet*). Note that "contemplated" (*visum* in Thomas's definition = seen, in the widest sense) indicates that which is known not by abstract concepts or reasoning but by direct intuitive perception of the thing in its unique existential singularity. Since in our present state of life we humans cannot directly intuit things outside ourselves by the intellect alone but must join with the senses (through the highest, integrating "cogitative sense"), which alone can directly intuit the individual existing singular thing, it follows that we humans cannot perceive beauty—it cannot shine out to us and give us delight—except as embodied in some sensory embodiment or symbol. Thus we can understand *that* God and spiritual things are beautiful in themselves, but we cannot with our natural knowledge in this life actually perceive and enjoy them as such, take delight in them, unless embodied in some way. (This applies to our natural way of knowing, not to a mystical, divinely infused mode of spiritual knowing. What about knowing the beauty of God, angels, in the next life?)

Relation of beauty to both intellect and will. The other relational transcendentals, truth and goodness, are each related to just one of the faculties: being as true to the intellect, being as good to the will. The uniqueness of beauty, which is one of the key arguments for including it as a distinct transcendental, is that it is related simultaneously to both intellect and will: that which gives delight to our wills precisely as intuitively contemplated by our cognitive faculties—not as possessed or physically united with us in its real being, as the good can be. It is the unique kind of delight that comes precisely from the disinterested contemplation of something in its existential wholeness, harmony, and "radiance." Understood thus, it has been called by many Thomists the synthesis of all the transcendentals, since all of them must be present in integration for beauty to appear. It is thus the full splendor of being in all its facets when related to the complementary world of spiritual intellects and wills, i.e., persons.

What are the defining characteristics of beauty? There has been considerable argument down the ages as to just what should be included. *Proportion* was long considered essential, but because it connotes some multiplicity of parts, it had to be dropped out when the notion was extended to God. The following have stuck as being more universally analogical in their spread:

1) *Unity:* extending from the pure simplicity of God to a certain integration, wholeness, completeness in composite beings: often called integrity (*integritas*).

2) *Harmony:* a certain apt fitting together (*consonantia*) of everything in the being to produce a kind of overall "harmony"—the analogy is drawn from music, the most spontaneously pleasing of all the arts to us humans, projected naturally into the spiritual world, e.g., the "choirs of angels"—which can be extended analogically even up to the perfect unity of God. This comes alive much more meaningfully when, enlightened by Christian revelation, we speak of God as Three Persons in One God. *Harmony* is of the essence here: the ultimate harmony between persons.

3) *Splendor or radiance (claritas):* A certain splendor or radiance that shines forth from the existing being to us, if we are attuned to receive it, deriving from its integrity, harmony, meaningfulness, etc., that somehow resonates deeply within us and elicits feelings of delight, awe, wonder, respect. Easy enough to recognize in the concrete experience, but very difficult to analyze conceptually! What is the deepest root of this mysterious "splendor" characteristic of the beautiful? *St. Augustine*, drawing from his metaphysics of form as the central metaphysical perfection spoke of it as "the splendor of form" (*splendor formae*) shining forth. *St. Thomas*, with his more profound metaphysics of existence (*esse*) as the ultimate root of all perfection (although he also refers to *splendor formae*) is able to deepen this into the splendor of existence shining forth through form in creatures; this becomes in God the unlimited splendor of pure existence beyond all form, pure light too dazzling for us to contemplate directly.

Thomas does not, I think, use these exact words, but he certainly could and equivalently does so when he often speaks of God as "*Pure Light*" (*ipsa Lux*) precisely because he is the pure fullness of existence, whereas creatures shine only with *reflected light* (they are "lit up," not pure "Light itself") precisely because they only participate in the light of existence from the Source: "Each and every thing is known by that which it is in act, and therefore the very actuality of a thing is like a light within it (*ipsa actualitas rei est quoddam lumen ipsius*)" (*Expositio in Librum De Causis*, lect. 6, n. 168); and "As much as a thing has of form and act, just so much does it have of light" (*Expos. in Timothy* 6:3, n. 268). This conjoining of existence with light is a very rich and seminal metaphor in St. Thomas, enabling him to join together the biblical description of God as Light ("God inhabits light inaccessible") with his own metaphysics of God as pure Subsistent Act of Existence. This conjoining of existence with light is also a peculiarly effective way of contrasting real being with non-being as light emerging out of darkness.

Centrality of splendor or radiance as signs of beauty. This seems to me the most profound and revelatory of all the three constituents mentioned above; it contains both the intrinsic aspect of a source of light plus the *relational dimension* of active shining forth or self-manifesting to any receptive spiritual intellect and will. It is also the one that applies most easily to God, though harmony can also be extended quite meaningfully, especially in view of God as Trinity of Persons. The "glory of God" is another way of describing the beauty of God.

Why should beauty be included among the transcendentals? 1) Every being, insofar as it exists in act, must have a certain inner coherence of unity and harmony—creatures through their intelligible forms— and shine forth with a certain splendor, radiance, light emanating from its act of existence, whose contemplation should give delight to any intellect and will apt and attuned to receiving it, simply because to know any real being, as a participation in being from God, is a good for any spiritual intellect, something to be approved of, appreciated, delighted in—not possessed—for its own goodness.

2) The argument of some, that beauty is merely a species of the good and so should not be made a separate property, is not cogent, since beauty is distinguished from all the others in that it signifies being as related to both intellect and will at once. And we all somehow intuitively recognize, it seems to me, that beauty is a unique and special dimension of our experience, irreducible to anything else we experience, and so it is appropriate for it to have its own unique rooting in being itself. It has a certain splendor of its own as the synthesis of all the transcendentals.

The fact that we humans cannot perceive all beings as beautiful is not due to any deficiency in being itself, but to the fact that we can have the intuitive contemplative experience of beauty only as embodied in some sensible expression, not through abstract, reasoning intelligence alone—in this life. One of the joys of the next life will be the liberation from this limitation and the opening to direct spiritual intuition of all beings—at least through sharing in the direct intuitive vision of God himself, who knows intuitively and delights in all his creatures, not to mention his own being. Then we too shall see not only how good, but how beautiful it is to *be* anything at all, and delight therein. That's what I am looking forward to!

Cf. *Transcendentals:* Josef Pieper, *The Truth of All Things,* reprinted in *Living the Truth* (San Francisco: Ignatius Press, 1989); Jan Aertsen, *Medieval Philosophy and the Transcendentals: The Case of Thomas Aquinas* (Leiden: Brill, 1996)—he does not include beauty on the list; Henri Pouillon, "Le premier traité des propriétés transcendentales," *Revue Néoscolastique* 42 (1939), 40–77.

Truth: Josef Pieper, *The Truth of All Things; The Silence of St. Thomas* (New York: Pantheon, 1957) ch. 2: The Negative Element in St. Thomas—very rich; creation as "the hidden key."

Goodness: Josef Pieper, *Reality and the Good,* reprinted in *Living the Truth* (San Francisco: Ignatius Press, 1989); Scott MacDonald, ed., *Being and Goodness: The Concept of the Good in Metaphysics and Philosophical Theology* (Ithaca, N.Y.: Cornell Univ. Press, 1990).

Beauty: Francis Kovach, "The Transcendentality of Beauty in Thomas Aquinas," in *Miscellanea Mediaevalia II* (Berlin: De Gruyter, 1963), 386–92; Jan Aertsen, "Beauty in the Middle Ages: A Forgotten

Transcendental," *Medieval Phil. and Theology* 1 (1991), 68–97; G. Grisez, "References to Beauty in St. Thomas," *Modern Schoolman* 29 (1951), 43–44; Frank Kunkel, "Beauty in Aquinas and Joyce," *Thomist* 12 (1949), 261–71; Emilio Brito, "La beauté de Dieu," *Revue Théologique de Louvain* 20 (1989), 141–61.

QUESTIONS FOR REVIEW AND DISCUSSION

1. What is the aim of this chapter?

2. What is the meaning of a "transcendental property of being"? Its relation to being?

3. How many such properties are there? Opinions: Neoplatonism? Aristotle? St. Thomas and the Scholastics?

4. Being as One. See Chapter 4; this is just a summary.

5. Being as Active. See Chapter 2; this is just a summary.

6. Being as True. What is the meaning of ontological truth vs. epistemological? Explain the diverse relations of truth to divine and human minds. What are the implications for understanding creatures and our knowledge of them?

7. Being as Good. See Chapter 16; this is just a summary.

8. Being as Beautiful. This is new. What is its status as transcendental in the tradition? What is the meaning of ontological beauty? What is its relation to both intellect and will? What are its defining characteristics? Should beauty be included in the Transcendentals?

CHAPTER NINETEEN

The Great Circle of Being and Our Place in It

The Universe as Meaningful Journey

The Universe as Journey.   Having outlined the basic metaphysical structure of the universe, the fundamental laws governing it, and its final unification as proceeding from one Ultimate Source of all real being, we
are now in a position to look back on the whole process and try to pull
it together in a single great synoptic vision of what this universe of ours
is all about. In this, our last chapter, we should like to do that by drawing
upon the resources of the imagination with the help of an ancient and
powerful archetypal image, that of the whole created universe as
journey.

I. STRUCTURE OF THE JOURNEY

Its two main phases are:
  1. The Journey of the Many (all finite beings), *projected outward
from the One,* their Infinite Source, by creation: the work of efficient
causality. This can be called the *Journey away from Home,* where creatures
actively unfold their diverse dynamic natures as finite participations
in the divine perfection and as centers of self-expressive and self-
communicating action and interaction with each other, thus forming a

universe (*uni-versum* in Latin = turned toward unity), that is, a system of many real beings joined together by their interaction to form the community of all existents—the ultimate of all communities. This part of the journey was called the *exitus* (journey out).

2. *The Journey of the Many back again towards reunion with the One,* their Source, drawn by this same Source through the pull of the Good built in to the very nature of every being through the mediation of final causality, which draws each being toward the fulfillment of its own nature, as far as it can, as toward its own good. But since each finite good is only a participation in and hence image of the infinite Divine Goodness, each one's search for the good is implicitly a search, St. Thomas says, for union with the ultimate fullness and Source of all goodness, which is God himself. This innate implicit longing of all creatures for union with the Good can be called the *Journey back Home,* back to where each came from in the first place. This part of the journey was called the *reditus* (journey back).

Thus God as the ultimate One now appears as both the *Alpha* and the *Omega,* the Beginning and the End, at once the Source and the Goal of the restless dynamism of all of nature, of all finite beings. As St. Augustine says of human beings, in whom the longing becomes conscious, "Our hearts are restless, O Lord, until they rest in You." And since the journey Home, back toward the Source again, can never be the same as the journey away from Home, the structure of the total journey was aptly imaged in the form of a *circle*—considered by the ancients as the most perfect of all figures, since its beginning joins its end. That is why the Journey of the Universe is called by St. Thomas "The Great Circle of Being": "In the emergence of creatures from their first source is revealed a kind of circular movement (*circulatio vel regiratio*), in which all things return, as to their end, back to the very place from which they had their origin in the first place" (*Expositio in Libros Sententiarum,* Book I, Dist. 14, q. 2, art. 2). St. Thomas actually uses the same structure of the emanation and return of all creatures from and to God as the basic organizing plan of his whole *Summa Theologiae,* his greatest work.

The image of the universe as journey, as the Great Circle of Being, is a very ancient one. Though rooted in older sources, Plotinus gives it explicit formulation as an image of the basic dynamism of his universe, the emanation of all things from the One-Good and their return thereto by the pull of the same ultimate Good, which pull actually holds them in existence for him. St. Thomas, with many medieval Christian thinkers (St. Bonaventure, etc.), adapts it to the Christian universe as emanating from God, not by a *necessary law of being*, as for Plotinus and the Neoplatonists, but by a gracious *free act* of loving self-communication by a personal God. But this basic image of the universe and all life, including human life, as a journey is a very old and very rich one, an archetypal image that shows up everywhere in cultures around the world, in their mythology, poetry, wisdom stories, art, philosophy, religion, etc.—and for very good reasons, since we all instinctively recognize the *journey* as the basic form of all human lives, a journey that can only be adequately described in a *story*. Thus in most religions throughout history first comes the story, only later come all the philosophical and theological reflections, commentaries, clarifications, explanations. Even in Christianity, first comes the Story, only afterwards the Creed. One of the favorite descriptions of the human being for St. Thomas and all medieval thinkers was *Homo Viator,* Man the Traveller.

Role of the Imagination in Philosophy.   It plays, in the great thinkers, an unobtrusive, behind-the-scenes, but still important and perhaps indispensable role. An image cannot be by itself the source and justification of a rational argument—it is always dangerous for a philosopher to think in images, or tie his thought too closely to images. But creative images can be a stimulus and pointer both toward significant problems and their solution; and especially, as in the case of the seminal image of the Universe as Journey, as the Great Circle of Being, a single pregnant image can sum up with striking vividness a whole philsophical investigation and its conclusions. Thus our long metaphysical search for the full intelligibility of our universe carried on through eighteen chapters of conceptual reasoning, can now be captured and concentrated in the single powerful image of the *Universe as Journey* and the *Great Circle of Being,* the *Journey away from Home* and the *Journey Back Home* again. Only an image, it seems, can hold together many distinct concepts and arguments in a single whole that resonates on many levels of our unique status in the hierarchy of being as embodied spirits.

II. The Place of the Human Person in this Journey

As we have seen, all creatures are drawn implicitly back toward union with the Infinite Good from which they originated, which is at once the

Alpha and the *Omega*. But we human beings play a unique role in this Great Circle of Being. Only beings endowed with spiritual intellects and wills, like ourselves, can actually achieve direct union with God, since they alone can self-consciously know and freely choose to love God. But the rest of the vast material universe below the human is incapable, by its very nature, of attaining union with God, of completing its journey back to the One, its Source, by itself. It needs a *mediator* that can take it up into itself and somehow carry it back Home with itself.

This is precisely what we human beings can do, and we alone. Angels cannot do it; they cannot speak for the material world. But we are *microcosms:* our bodies contain in us all levels of matter from the lowest atoms—blown out from exploding stars in the early stages of the universe's journey—to the highest animal life; these are part of us, part of our very being. We also reach up through our spiritual intellects and wills into the whole realm of the spirit—the "lowest of the spirits," St. Thomas calls us—able, with God's help, to know, love, and be personally united to the supreme Source of all being. Thus we can take up the whole material world into our human consciousness, using both sense and intellect, bring it into the light of self-consciousness in us, and offer it back to the Source whence it came with acknowledgment, gratitude, love for this gift. Thus we can take the whole material world with us as part of our own journey Home to the Source, and so fulfill the implicit longing of this subrational world to find its way back Home and not be left in the darkness of unconsciousness.

Human persons, therefore, are the sole mediators between the material universe and God, the Source of both, and this is a fundamental part of our mission, our vocation as humans on this earth, to respond to this God-given call, not just to focus exclusively on our individualistic journeys to God. We are more than just human individuals, even joined in human communities. Each one of us is also a *microcosm,* partaking within us of all the levels of being, matter to spirit, and divinely commissioned by this very fact to speak for this whole subrational universe beneath us—beautifully symbolized in *Genesis,* when Adam calls all the animals before him and gives them all names, corresponding to their natures. Thus there is an indispensable service we can do, and we alone, for our whole 15 billion-year-old material cosmos, without which it can never fully complete its part of the Great Circle of Being, the Journey Home of the entire created universe.

The Role of Science here takes on its full intelligibility, dignity, and indispensable role within our human development as mediators for the material world. In doing science, we are trying to gather up into conscious understanding the whole history of this material cosmos, its origin, extent, how it operates, all its deepest secrets—which really means we are striving to rethink in our own human way, as images of God, the original creative thoughts of God himself, "striving to know the mind of God," as the great physicist, Stephen Hawking, himself said in his *History of Time*. For those who understand its full meaning for the human person, therefore, human science is an enterprise that is both humanistic and potentially religious.

The Role of Art, in all its forms, also shines forth in a new light. All real beings, through their self-manifesting action, project a partial image of themselves; but we humans alone can make *images*—a unique synthesis of spirit and matter—that symbolize, not only ourselves, but the entire universe and its journey, together with us, back to the Source. This, too, is a uniquely human way of taking the entire material cosmos back with us to God. Art, too, has both a humanistic and a potentially religious finality.

This is part of the essential work of *Religion*, too (which means the binding of humans to God), i.e., to bind ourselves and the whole human race, together with the whole material world, to their Source and ultimate Goal with gratitude, reverence, and love. And Christian revelation adds on a philosophically unpredictable and astonishing new chapter to this great cosmic story, by telling us that the Source itself has graciously come down among us, in the person of the God-man Jesus Christ, to share our journey with us, to show us the best and surest way to walk it, and to insure its final transcendent success beyond this present world. This *God-with-us* now becomes the great, perfect Mediator and High Priest (the *Pontifex Maximus* = supreme Bridge-Builder) between the entire created world and its Ultimate Source and Goal.

Conclusion. This, in sum, is what it means to be a human being, to be a *traveler*, each one on his or her own unique journey, but also an inseparable part of the journey of the whole cosmos, with responsibility not only for our individual selves but also for each other and for the whole world beneath us, in our common journey in and through the world of matter, a journey from time to eternity, from the lowliness of matter to the fullness of spirit in transformed matter. A whole basic philosophy and theology of *ecology* is contained in germ here.

Such is the great cosmic vision animating the whole philosophy and theology of St. Thomas Aquinas—and of many others of the great medieval thinkers (St. Bonaventure, etc., each by his own metaphysical path, analogous but not identical to that of Aquinas). The Great Circle of Being, the Universe as Journey, is finally what the whole metaphysical quest is about. The message of this book: Get on with the Journey, as a fully self-conscious Traveler!

Homo Viator!

On the Great Circle of Being in St. Thomas: the text above is from *In I Sent.,* d. 14, q. 2, a. 2; *In II Sent.,* d. 12, q. 1, a. 3, obj. 5. On man as microcosm: *Summa contra Gentes,* II, 68, n. 6; II, 81, n. 12. See also my article, "Living on the Edge: The Human Person as 'Frontier' Being and Microcosm," *Internat. Phil. Quart.* 36 (1996), 183–200.

THE MEANING OF THE UNIVERSE:
VIEW FROM THE TOP DOWN

Point of view.   Now that we have reached the end of the mind's search for meaning with the discovery by reason of the Ultimate Source of all being, it will be helpful to look back from the top to view again the whole terrain below, seen from this new vantage point. Certain key points will now emerge more clearly into the light, so that we can finally see not only *that* we must accept them as true, under pain of crippling any further use of our minds, but also *why* they are true. This vision was obscured from us on the way up by the mists hiding the summit. What difference does it make once we understand that the entire universe of real beings was created by an Ultimate Source that is infinitely wise and loving, that creates freely out of gratuitous self-communicating love? Let us select a few examples.

I. THE INTELLIGIBILITY OF BEING

We can now see why all being must be intelligible: because it has been thought-created by an Infinite Mind. Two things follow, as Josef Pieper has beautifully brought out: (1) All creatures are intelligible through and through in themselves, because they have been thought-created by an Infinite *Mind.* (2) But they are also by the same token never fully, exhaustively intelligible for us, because they have been thought-created by an *Infinite* Mind. As such they are all images in some way of their Source, with its infinite fullness of perfection. But it is impossible to know fully an image unless we know fully the Original. The latter is impossible for our finite minds; we cannot sound to its depths the infinity of God; there is always a surplus of light too bright for us to see or "get to the bottom of." It follows that there is a depth of intelligibility in every creature, where and how it connects up as image to Original, that we cannot plumb or exhaust. Hence neither God, the Source, nor any of his creature-images are fully intelligible to us with our finite minds, at least in this life as weighed down with our present bodies. All creatures, therefore, have a certain depth of mystery, are *known-unknown* to us now, though fully intelligible in themselves as coming from the creative Mind of God. It follows that the structure of our human knowing in this life is what Pieper calls "the hope-structure of human knowledge," looking forward hopefully to further fulfillment from the side of God himself.

II. PURPOSE OF THE CREATED UNIVERSE

I suggest, then, that the only adequate meaningfulness of the universe is as a gift of its Creator to rational creatures, who are endowed with intelligence to understand consciously the gift and free will to accept it with appreciation and grateful love in return. God, as we have seen, is already infinitely rich in perfection and needs nothing to complete himself; creatures lacking intelligence and free will are sunk in the darkness of unconsciousness and can neither know nor enjoy the fact of their existence. Hence I suggest that it would be a waste of time for God to create a material universe with no rational beings to appreciate it, beings capable of recognizing it as a person-to-person gift and responding appropriately with gratitude and love to the Giver. It follows that the intelligibility of being—all being—is inseparable from the context of persons: it is rooted *in* personal being, flows out *from* it, *to* other persons, who complete the circle by returning it back again to its personal source. In a word, the ultimate meaning of being is: Person-to-Person Gift!

This opens up a whole new personalized interpretation of that most universal of metaphysical structures: the *essence-existence* composition in all finite beings, i.e., the participation of all beings outside of God, through their diverse limiting essences, in the central perfection of the act of existence, which in its unparticipated fullness is the very nature of God. What might have appeared earlier in the course as an abstract, impersonal metaphysical exigency now turns out to be a love-inspired sharing by God of his own personal perfection in some distinctive way with each one of his creatures. This entails a profound relation of intimate personal presence of God as sharing and caring in each creature. And this reaches its full perfection (and intelligibility, as I see it) only in the divine presence to created persons, who alone can close the circle of gift-giving by a conscious response of gratitude and love and final personal communion with the Giver—the ultimate goal of all creation. Thus the ultimate answer, the ultimate key to the mystery of being— why is there a universe of real beings at all?—turns out to be nothing less than interpersonal love!

III. THE UNIVERSE AS BOTH GIFT AND TASK FOR HUMAN PERSONS

Since our material universe is a dynamic evolutionary one, still in process of unfolding—a still unfinished story—we humans who inhabit this earth and are an essential part of its story are now also the cutting edge of its development, through the self-conscious intelligence, freedom, and creativity that render us able to influence significantly the whole story itself, both for good and for evil. Thus we now find ourselves as stewards under God for this whole subrational world, most urgently for our own little planet earth. So the created universe has become for us both a gift and a task to be responsibly fulfilled: i.e., to care for our world as created co-creators with God of a not-yet-finished universe, as well as mediating its return to God with ourselves by acknowledgement, gratitude, and love. These are the full implications of the foundational image of St. Thomas: the Great Circle of Being.

CONCLUSION OF COURSE

This then is the final Meaning of the Universe: a gift from its Maker to us—and other created persons—intelligible through and through, full of rich and wonderful complexities, but also full of as yet unsolved mysteries for us; yet in its overall lines, despite pockets of local disorder, a work of profound order, harmony, and beauty for those who have eyes to see. A metaphysics like that of St. Thomas can be a big step along the way. A recent historian of science, Stephen Weinberg, in his enlightening book *The First Three Minutes* (New York: Basic Books, 1977), after laying out the amazing recent discoveries of science about the origins of the physical universe in the Big Bang, concluded with the sad comment that the more science discovers about how the universe works, the more it becomes embarrassingly obvious that the *why* of it all has eluded us—the existence and purpose of the universe remains in itself "meaningless"! This is quite true as far as science is concerned, which unfortunately for him is the only sure way of knowing. We should not expect more from science than it can give, with its chosen restrictive methods of empirical experiment and measurement, ordered by mathematical analysis. But from the higher viewpoint of metaphysics we can trace the entire system back to its Ultimate Source, and, looking back from this vantage point, our universe turns out to be not at all meaningless, but profoundly and luminously meaningful.

IV. BEYOND METAPHYSICS

This is as far as a metaphysics guided by the light of natural reason alone can take us. It points out to us the structure of the journey of the universe and the only adequate Goal toward which we humans are tending. But it cannot show us further how to actually get there, despite all the existential obstacles and our own weakness. For this, metaphysics itself bids us look further, into history and religion, to find out if the Source has revealed any further special plans for us, in this life and the next—including, perhaps, his coming down to join us in our journey and helping us bring it to fulfillment. But let us be grateful to metaphysics for bringing us this far in our journey, well beyond where science or any other human discipline can take us.

In the light of the above reflections, the whole enterprise of metaphysics itself which we have just completed, following the Thomistic path, now takes on a new existential and personal depth. I am inspired here by Eric Voegelin in his profound essay, "The Beginning and the Beyond" (posthumously discovered). Cf. Voegelin, *Collected Writings*, vol. 28: *Late Unpublished Writings* (Baton Rouge: Louisiana State Univ. Press, 1990).

Rather than being the work solely of an impersonal objective drive of the mind to fully understand the real as far as it can by the use of reason, the metaphysical quest now turns out to be at a deeper level but one expression of an existential pull from a Transcendent Source beyond us, drawing our whole being—intellect, will, imagination, emotions—in two primary directions, which ultimately turn out to be one: the *Beginning* (where it all comes from) and the *Beyond* (the ultimate Goal, which is also beyond all the levels of finite being). Thus metaphysics turns out to be not just a one-sided quest for the fullness of truth, but more profoundly a hidden existential encounter with the Transcendent Source itself, the Alpha and the Omega, drawing us to itself by its own initiative, expressed through our own faculty of spiritual intelligence—which, as St. Thomas often says, is *capax Dei* (with a capacity for God) precisely because it is *capax entis* (with a capacity for being).

QUESTIONS FOR REVIEW AND DISCUSSION

1. What is the point of this final chapter and its recourse to the imagination?

2. Summarize the two great phases of the universe's journey. Why is this journey called the "Great Circle of Being"?

3. What is the difference between the Great Circle as understood by St. Thomas and other Christian thinkers and Plotinus who originated the image?

4. What is the role of the imagination in philosophy and metaphysics, which seems to be such a highly abstract and intellectual discipline?

5. Explain the place of the human person in this journey? What is his dual role as microcosm and mediator? Why is it that only human beings can fulfill this role? Why not angels?

6. What is the role of the sciences, the arts, and religion in fulfilling our role in the journey? The role of human work?

7. What new dimension does the Christian revelation add to the notion of the universe as journey?

8. Explain what new understanding of the universe of being is gathered from looking back on the universe from the point of view of its Creator—a top-down view, rather than the bottom-up order we have followed thus far: a) The Intelligibility of Being? b) the Universe as Gift and Task?

9. What should be the fundamental response of the mind-heart of the metaphysician to the mystery of being as gift?

10. Explain the meaning of the formula: "We human beings are created co-creators with God of a not-yet-finished universe"?

11. What are the limits of how far metaphysics can take us in comprehending the human journey in the Great Circle of Being? What else is there we need to know, and where do we find the answer?

Glossary of Terms

Note. Many of the following key terms in the metaphysical structure of finite beings are defined together in a limited Glossary at the end of Chapter 10: The Metaphysical Structure of Finite Being: An Interlocking Synthesis: *accident/ substance, essence/existence, form/matter, act/potency.*

Abstract, abstraction = an attribute of ideas or concepts which signify in their content some aspect of their objects but leave out others. Most commonly used to describe universal ideas that abstract the essence or central meaning of something and omit the concrete individual details: e.g., man—Socrates.

Accident = see Glossary at end of chapter 10; also chapter 8: Substance and Accident.

Act, actuality. Act in its ordinary meaning = the action of some agent. In its technical meaning = actuality as correlated with potency, see Glossary at end of chapter 10; also chapter 7: Act and Potency.

Analogy, analogous = the property of a concept or linguistic term (not a real being) by which a concept or term is predicated of several different subjects according to a meaning partly the same, partly different in each case: *strength* of muscles—*strength* of will. *Analogate* = the subject of an analogous predication. Types:

1. *Analogy of extrinsic attribution:* where the analogous term is predicated properly (literally) only of one primary analogate and of the secondary analogates only because of some relation (causality, etc.), not because of any inrinsic similarity: e.g., a healthy woman—healthy food.
2. *Analogy of proportionality* = where the analogous term is predicated because of some proportional similarity between the analogates. a) *Metaphorical* (or

Improper) proportionality = where the analogous terms is predicated properly only of one analogate and of the others only by metaphor: e.g., an angry man—an angry sea. b) *Proper (literal) proportionality* = where the analogous term is predicated properly of all the analogates: e.g., a man knows; God knows. Cf. chapter 3: Analogy.

Beauty = that whose contemplation gives delight. Can be *ontological* = the beauty of beings in themselves, or *aesthetic* = the beauty of works of art: e.g., a beautiful woman—a beautiful painting. Cf. Chapter 18: The Transcendental Properties of Being.

Being = that which is. When used without qualification = a *real being* = that which actually exists with its own act of existence outside of an idea. When specified as a *mental being* = that which is present not by its own act of existence but only inside an idea; its being is its to-be-thought-about: numbers, possibles, abstractions as abstract, hypotheses, etc. chapter 2: The Meaning of Being.

Cause = that which contributes positively to the being of another. a) *Efficient* = that which contributes . . . by its action. b) *Final* = that which contributes . . . as the end or goal for the sake of which something is done. c) *Formal* = that which contributes . . . as that in a being which determines it to be this kind of being and not another. d) *Material* = that which contributes . . . as that in a being out of which something is made. e) *Exemplary* = the exemplar or model in the mind of its maker that corresponds to the formal cause in the being. Cf. chapter 12: Efficient Cause.

Composition = a complex unity formed by several composing elements. *Real metaphysical composition* = a composition in some real being wherein the composing parts are not complete real beings in themselves but only incomplete, correlative, interdependent co-principles that are really distinct from each other (= irreducible to each other) but cannot exist without their correlative co-principles: essence-existence; form-matter; accident-substance.

Creation. In its *philosophical* meaning = the production of a being out of nothing, i.e., out of no preexisting subject or material; or, the production of the total being of something. In its *theological* meaning (Christian, Jewish, Islam) = the production of a being out of nothing with a beginning in time. In both meanings creation is proper to God alone as the unique Ultimate Source of all being.

Essence = that in a being which makes it to be what it is, this being and not some other. See the Glossary at end of chapter 10; and chapter 5: Being as One and Many.

Existence = that in a being which makes it to be a real being. For St. Thomas it is not just a form or essence or anything static, but the act of existence (*esse*), which makes an essence to be actually present in the real world and actively present to other real beings. See Glossary in chapter 10, and chapter 13.

Eternal = that whose existence never ends. Cf. chapter 14: The Ulimate Source of All Being.

Evil = the privation of some good due to something. a) *Moral* = contrary to the good of personal beings in the moral or ethical order: e.g., murder. b) *Physical* = contrary to the ontological good of something considered in itself: e.g., blindness. Cf. chapter 17: Evil and Being.

Evolution = the process of emergence over time of the various species of living things from each other and originally from non-living beings. Does not it-self specify *how* species evolved, on their own or with the help of some higher cause, such as God. Cf. chapter 15: The Metaphysics of Evolution.

Finality, final cause = see chapter 13: Final Cause. Also above under *Cause: final.*

Form = see Glossary at end of chapter 10; also chapters 6 and 9 on Form and Matter.

Good, goodness = that which has some positive quality or perfection in itself ren-dering it apt to complete or be perfective in some way of some being (including its own being), thus rendering it apt to be desired, loved, ap-preciated by some being. It is correlated with some appetitive power in a being—sense appetite or rational will, just as being as true is correlated with the intellect. Cf. chapter 16: Being as Good.

Hylemorphism = the Aristotelian doctrine, adopted (and adapted) by St. Thomas and other Scholastic thinkers, of the composition of all material beings by matter (*hylé* in Greek) and form (*morphé* in Greek).

Law (metaphysical) = a relation binding together in a necessary connection of intelligibility two or more aspects, elements, or types of entities in the order of being: Every finite being must be a composition of essence and exis-tence; every being that begins to exist requires an efficient cause.

Matter (Primary) = see Glossary at end of chapter 10 under form/matter. It is formless matter, with no form of its own, and can exist only under some form. *Secondary matter* is some material being that already has its own essen-tial form, but is open (potential) to further formal determinations: e.g., molten iron. For matter as the non-formal principle allowing the multipli-cation of the same specific form in many members of the same species, see chapter 6: Form and Matter I. For matter as the principle of continuity in the transition from one essential form to another in essential change see chapter 9: Form/Matter II.

Metaphysics = that part of philosophy that studies all real beings insofar as they *are*, as they belong to the all-embracing community of real existents. It seeks to discover the basic properties, principles, and laws that govern all beings in our universe insofar as they exist. Aristotle and Aquinas called it the science of being *qua* being, i.e., of all beings insofar as they are.

Nature = see Glossary at end of chapter 10. It signifies essence considered under the aspect of its action. *Nature* = the essence as abiding center of acting (and being acted upon) in a being. It answers the question: What are the characteristic actions of this essence?

Participation (in the order of real being) = a structure or order of relationship between beings such that they all share in various degrees of fullness in some positive property or perfection common to them all, as received from the same one source: all finite beings participate in existence from God. A Neoplatonic (not Aristotelian) doctrine adapted by Aquinas to express his own essence/existence metaphysics.

Potency = see Glossary at end of chapter 10. It means that principle within a being which limits some act or actual perfection possessed by the being and is the root of its capacity for change. *(a) Passive potency* = the capacity to receive some actual perfection. *(b) Active potency* = the power to act, to do something, given the proper conditions. The former implies some incompleteness on its own, hence cannot be found in God; the second implies no incompleteness or imperfection, hence can be found in God: God has the power (active potency) to create the world or not. Cf. chapter 7: Act and Potency.

Principle = a primary root or source from which other things flow or take their beginning and on which their intelligibility depends. Can be *(a) a basic principle (or law) governing the order of knowing*, e.g., the Principle of Non-Contradiction: Nothing can be and not be (or be thought) at the same time under the same aspect; or *(b) a principle (or law) governing the order of being*, e.g., the same Principle of Non-Contradiction, or the Principle of Sufficient Reason: Every real being must have the sufficient reason (grounding its intelligibility) either in itself or in some other real being; or the Principle of Causality, etc. *Principle* as understood here means the same as *metaphysical law* (see above) = necessary connection, except that principle means a primary or absolutely basic law on which many others depend. Principle can also mean c) some individual element in a metaphysical composition on which a whole basic metaphysical structure of being depends: essence and the act of existence are metaphysical co-principles at the root of all finite beings; so, too, form and matter for substantial change. This meaning of principle runs all through metaphysics.

Property = an attribute or characteristic of something that does not signify the essence itself of the thing but something that follows immediately from the essence and is necessarily connected with it (proper to it): Every being is one, true, etc.

Substance = the opposite of accident; see Glossary, end of chapter 10. Substantial = in the order of substance. Cf. chapter 8.

Truth = the conformity between mind (judgment) and being. *Epistemological truth* = truth as located in the mind as true to the being of its object. The concern of Epistemology or theory of Knowledge, not of Metaphysics. *Ontological truth* = the truth as located in beings themselves towards minds, our concern here. *Two types of relation,* corresponding to two types of minds: *(a) To the divine mind:* created things are conformed to the idea in God's mind according to which they were created and are always actually known by God. As Aquinas puts it, they are "measured by the divine mind." (*b*) *To human minds:* since we did not create the beings we know, we do not measure them; they "measure our minds," make themselves known to us by their actions. Hence created beings stand in the middle between the divine and human minds: *measured* by the divine, *measuring* human minds. Hence *ontological truth* = the innate intelligibility of beings—actually known by God, apt to be known by human minds. Cf. chapter 18: The Transcendental Properties of Being—3. Truth.

Transcendent = that which leaps over all boundaries and categories of being; more particularly and usually refers to what is above all limitations of lower levels of being: spirit transcends matter; God transcends all finite beings.

Transcendental = technical term signifying one of the basic properties belonging to all beings as beings, hence transcending all particular categories, like being itself: Every being is one, good. Cf. chapter 18: Transcendental Properties of Being. Special meaning in Kantian tradition: "transcendental method" = the analysis of human knowing according, not to its content, but to the a priori necessary conditions of possibility of all human knowing. Used also by Transcendental Thomists like Maréchal, Rahner, Lonergan. Controverted among Thomists as to whether legitimate or too dangerously close to some form of idealism.

Unity = that property of inner coherence that makes something to be undivided in itself and divided from every other. It is one of the transcendental properties applying to all beings. As such, it is applied analogously to different kinds of being, like being itself. Like being, it signifies not something static, a mere state, but an act, the inner act of cohering together to form an intrinsic unity, each being in its own way. Two main types: *(a) Intrinsic unity* = that proper to a real being as possessing one single act of existence and one center of action. *(b) Extrinsic unity* = that proper not to a single being but to a collection or aggregate of several real beings bound together by some kind of relation, like a common purpose or goal, same location in space, etc.: an army, a family, a college, a city, etc. Cf. chapter 4: Unity as Property of Being.

Index of Names